I0828370

HISTORIC BRIDGES OF SOUTHEAST MINNESOTA

HISTORIC BRIDGES OF SOUTHEAST MINNESOTA

STEVE GARDINER

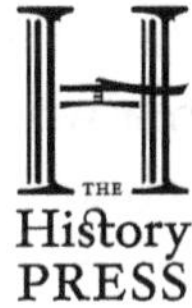

Published by The History Press
Charleston, SC
www.historypress.com

First published 2023

Manufactured in the United States

ISBN 9781540258458

Library of Congress Control Number: 2023937775

Notice: The information in this book is true and complete to the best of our knowledge. It is offered without guarantee on the part of the author or The History Press. The author and The History Press disclaim all liability in connection with the use of this book.

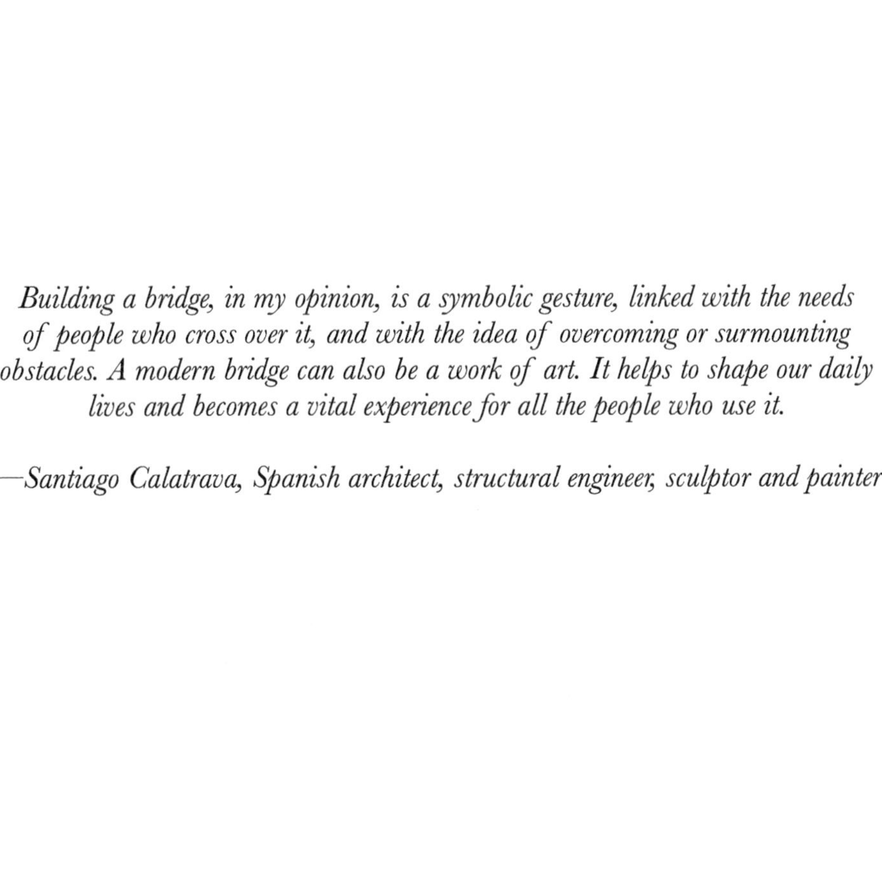

Building a bridge, in my opinion, is a symbolic gesture, linked with the needs of people who cross over it, and with the idea of overcoming or surmounting obstacles. A modern bridge can also be a work of art. It helps to shape our daily lives and becomes a vital experience for all the people who use it.

—Santiago Calatrava, Spanish architect, structural engineer, sculptor and painter

To those who plan, fund, design, construct and use the thousands of bridges in Southeast Minnesota

CONTENTS

PREFACE

Minnesota has long been known as the "Land of 10,000 Lakes." It could also be called the "Land of 20,000 Bridges," according to the Minnesota Department of Transportation. A state that has that many lakes, as well as the network of rivers and tributaries that accompany them, will need to have a significant number of bridges. Those bridges, developed throughout the history of the state, affect the transportation, economy and lifestyle of the region. This book will look at some of the bridges that have influenced the southeastern portion of the state.

Minnesota is not a square state with a clearly defined southeast quadrant, so there are two geographic considerations to make regarding the framework of this book. The first is that the term *Southeast Minnesota* is somewhat arbitrary, not neatly divided or defined, but for the context of this project, I'll define it as covering the area from the Twin Cities east to Stillwater at the Wisconsin border and from the Twin Cities south roughly along I-35 to the Iowa border.

While the Metro area would often not be included when referring to Southeast Minnesota, including the Twin Cities is still far less than one-quarter of the state, and it makes sense for the purpose of this book. There are many important bridges in the Metro area, and the history of those bridges determined what happened throughout the rest of the state and country. I'll include a few bridges from the cities in the first chapter, because they are a significant part of the culture, history and fabric of the region. That historical influence continues today.

A traveler in this region would be a two-hour drive or less from any other part of the area, so the variety and beauty of the bridges included here would be easily accessible if anyone wants to see them. A person could see many of the bridges included in this book in a single day.

Using these criteria, I'll include a selection of bridges from the Twin Cities as well as bridges across the Mississippi River in several towns and cities downriver. I'll also include inland bridges in rural areas, several smaller communities and in the Rochester area.

For easy understanding, I've divided the southeast region into seven smaller units that form the chapters of the book. Six of those are based on major bridges crossing the Mississippi River, and the other centers on bridges in or near Rochester.

While most chapters focus on a town with a major bridge, there are other smaller bridges in towns nearby. How to organize those smaller towns and rural bridges is also an arbitrary decision. I've grouped those bridges in smaller towns with what seems to be the best chapter, the closest geographically. They are grouped for convenience more than any other factor.

For most of the major bridges across the Mississippi River, the Minnesota town is the larger and the bridge is commonly referred to by that name, such as the Red Wing Bridge or the Wabasha Bridge, even though they all have an official name. I will give both official names and common names when both exist.

There are thousands of bridges in Southeast Minnesota. For the sake of this book, I had to select a limited number of bridges that represent the variety and scope of the bridges that exist throughout the region. Choices had to be made, so a reader's favorite bridge might or might not appear here.

Although bridges may often seem like a cornerstone of a community, they are in a perpetual state of evolution. They are built. They are rebuilt. They are torn down and replaced. They are abandoned. In the case of the latter, more than once I went to visit a bridge and found it fenced off. Some had warnings about safety. Some had No Trespassing signs. To avoid danger or illegal activity, I chose to leave those bridges out. Other abandoned bridges are easily accessible and are included.

The larger bridges drew more attention during their planning and construction. There was more coverage in media at the time they were built, so there is more extant information on them now. Their impact is greater; they cost more, take more time, handle more traffic and affect more lives. With that in mind, the larger bridges get more coverage in this book and form the basis of each chapter. I include information on the smaller bridges in each appropriate chapter.

Some bridges, especially those in rural areas and on private farms, may have little or no information published about them, yet they are included here because they represent a different type or use of a bridge. For a few, the caption information included with the photo is the only historical background that was available, so they cannot be explained in depth.

This book is not a lecture on bridge design or construction. It is not a lesson in architecture. There are other books, videos and classes for that. Those topics are touched on in relevant chapters to help show the variety of types and materials, as well as the uses of bridges built for pedestrians, bicycles, cars, trucks or trains.

The goal of this book, then, is to express a sense of gratitude for the bridges of Southeast Minnesota, the valuable services they provide and the beauty they add when combining the work of human beings and nature. Bridges help us save time, move people and goods, support the economy and connect people to places. I hope that after reading this, the reader has a better appreciation of the roles that the bridges of Southeast Minnesota play in our lives.

ACKNOWLEDGEMENTS

After teaching high school English and journalism for thirty-eight years, I retired and moved to Minnesota to be closer to family. Not long after moving here, I had the chance to fulfill a longtime goal of working as a newspaper reporter. I worked for three years at the *Red Wing Republican Eagle*, part of RiverTown Multimedia, and near the end of that stint, the editor, Anne Jacobson, assigned me to write a few articles about bridges in the area. I started driving around to see them and talking to people who built them, supported them and used them. My whole perception of bridges changed, and even after I finished the articles, I continued to look at bridges and take pictures of them. Any trip I took around the state became an opportunity to see and photograph more bridges. I amassed a large collection of photos based on that brief beginning I got at the newspaper. Thank you, Anne, for sparking my interest in the area's bridges.

When I started working on the bridge articles for the *Republican Eagle*, I needed help locating bridges around the area. I found that and more in Bruce Ause, former director of the Red Wing Environmental Learning Center. His decades of exploring the backroads of Minnesota made him the perfect source for directions to interesting and scenic bridges. Thank you, Bruce, for your help locating bridges and for many wonderful hours spent together canoeing and cross-country skiing.

Thanks to John Rodrigue, acquisitions editor for The History Press. He saw an article I wrote about the 1965 flood on the Mississippi River and contacted me. That led to my book *Historic Disasters in Southeast Minnesota.*

When that book was finished, I contacted John again and proposed this book on bridges. He liked the idea and carried the proposal to the editorial board, and they approved. Thank you, John, for your continued support.

Hilary Parrish, senior editor at The History Press, provided excellent copy editing on the manuscript.

While I took the majority of the photos in this book, there are many that are from the archives of historical centers in the region. These centers also provided hundreds of articles that form the basis of the text of this book. These historical societies are amazing resources.

I want to thank each of the following persons and organizations for assistance with photos and/or information that helped make this book: Afton Esson and Liz Schmidt of the Goodhue County Historical Society in Red Wing; Walt Bennick with the Winona County Historical Society in Winona; Krista Lewis at the History Center of Olmsted County in Rochester; Margaret Peterson of the Wabasha County Historical Society in Reads Landing; Mary McLaughlin at the La Crescent Historical Society; Rebecca Snyder with the Dakota County Historical Society in South St. Paul; and Mary Fuller with the Oronoco Area History Center. The *Wabasha County Herald* and the *Red Wing Republican Eagle* gave permission to use materials from their archives. Thanks to each of those people and their corresponding organizations for providing help.

Stacy Bengs, owner of Stacy Bengs Photography in Eau Claire, Wisconsin, grew up in Red Wing and was at the University of Minnesota the day the I-35W bridge collapsed. A student in the journalism department, she was one of the first on the scene with her camera. Thank you, Stacy, for sharing your story and photographs of that historic bridge event.

I drove hundreds of miles in search of information and photographs of the bridges included in this book. My wife, Peggy, accompanied me on many of those journeys and waited patiently while I searched for the best angle to photograph a bridge. Thank you, Peggy, for traveling with me, not only on the backroads of Southeast Minnesota, but through more than four decades of marriage as well.

INTRODUCTION

For most of us, it happens so often we don't even notice it. We are walking, cycling or driving, and we cross a bridge. It is so easy, so normal, but getting to this point in time where country lanes, city streets, state roads, interstate highways and railroads cross rivers, canyons and each other was a long process.

The Minnesota Department of Transportation noted that the bridges of the state "range from small, nondescript spans over local streams, to the monumental structures that carry our trails, roads and railroads over the Mississippi River. Bridges are not only a key component of our transportation system, they also tell many overlapping stories of the state's development. They represent complex interrelationships of topography: settlement; evolving modes of transportation; advancements in engineering, materials, and construction; changes in social trends and aesthetics; and changes in local and national economics."

Bridges are an impressive human achievement, a place where engineering meets art, where function meets beauty, where practical meets grace.

The history of bridges is filled with ingenuity. New designs, new materials and new methods have made the evolution of bridges capture the human imagination.

Throughout the long history of bridge building, different styles of bridges have developed. While each bridge has to be built based on its purpose and the unique features of its location, bridges throughout history have tended to fit into six basic design categories.

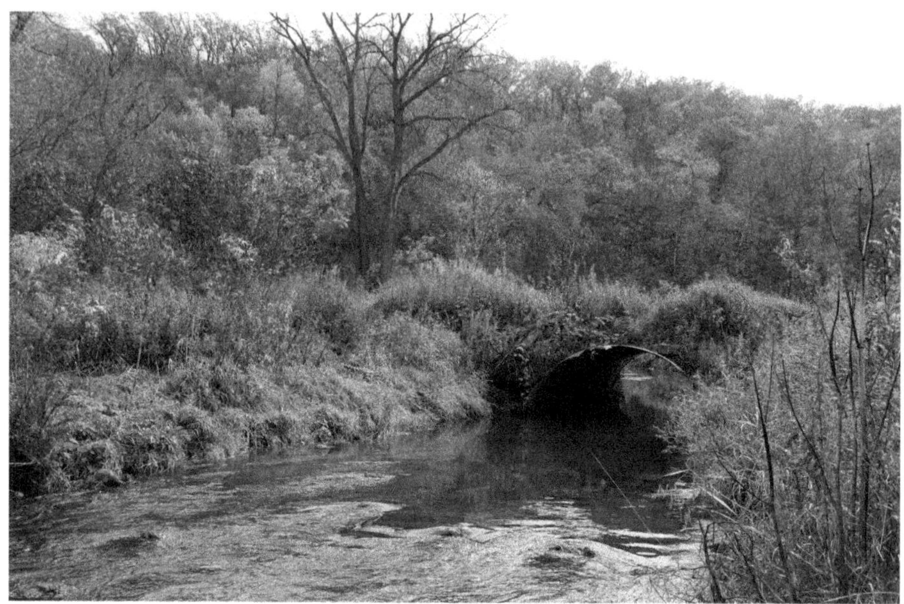

Bridges of all shapes and sizes have been made to meet the needs of those who use them. This culvert bridge is on a farm road just off Highway 58 south of Red Wing. *Photo by Steve Gardiner.*

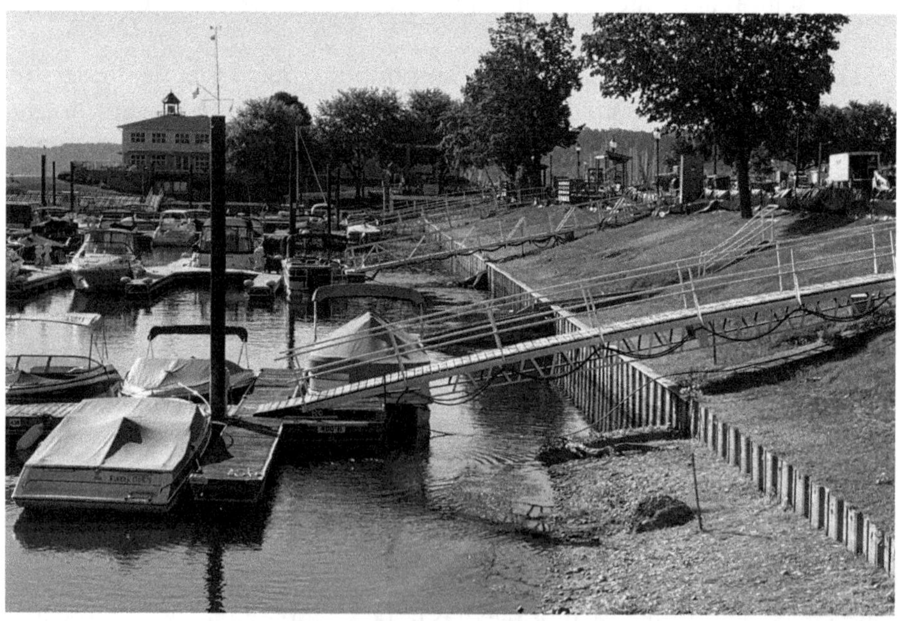

One common use for small bridges in Minnesota is to get to floating boat docks that rise and fall with the water level, such as these at the Lake City Marina. *Photo by Steve Gardiner.*

BEAM BRIDGES

A log across a stream, supported on both ends by the banks, is an example of a beam or girder bridge. They are the most common type of bridge and may consist of a single span or multiple spans running continuously from one support pier to another and are generally best used to span short distances. The beams or girders can be made from many types of materials, including wood, iron, steel or concrete. Steel girders are often in the form of I-beams. Concrete girders are frequently shaped as T-beams and are generally made using reinforced or prestressed concrete. Weight on a beam bridge creates compression on the top of the beam, tension on the bottom of the beam and vertical force downward on the supports at both ends of the beam into the piers and the ground.

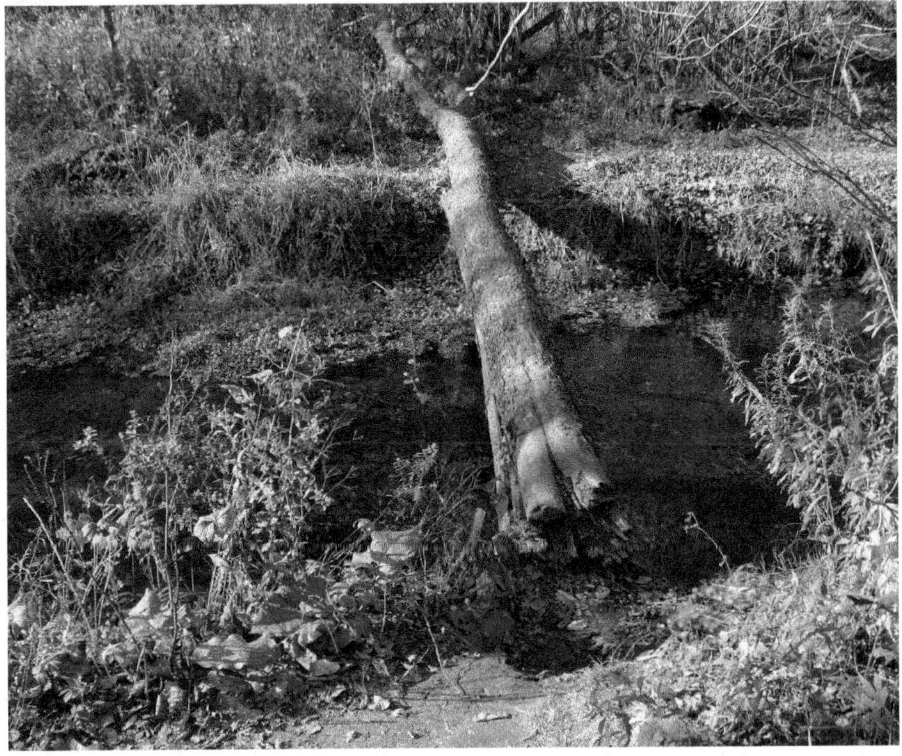

A log across a stream is one of the earliest forms of bridges in this region, and this one shows the trails of fishermen who have used it. *Photo by Steve Gardiner.*

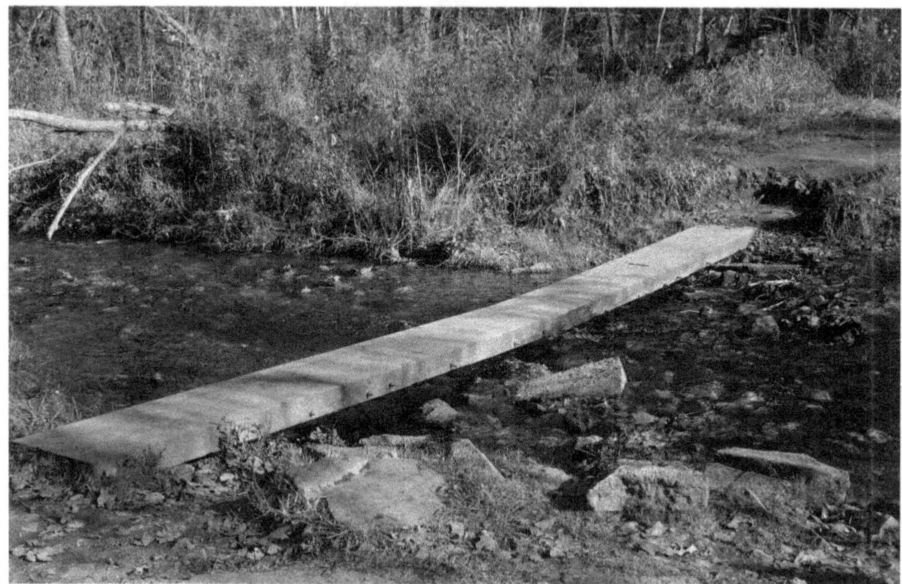

Complex bridges like those that cross the Mississippi River and simple ones like this plank across a creek help us traverse terrain that would be more difficult without them. *Photo by Steve Gardiner.*

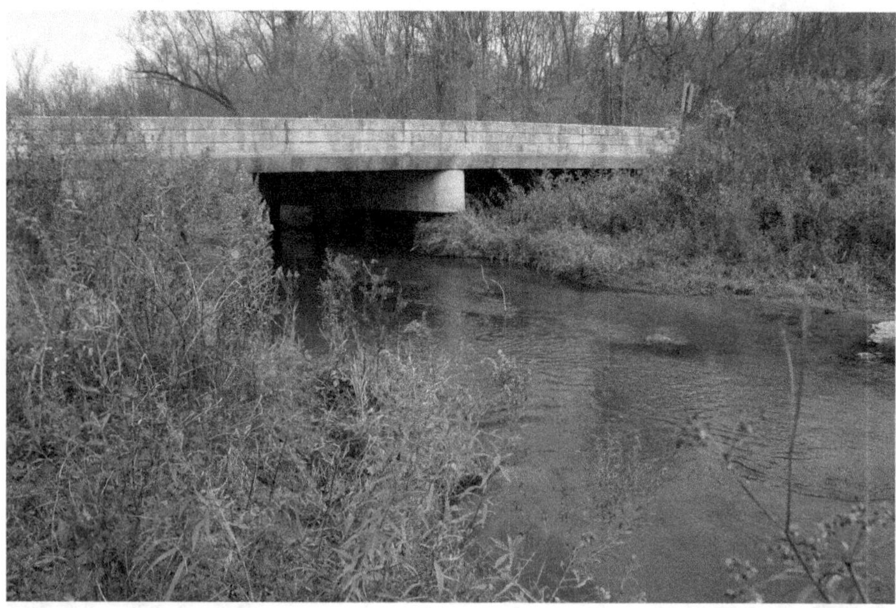

Concrete beam bridges, like this one on Hay Creek Trail south of Red Wing, are very common for country roads, highways and interstates throughout the nation. Their simple design keeps costs down, and the reinforced concrete makes them last for decades. *Photo by Steve Gardiner.*

TRUSS BRIDGES

These bridges feature a framework either above or below the bridge deck. The frame often uses triangular shapes to stabilize the bridge and add strength to the spans. A frame that is above the bridge and connects across the top is called a through truss because the traffic passes through the framework. Many times, a through truss connects over the top of the deck, forming a sort of tunnel. Other times, the truss work is only on the sides with no top bracing, which is called a pony truss. A truss frame that is below the bridge is called a deck truss. There are many different formations for assembling the structure of a truss bridge, and the style often reflects the designer's name, such as Warren or Pratt trusses. Truss bridges are popular because they can use a relatively small amount of materials to support a substantial amount of weight. By using trusses, the weight of the load on the bridge is spread out from the point of the weight across a wider area. Trusses are also used as secondary elements on arch, suspension and cantilever bridges.

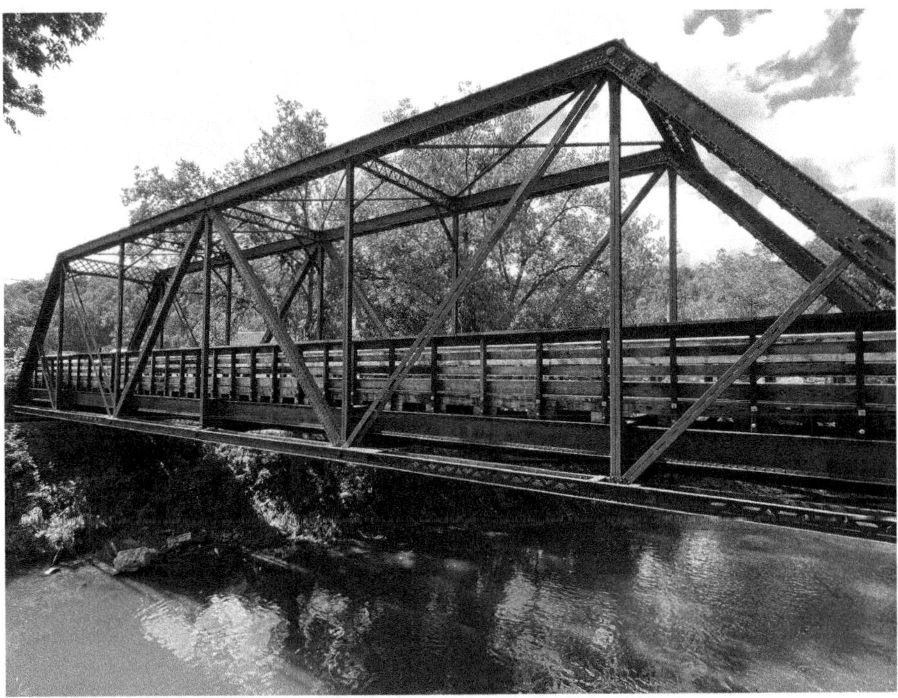

The Root River Trail Pedestrian Bridge in Lanesboro illustrates the use of trusses above the bridge decking to support the bridge span. This is called a through truss because traffic moves through the trusses. *Photo by Steve Gardiner.*

Arch Bridges

Arch bridges have been around since early Roman times and have been used in many different locations and settings. With beam and truss bridges, the load is supported by compression on the top of the bridge and tension on the bottom. With an arch bridge, the forces are downward on the arch, making it press against itself, putting the full arch into compression but adding a horizontal force to the foundations that must be accounted for in the bridge design. An arch bridge may be constructed of a large single arch or of a series of smaller arches, which allows greater length for a bridge that is capable of having several piers or foundations in the middle.

Suspension Bridges

Cables that curve down from vertical towers give suspension bridges an elegant profile. The load is supported with tension through the cables and compression in the towers, causing some designers to suggest that the suspension cable works as an upside-down arch. The deck of a suspension bridge is hanging in the air, so some early suspension bridges suffered damage when windstorms twisted the decks. Designers had to find ways of holding the decks in place, which can be done with added weight or with trusses that keep the deck from flexing. Suspension bridges have frequently been used when the distance of the span is longer than could be supported by a beam or truss bridge.

Cantilever Bridges

The beams of a cantilevered bridge are supported on only one end and extend outward in much the same way as a diving board reaches out over a swimming pool. Some cantilever bridges are made of two cantilevered arms that connect in the middle. Others are made of three parts—the two cantilevered arms stretching out horizontally and a third section that serves as a span between the two anchored arms. The central section could be a beam or is often a truss bridge used as a connection between the two cantilevered arms. Steel and prestressed concrete are common materials used in constructing these bridges.

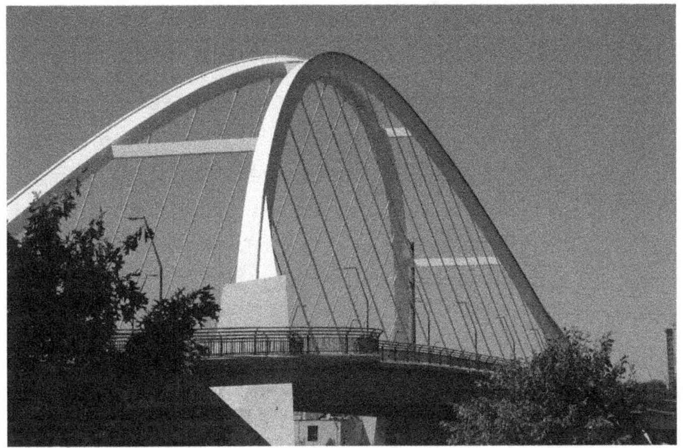

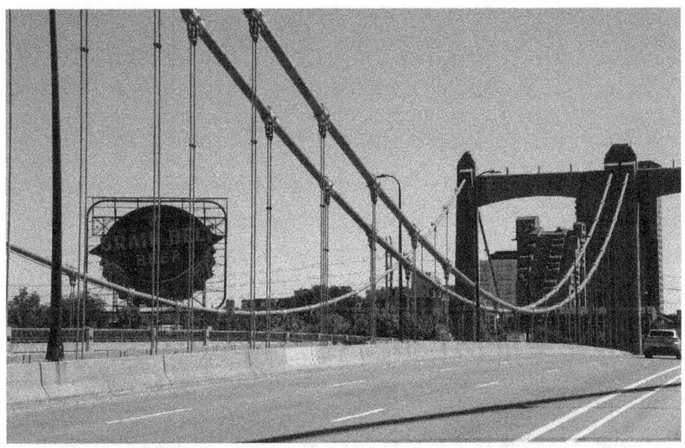

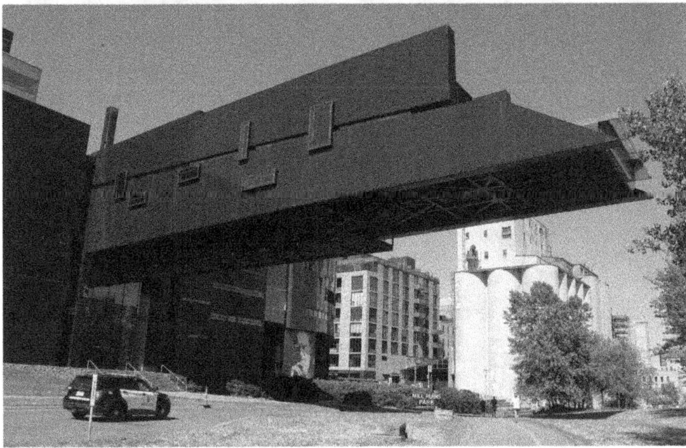

Top: Arches have been used for centuries because of their strong support. The Lowry Avenue Bridge in Minneapolis shows the use of two arches connected at the top for additional strength. *Photo by Steve Gardiner.*

Middle: The Hennepin Avenue Bridge in Minneapolis is a classic suspension bridge. *Photo by Steve Gardiner.*

Bottom: A good example of how a cantilever works is the Endless Bridge, part of the Guthrie Theater in Minneapolis. The cantilever extends out 178 feet and is 55 feet above the roadway. *Photo by Steve Gardiner.*

Cable-Stayed Bridges

Like suspension bridges, cable-stayed bridges employ a vertical tower and cables that support the bridge deck, but instead of having the cables curve down toward the bridge deck and back up to the next tower as they do on a suspension bridge, the cables on a cable-stayed bridge connect the tower directly to several locations on the bridge deck in straight, diagonal lines. The cables may run parallel to each other or may look more like a fan spreading out as they approach the bridge deck. This leaves the cables in tension with compression on the towers. The tension in the cables can also put the deck into horizontal compression. A combination of girder bridge and cable-stayed bridge is sometimes used and is referred to as an extradosed bridge.

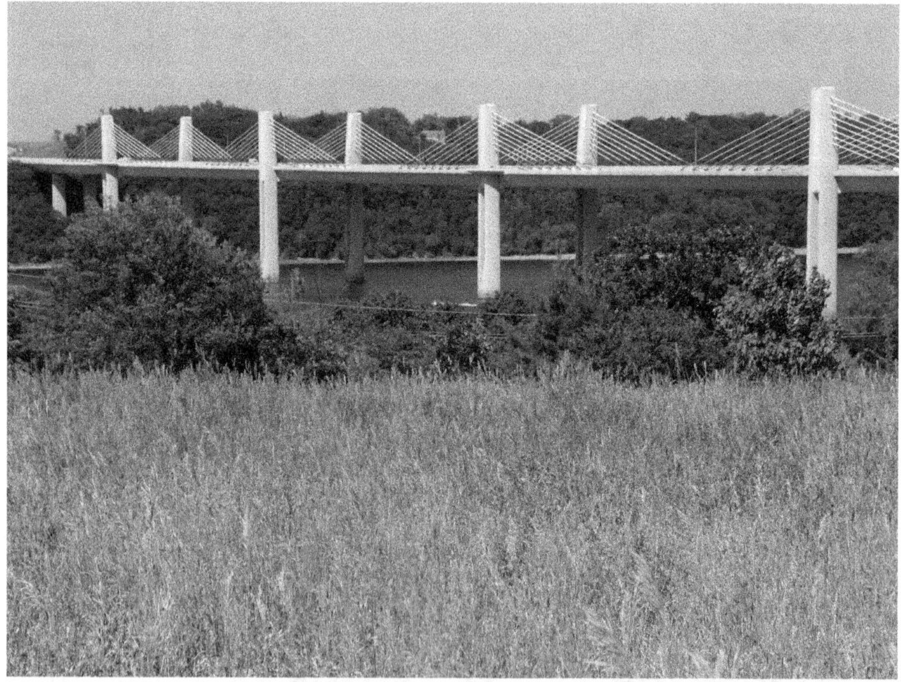

Cable-stayed bridges use cables extending down from a tower that attach directly to the bridge decking. While the St. Croix Crossing bridge near Stillwater is an extradosed bridge—which means it has features of both a girder bridge and a cable-stayed bridge—the cables give a good view of how a cable-stayed bridge is supported. *Photo by Steve Gardiner.*

SUPERSTRUCTURE AND SUBSTRUCTURE

All of these bridge types have two things in common: a superstructure and a substructure. The superstructure is the part of the bridge that actually carries the weight of the pedestrian, bicycle, car, truck or train that is passing over it. The superstructure includes the girders or trusses as well as the deck of the bridge.

The substructure contains the elements that support the superstructure and transmit the weight of the bridge and its load to the ground. Piers, abutments, footings and foundations are parts of the substructure.

LIVE LOAD AND DEAD LOAD

All of these bridge types also need to consider live load and dead load. Dead load is the weight of the bridge itself, and live load is the weight of the traffic that will cross that bridge. Engineers must consider these weights as they decide what materials and what type of bridge to build in a location.

For shorter spans, the dead load is often less than the live load, but as the length of the bridge increases, the dead load often becomes greater than the live load.

Engineers must also consider the direction of forces on a bridge. The live load and dead load of a bridge are vertical forces moving downward into the substructure of the bridge and into the ground. Forces of nature, such as winds and floods, can create horizontal forces against the bridge and must be accounted for in the bridge design. In some cases, horizontal stabilizing needs to be added to a bridge.

A LONG HISTORY

Evidence of arches and primitive suspension bridge techniques has been found dating as far back as 2,500 years ago in China, India and Egypt. By the second century BC, the Romans were building masonry bridges and aqueducts. Julius Caesar built a timber trestle bridge across the Rhine in 55 BC. Rope suspension bridges have existed for hundreds of years in places like Nepal and Peru. The famous Old London Bridge was built in AD 1210, and the picturesque Rialto Bridge in Venice was completed in 1591.

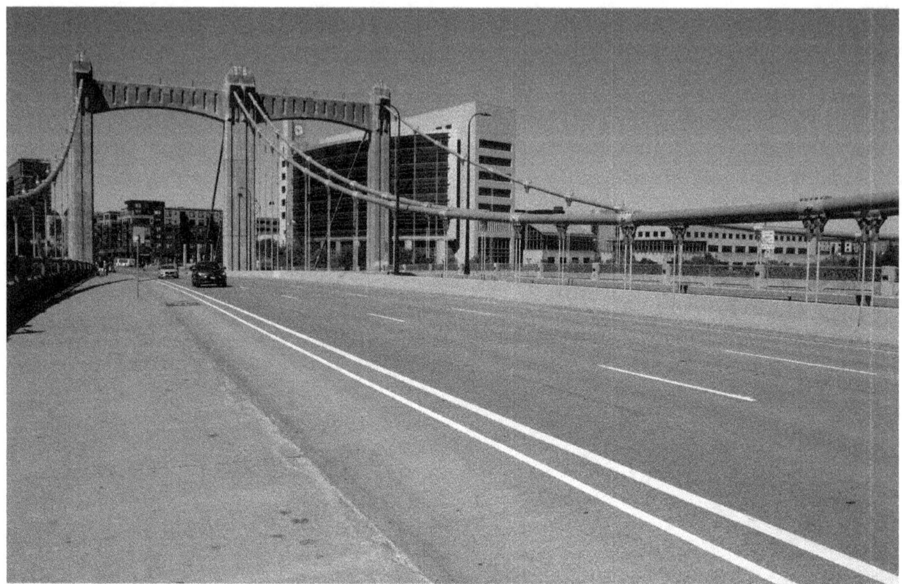

The view looking south going into downtown Minneapolis on the Hennepin Avenue Bridge. *Photo by Steve Gardiner.*

Closer to home on the Upper Mississippi River, the land that is now Minnesota was filled with endless forests. Native Americans and early settlers used the logs from these forests as simple bridges, sometimes singly and at other times placing two or more large logs side by side and crossing them with smaller logs to provide a deck. Similarly, flat stones often served as the foundations and structures for basic bridges.

As communities of settlers formed, residents often built wooden bridges over smaller streams and rivers to connect with another town. Various boat owners provided ferry services over wider rivers and lakes. But it wasn't long before the number of people moving into the region required more advanced structures to be built.

By the time Minnesota became a state in 1858, the need to move passengers and goods was great enough that serious bridge building began. New York engineer Thomas Musgrove Griffith constructed the Hennepin Bridge, the first bridge across the Mississippi River, in 1855. It was a suspension bridge from Nicollet Island to what is today Hennepin Avenue, even though Minneapolis hadn't been incorporated yet.

With businesses like the Minnesota Bridge Company in place and settlers eager to expand opportunities, many new bridges were built. The early

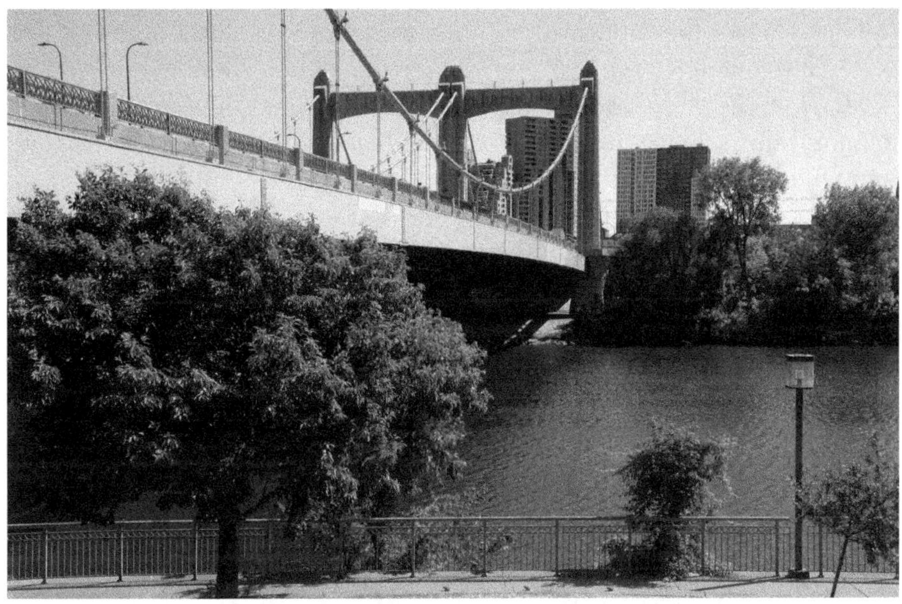

The Hennepin Avenue Bridge, seen from the riverwalk, was built on the site of the first bridge across the Mississippi River. *Photo by Steve Gardiner.*

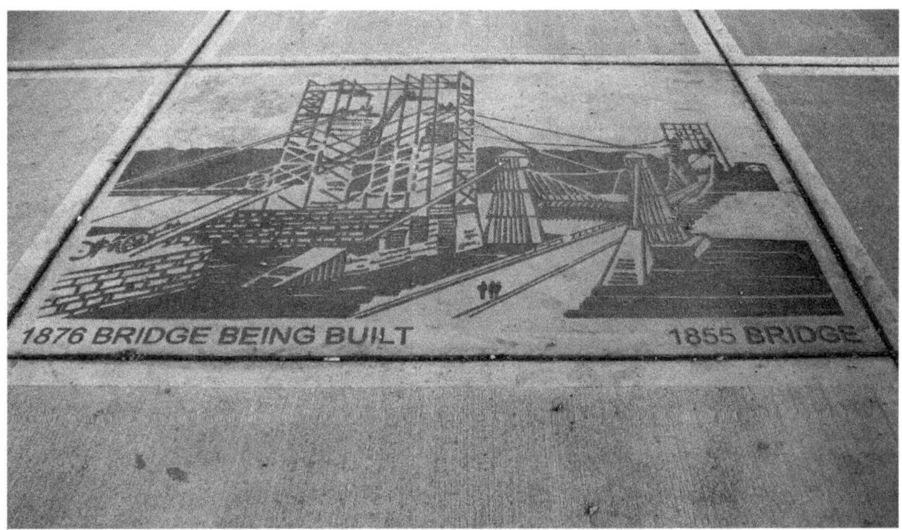

This plaque at the base of the south abutment of the Hennepin Avenue Bridge celebrates the original bridge, built in 1855, and the construction of its replacement in 1876. *Photo by Steve Gardiner.*

wooden bridges were replaced by stone structures, then iron and steel and eventually concrete.

Many of the early bridges were built privately, and the owners charged tolls for walkers, horses or wagons to cross. Later, communities, counties and states funded the increasing number and size of bridges.

With the arrival of the railroads in the 1860s, a new type of bridge was necessary. Railroads sometimes used wooden trestle bridges, but steel truss bridges soon became the norm for train traffic.

One of the most famous bridges in Minneapolis came out of this era. The Stone Arch Bridge was built in 1883 by James J. Hill for his Great Northern Railway. It was listed in the National Register of Historic Places in 1971 and was used as a railway bridge until 1978. After that, it sat unused until it was repaired and repurposed by the Minneapolis Park Board as a cycling and walking bridge, making it a focal point in downtown Minneapolis.

Bridges across the Mississippi River also had to accommodate the transportation that happened beneath them. Bridges had to provide some way for steamboats and, later, tows and barges to move upstream and downstream. Many were built high enough that boat traffic could pass below them. Some were built with a section that pivoted on a pier so that the

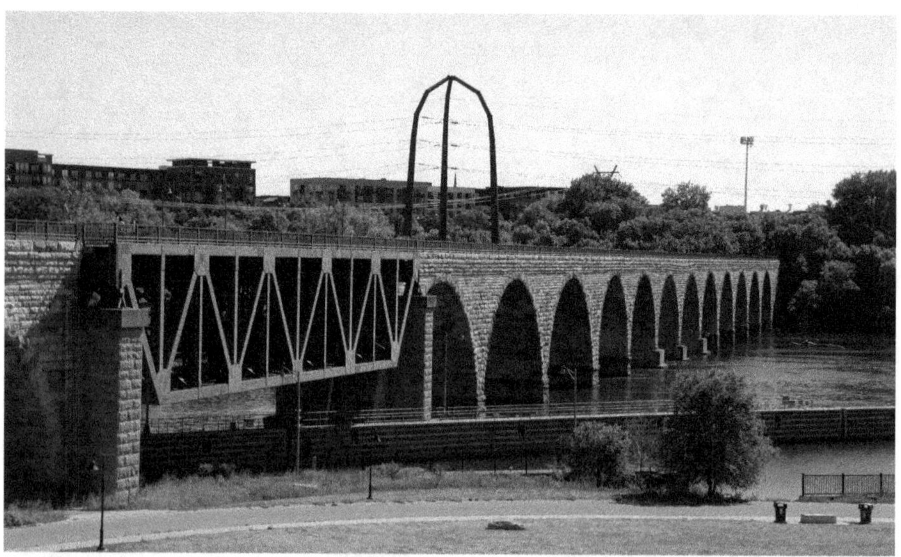

One of the most popular sites in downtown Minneapolis, the Stone Arch Bridge features a series of namesake arches as well as a span of steel truss bridging in the left of the photo. Because the truss is below the deck, the span is known as a deck truss as opposed to a through truss, which is above the deck. *Photo by Steve Gardiner.*

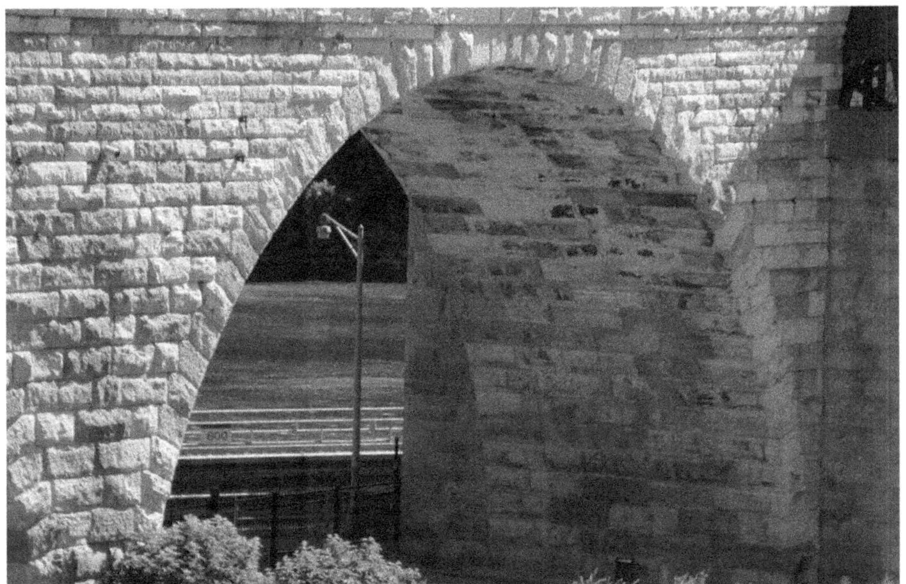

This photo gives a closer view of one of the arches on the Stone Arch Bridge, which opened in 1883. *Photo by Steve Gardiner.*

section ran parallel to the river, allowing boats to move through the opening created by the "swing" section. Others had a central section that could be lifted by two towers to raise it high enough that boats could pass underneath. A few were designed as drawbridges or bascule bridges, which had sections that were able to raise and separate, leaving a passage through the bridge.

As Minneapolis and St. Paul developed, and as hundreds of other communities spread out across the Upper Mississippi River region, the construction of numerous roads and railroads required that thousands of bridges be built to meet the needs of the people.

More bridges were built across the Mississippi River, and that process continues today with new bridges being opened in Wabasha in 1988, La Crosse in 2004, Hastings in 2013 and Red Wing in 2020.

A traveler today, driving across the I-35W bridge in the Twin Cities, can easily look upstream and see the Stone Arch Bridge, the Third Avenue Bridge and the Hennepin Avenue Bridge, each distinct in style and form. What is hard to imagine is a time when they, and the many other bridges across the Mississippi River and its countless tributaries, did not exist. The river would have been a dangerous and overwhelming obstacle, a huge barrier, a powerful opponent that today is a scenic view captured from the crests of the bridges that span the Great River.

Chapter 1

TWIN CITIES

A Bridge Gone Down

It was rush hour on a Wednesday—just after 6:00 p.m. on August 1, 2007—on the I-35W bridge over the Mississippi River near the University of Minnesota in Minneapolis. Officially known as Bridge 9340, the bridge, which handled 140,000 vehicles per day, was scheduled for some repair work, so heavy construction equipment and materials were loaded onto the bridge.

Suddenly, the bridge gave way, with the central span falling into the river. Cars and trucks, concrete and steel, plunged into the waters of the Mississippi.

According to the National Transportation Safety Board in an accident report, the bridge "experienced a catastrophic failure in the main span of the deck truss. As a result, 1,000 feet of the deck truss collapsed, with about 456 feet of the main span falling 108 feet into the 15-foot deep river. A total of 111 vehicles were on the portion of the bridge that collapsed. Of these, 17 were recovered from the water. As a result of the bridge collapse, 13 people died, and 145 people were injured."

On the Scene

On the day the I-35W bridge collapsed, Stacy Bengs was a photojournalism student at the University of Minnesota. She lived in an apartment four blocks from the bridge. Around dinnertime, she and her roommates heard a noise, but with all the recent construction in the area, they ignored it.

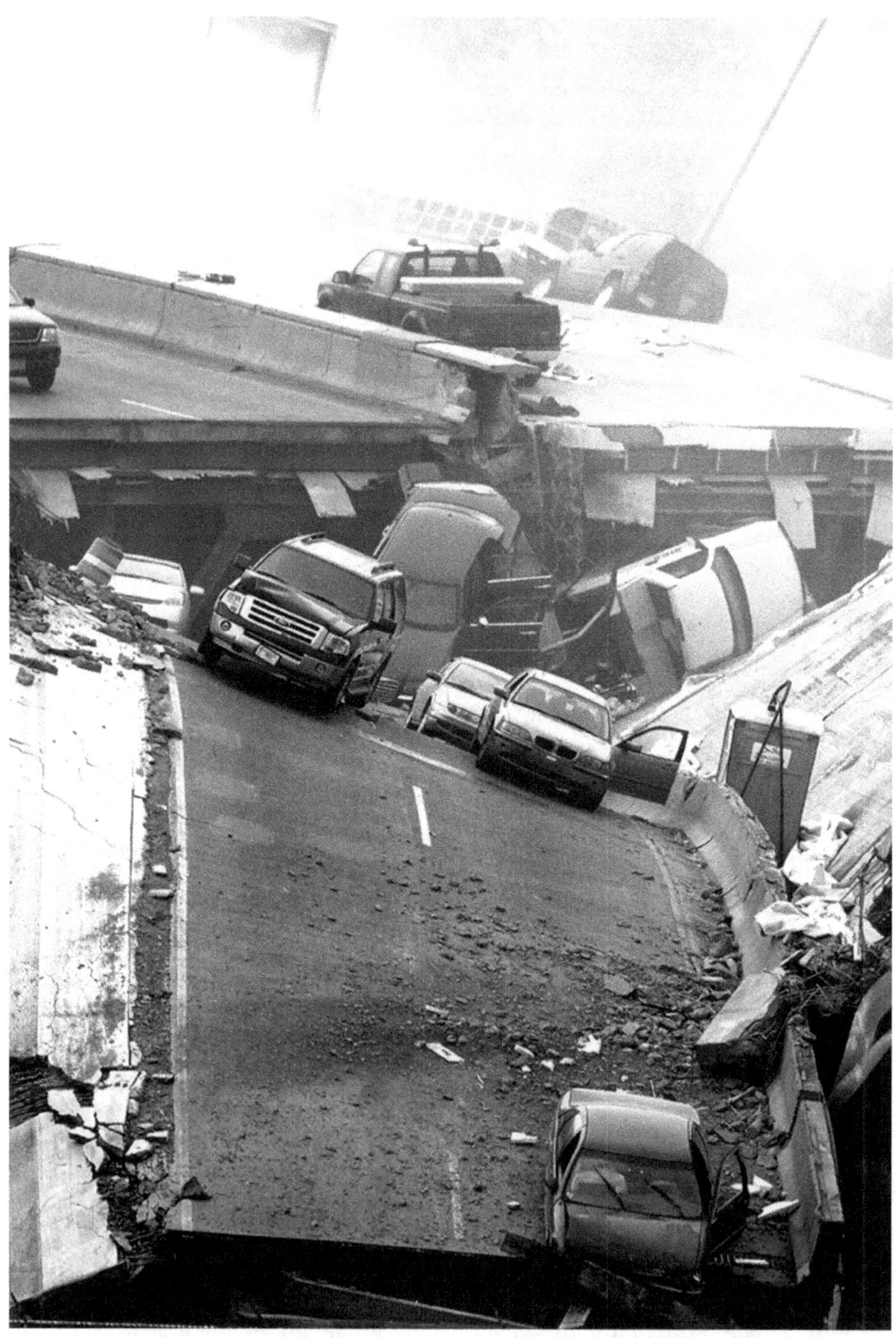

The I-35W bridge gave way shortly after 6:00 p.m. on Wednesday, August 1, 2007. *Photo by Stacy Bengs.*

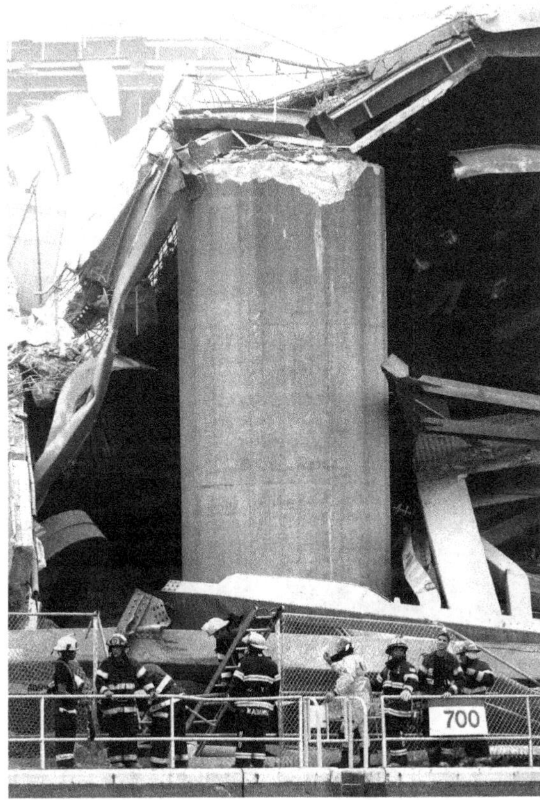

Left: Firefighters gather near the wreckage of the I-35W bridge. *Photo by Stacy Bengs.*

Below: A helicopter hovers over what was the steel-arched I-35W bridge in Minneapolis. The bridge rose 64 feet above the Mississippi River and stretched 1,900 feet across the water. *Photo by Stacy Bengs.*

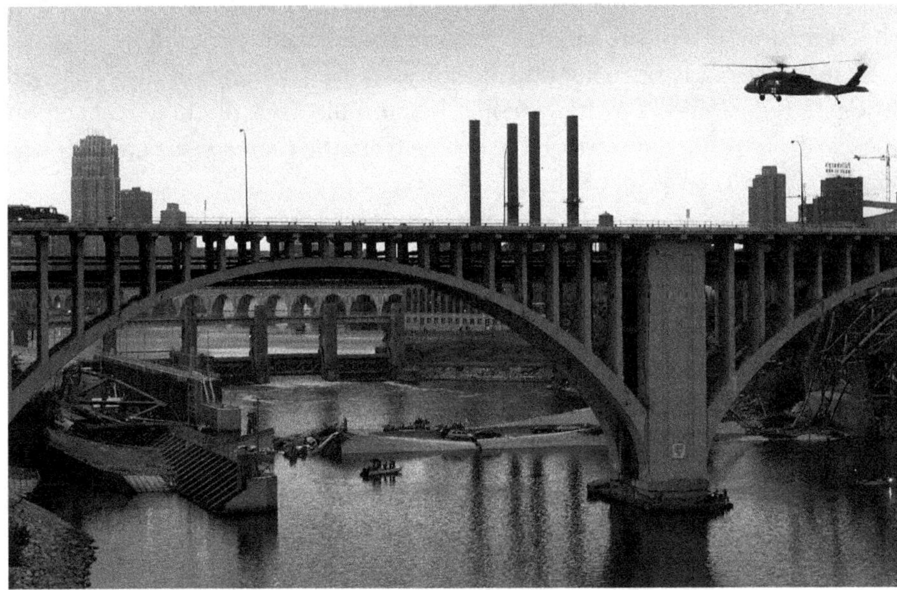

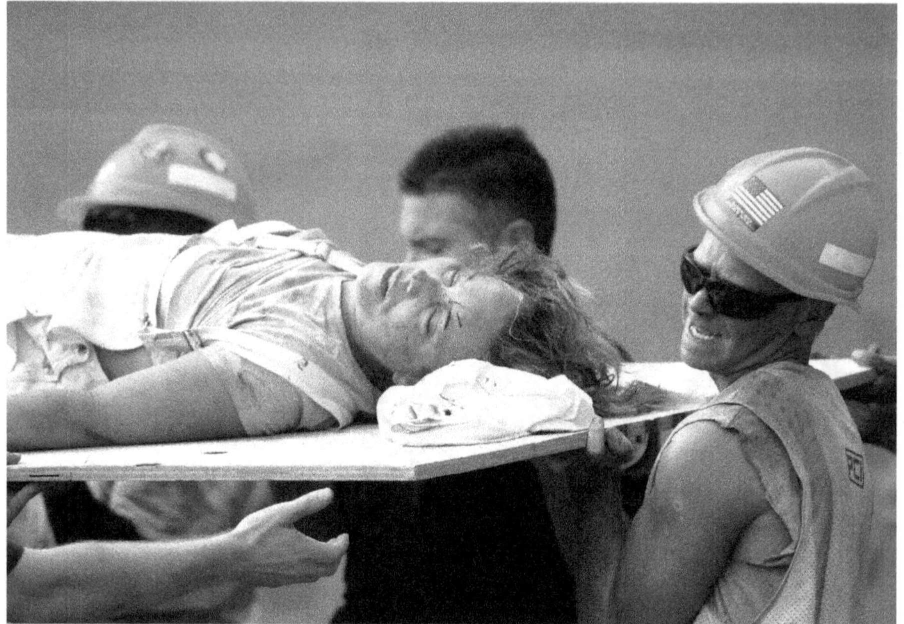

Construction workers use a plywood board to carry a woman to safety after the I-35W bridge collapsed into the Mississippi River on August 1, 2007. *Photo by Stacy Bengs.*

Then Bengs's phone rang. The caller told her that the I-35W bridge had fallen into the Mississippi River. Bengs grabbed her camera and headed in that direction, where she ran into another student photographer.

"He and I made our way down until we were standing on the collapsed bridge," Bengs said. "We saw people being pulled out of the wreckage on pieces of plywood that were on the bridge from the road construction. It was kind of surreal to see all of that."

As one of the first people to arrive, Bengs was able to walk right into the middle of the scene. Soon after, officials put up warning tape and moved Bengs and the others who had gathered there farther away. She stayed nearby for four hours, moving around and shooting photos the whole time. Then she went to the university newspaper office.

She and other photographers were putting their photos online when they received a message from the Associated Press in Washington, D.C., asking them to post photos on the AP wire. It was an energizing time for a group of student journalists.

Fifteen years later, Bengs is still a little stunned when she remembers that August evening when she was frontline to a worldwide news event.

"You don't forget it," she said. "I made some split-second decisions, and I'm glad I made the decisions I did. I just went with my instincts. You are a journalist, so you go."

Now, as a married mother of three children, she said her decisions might be different, but on that evening, her knowledge of the area, of a shortcut down the hill to the edge of the river, put her in position to get firsthand photos of the disaster.

The I-35W bridge supported eight lanes of traffic, four in each direction. Two lanes on each side were closed in preparation of moving on the construction materials and equipment for a scheduled concrete pour at 7:00 p.m. The materials were in place by 2:30 p.m., and when the bridge collapsed, twenty-five of the vehicles that fell were either construction vehicles or vehicles owned by construction workers.

A caller on 911 notified the Minnesota State Patrol about the bridge collapse at 6:05 p.m., and dispatchers sent out calls to Minneapolis fire and

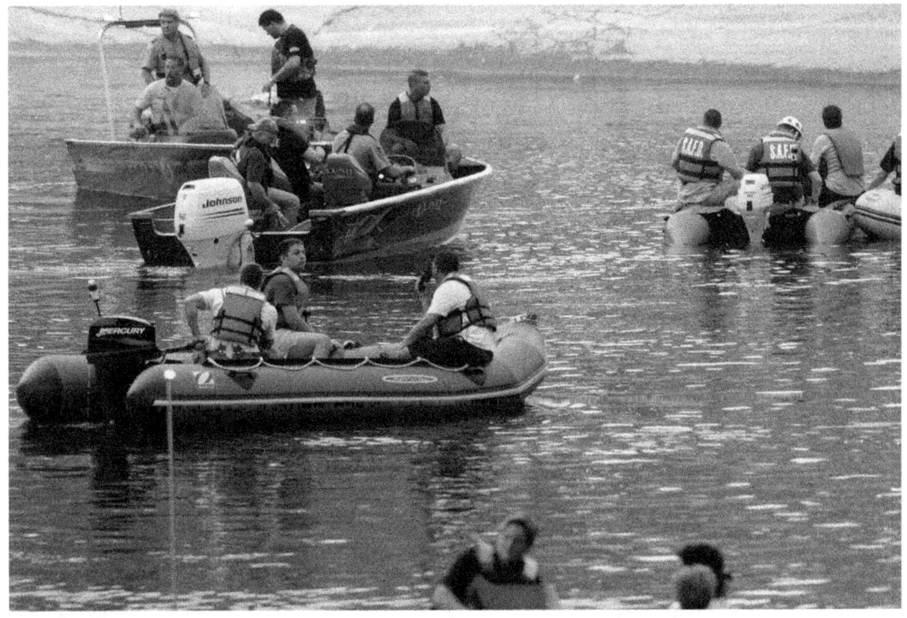

First responders scour the river for survivors of the I-35W bridge collapse near the University of Minnesota in Minneapolis. *Photo by Stacy Bengs.*

police departments. At 6:08 p.m., Minneapolis 911 made a distress call requesting all available emergency responders.

"The Minneapolis police captain responsible for the on-scene investigation estimated that 100 citizens assisted in the total rescue effort," the NTSB reported. "These people included construction workers who had just left or arrived for shift change, passersby, a group of medical personnel who were in training at the nearby Red Cross building, and a number of University of Minnesota students and staff. He said that 30–40 of these individuals went into the river to pull drivers and construction workers to safety."

Ambulances, fire engines and other public safety vehicles arrived, and by 6:25 p.m., the sheriff's office had established a river incident command site near the University of Minnesota River Flats area. Within the hour, twelve other agencies responded with twenty-eight watercraft to participate in the river rescue operations. This remained active until 7:27 p.m., when the commander changed the water operations from rescue to recovery, according to the NTSB accident report.

The Aftermath

In the hours and days that followed, officials confirmed that 190 people were on or near the bridge at the moment of the disaster. Of those, 13 were killed, 34 received serious injuries, 111 received minor injuries and 32 were not injured or their status was unknown. Medical records show that 145 people were transported to twelve area hospitals, medical centers and clinics.

With one of the major bridges in Minneapolis down, fast action was needed to replace it. Within three days, Congress had authorized $250 million for replacement funds, and the Minnesota legislature set up a Joint Committee to Investigate the Bridge Collapse. This Joint Committee, in its report, noted, "When a bridge collapses, so does public faith in government. It is therefore essential that the role of government in maintaining and replacing our infrastructure be subject to the most rigorous and objective scrutiny, not to ascribe blame but to proscribe future disasters."

The Joint Committee investigation went on for several months and ended up with recommendations that the Minnesota Department of Transportation (MnDOT) as well as the Minnesota legislature could make to improve their policies in relation to bridges.

The National Transportation Safety Board conducted an examination, not of policies but of the wreckage of the bridge, and determined that "the probable cause of the collapse of the I-35W bridge in Minneapolis, Minnesota, was the inadequate load capacity, due to a design error by Sverdrup & Parcel and Associates, Inc. of the gusset plates at the U10 nodes, which failed under a combination of (1) substantial increases in the weight of the bridge, which resulted from previous bridge modifications, and (2) the traffic and concentrated construction loads on the bridge on the day of the collapse."

The gusset plates held major beams of the bridge together, and the investigation revealed they were half as thick as they should have been. Sverdrup & Parcel and Associates, Inc. of St. Louis, Missouri, designed the bridge in the early 1960s, and work began on some of the piers in 1964. Hurcon, Inc. built the bridge, and it opened to traffic in 1967. It was inspected every two years by the Minnesota Department of Transportation until 1993 and then annually after that.

Following the incident, concern for other bridges was high, both among officials and the public. Funding to increase inspections and infrastructure improvements became a prominent issue and led to many discussions, including one in the 2008 state legislature regarding a proposal to raise the gas tax. The bill passed both houses, but then-governor Tim Pawlenty vetoed it, and the legislature passed an override of the veto. It had become a

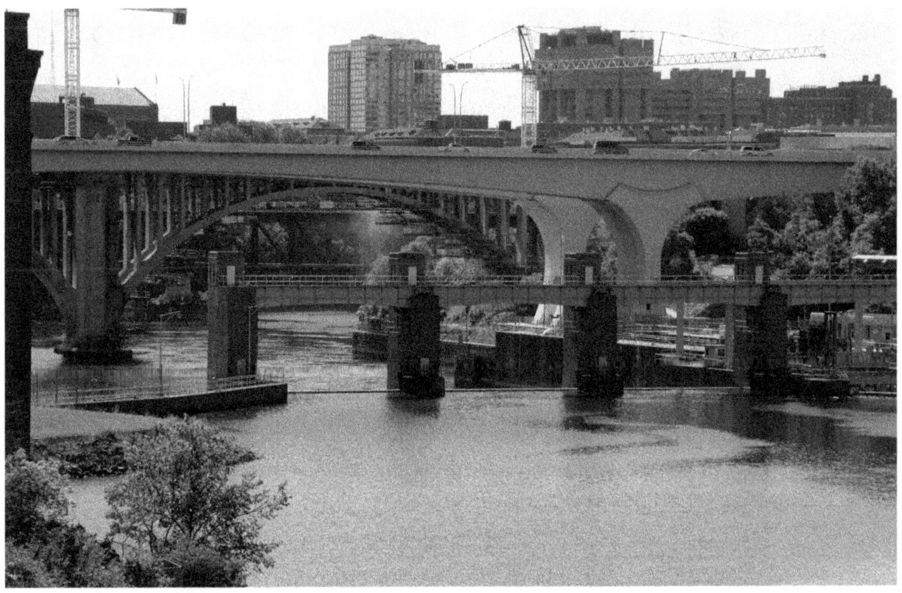

Several cars and trucks make a midday crossing of the new I-35W bridge on July 30, 2021. *Photo by Steve Gardiner.*

difficult topic, but the issue of bridge and infrastructure safety and funding had grown into an important part of public discourse.

On September 19, 2007, MnDOT announced that Flatiron Constructors and Manson Construction Co. would rebuild the bridge for $234 million. The new bridge was built, and it was opened to traffic on September 18, 2008.

During the year that the bridge was down, a major transportation route in the Twin Cities was missing, and thousands of people had to restructure their daily routines. Each time they took a detour, they were reminded of the tragedy and of the disruption in their lives.

"Bridges are about not having to deal with rivers," wrote John O. Anfinson in *The City, the River, the Bridge*. "By crossing over a river on a bridge, people do not have to think about how far down it is, how steep the banks are, how fast the water is flowing, or how deep it is. They do not have to consider how clean or dirty it might be, or whether it is fit for aquatic or human life. The Great River entered a person's life for only seconds when crossing the old I-35W bridge, if they were aware of it at all. Only when the bridge fell into the river did these aspects become relevant."

Concern for Safety

That fall caused many reactions regarding bridge safety. MnDOT now requires that bridges be inspected every other year.

"We inspect half of them one year, and half of them the next year," said Gary Lovelace, district structures engineer for MnDOT District 6, in an article in the April 17, 2021 issue of the *Red Wing Republican Eagle*. "We want to make sure that the bridges are maintained in a safe manner, and that the public can know that things are safe for them to travel across the bridge."

Lovelace is in charge of a team of six inspectors and three teams of maintenance crews. If the inspectors find minor problems, one of the maintenance teams goes out and fixes the problem. If a larger problem, what Lovelace calls a "critical find," is encountered, he and his team may have to shut down the bridge and bring in a construction crew to complete the repairs.

Safety starts with constructing a solid bridge from the beginning. That means meeting all the current construction codes and design criteria and having all the plans reviewed by engineers for accuracy.

"Bridge construction experts will look at the plans to minimize the number of issues encountered during construction," Lovelace explained. "They want to make sure that the bridge is supported on a good foundation. From the

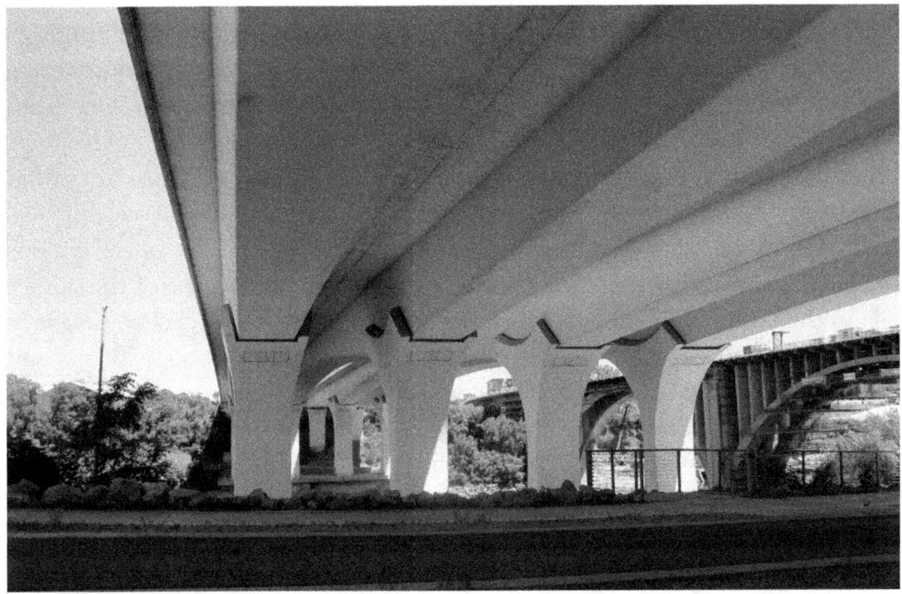

The substructure of the new I-35W bridge provides a solid base for thousands of vehicles every day. *Photo by Steve Gardiner.*

foundation, they build up the substructure which is the piers and abutments. Then they have the superstructure which could be beams, girders, and fancier things like suspension type bridges. Then you put the deck on the bridge which is what transports the traffic across whatever element you are trying to bridge."

Lovelace said that bridge designers also look at all the factors around the site of the bridge. For example, when MnDOT was planning the Eisenhower Bridge of Valor in Red Wing, they had to consider the length of the span across the Mississippi River and the railroad tracks, the height above the water to allow tows and barges to pass underneath and the width to allow it to pass through the space between existing buildings and the bluff.

"All of those things were taken into account in that situation," Lovelace said. "We look at the cost, based on the design and the materials that are selected."

One other safety factor built into the design is what Lovelace called "redundancy."

"That is the ability of the structure to carry the load through multiple paths," he said. "You don't want to have just one beam. You want to have several beams that can carry the load, so if one has a problem, the other ones will support the load."

Most bridges on Minnesota roads are not as complex as the Eisenhower Bridge. They span shorter distances and are made of prestressed concrete beams. "Prestressed concrete beams are cast in a factory," Lovelace said. "There are steel cables that are embedded in the concrete. They are tensioned and then the concrete is poured, and that helps create strength in that beam. They carry the load really well. They have a long service life."

As might be expected, the weather in Minnesota can cause serious problems for those people in charge of bridges. "That's because of the salt we use in the winter time and also because of the freeze-thaw cycle," Lovelace said. "If you get cracks in the concrete, which you do, water with the salt gets down into the concrete and that will corrode the steel. In the Red Wing bridge, we used stainless steel, because that is resistant to corrosion."

Because Minnesota and Wisconsin share a border along the Mississippi River, they need to work together to maintain safe bridges between the two states.

"We have cooperative agreements with Wisconsin on all the bridges on the border," Lovelace said. "We have a meeting with them every year and talk over issues along the border between the two states. We cooperate with them to make decisions on who is going to do the work."

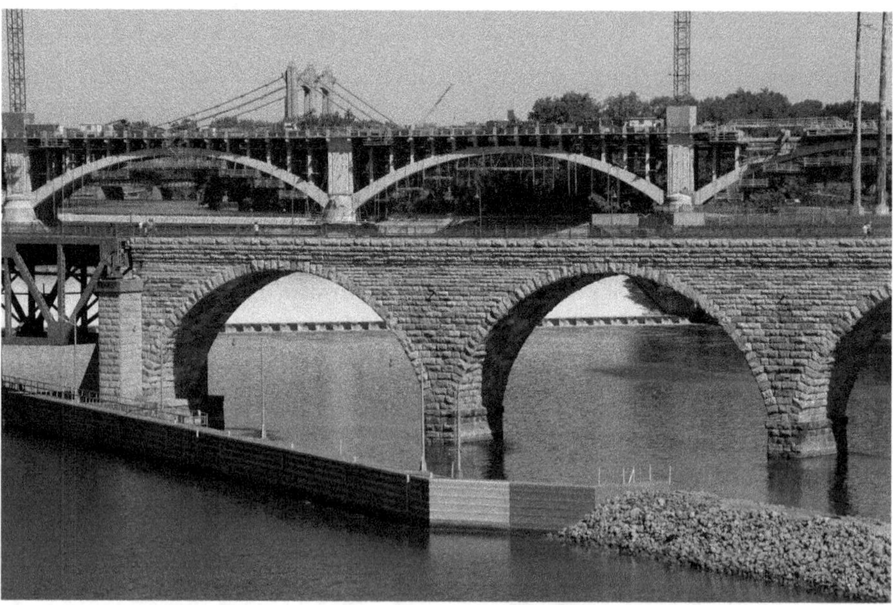

This view shows the arches of the Stone Arch Bridge and the Third Avenue Bridge, as well as the suspension towers and cables of the Hennepin Avenue Bridge. *Photo by Steve Gardiner.*

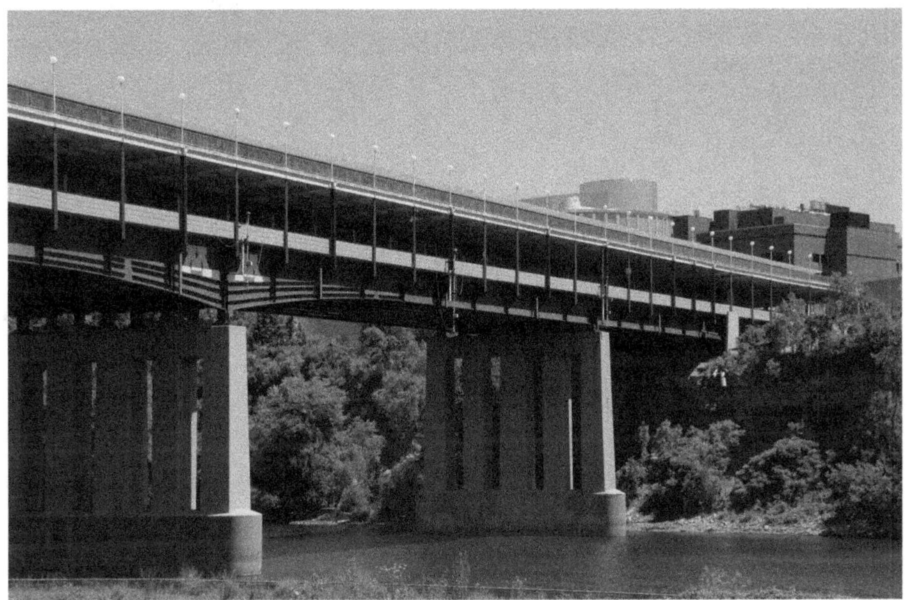

The Washington Avenue Bridge is a versatile structure carrying bikes and pedestrians on the upper level and the Metro Green Line light rail and two lanes of traffic, one in each direction, on the lower level. *Photo by Steve Gardiner.*

In addition to considering materials and structural elements of a bridge, designers must also consider other factors.

"You have to be sensitive to the natural environment such as wetlands or any historic site or cultural site," he said. "We also get input from the community, the stakeholders, about what they like and what they don't like."

New Policies and Procedures

When the I-35W bridge in Minneapolis collapsed in 2007, Steve Murphy was the state senator for the district that included Goodhue County, Wabasha County and part of Winona County. He was first elected in 1992. By 2007, he was the chairman of the Transportation Committee, and he visited the accident site.

"It really bothered me standing there looking down," Murphy told the *Red Wing Republican Eagle*. "I could see the rescue workers, although by that time, it was recovery. That is something you never forget."

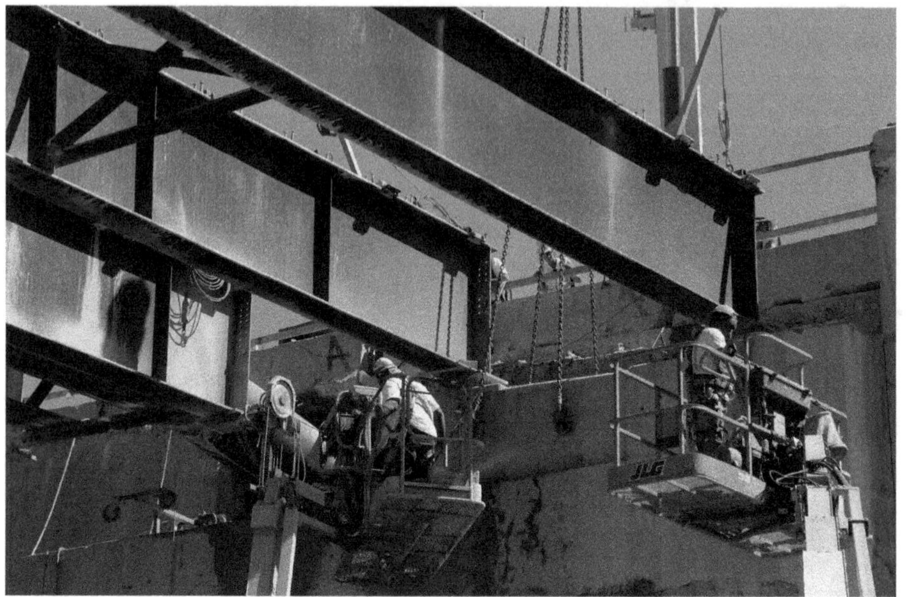

Bridge construction and repair is a challenging and difficult process. In this photo, the Third Avenue Bridge in Minneapolis is shown on June 14, 2021, midway through a multiyear renovation project. *Photo by Steve Gardiner.*

After the bridge collapse, Murphy became the chairman of the House-Senate Committee that investigated the incident.

"Minnesota was held up as the gold standard nationwide for bridges," he said. "Then we had this bridge collapse. Simple math says that bridge should have still been standing there, but it wasn't anymore."

The committee's investigation agreed with the report by the National Transportation Safety Board that the primary cause of the collapse was the undersized gusset plate, but Murphy said his committee also determined that bridge inspections were lacking in some areas.

"We weren't measuring rust pack," Murphy said. "You get rust and pretty soon it starts swelling and then it pops bolts out of place. Then the gusset plate sheared. It was a combination of things that led to the tragic accident."

In the aftermath, Murphy was a key player in helping bring about legislation to require more inspections of bridges and replacement of any bridges determined to be fracture critical, meaning if one component of a bridge failed, the entire bridge would be unsafe or collapse. The law required all those updates to be completed by 2020, one reason for the updates or replacements of several bridges in the area.

That legislation also added a gas tax that could be used to pay for the replacement bridges as well as road repair and maintenance, according to Murphy.

"We wanted to guarantee to the people of the state of Minnesota that no other families would have to go through what happened to those people who died or were injured on the bridge that day," he said.

Chapter 2

HASTINGS

A Bridge with Identity

Many cities around the world identify themselves with a local bridge. New York prides itself on the Brooklyn Bridge. San Francisco adores the Golden Gate Bridge. Venice loves the Rialto Bridge. London reveres the Tower Bridge.

Closer to home, bridges provide a local identity as well. One of the most unique bridges ever built in Southeast Minnesota was the Spiral Bridge, Hastings's first permanent bridge across the Mississippi River.

It happened because in the 1890s, Hastings was a growing town. Businesses lined both sides of Second Street, and river traffic was increasing. When steamboats stopped at the levee, they were a short distance from the stores, a good boost to the local economy.

Getting across the river was more difficult then. A rope ferry made it possible, but with more people, wagons and boats arriving, the people of Hastings needed a better way to cross the Mississippi. They needed a bridge.

There was one problem. The bridge needed to be high enough to allow the steamboats to pass under. With that much height, the ramp down on the Hastings side would extend far into the town, well past the business center on Second Street. No one wanted the wagons and horses bypassing downtown.

The solution came in the form of a bridge with a spiral on the southern end. After crossing the river, the bridge would circle north and pigtail around under itself, depositing travelers on Second Street. The bridge would eliminate the rope ferry and give Hastings residents better access to the road

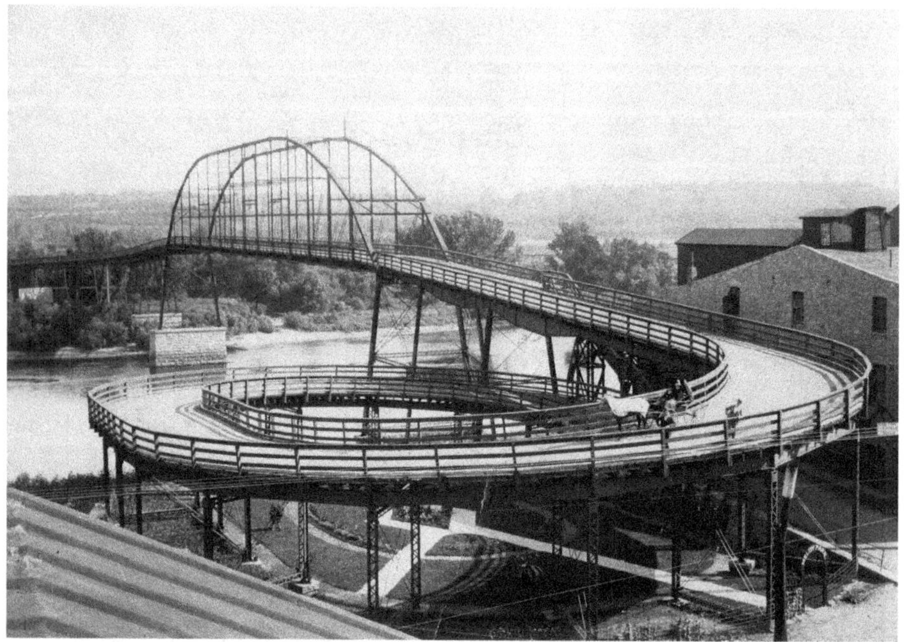

The Spiral Bridge was a Hastings landmark for fifty-six years. *Courtesy of Dakota County Historical Society.*

north, a dirt passage called the St. Paul–Hastings Wagon Road. It was still gravel when it was renamed U.S. Highway 61 in 1926.

Constructed at a cost of $39,050 in 1895 by the Wisconsin Bridge and Iron Company and supervised by Oscar Claussen, who is often given credit for the unique design, the spiral was on the north end of Sibley Street where the American Legion Post 47 now stands. The bridge was 1,987 feet long and 14 feet wide, with a 4½-foot sidewalk on the east side. The main channel span was 380 feet long and featured a Baltimore through truss with a curved top chord.

When automobiles arrived in the area, they started using the Spiral Bridge, even though it was designed for wagons, horses and pedestrians. The increased wear on the bridge raised concerns about its safety. Several attempts were made to repair the bridge, but eventually, officials determined that it needed to be replaced, although not everyone agreed.

"The sad tale of the bridge's demise spanned many years and ended in a pocket veto by Governor Luther Youngdahl in 1951. The Dakota County Historical Society retained attorney David Grannis, Jr., who presented a resolution to the State, asking to take title and preserve the approach. A

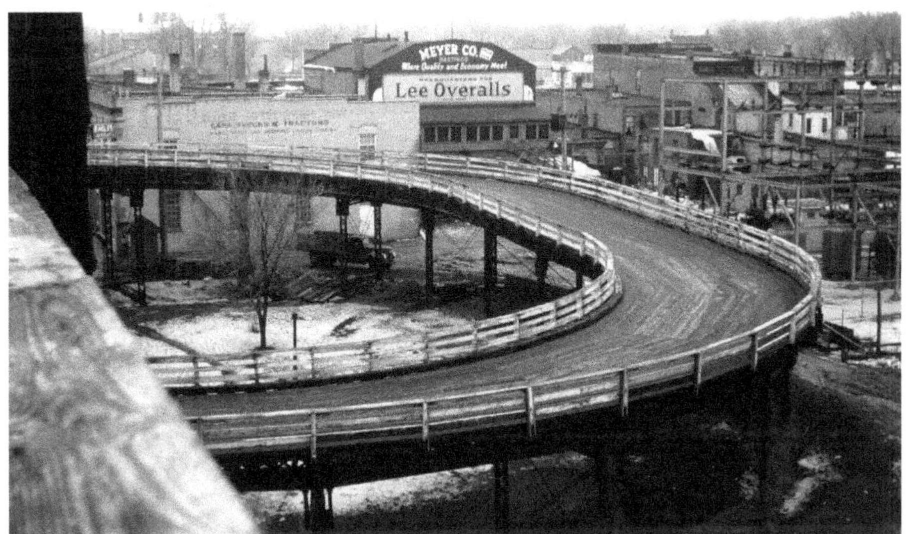

The Spiral Bridge was designed for wagon and horse traffic and was only fourteen feet wide. *Courtesy of Dakota County Historical Society.*

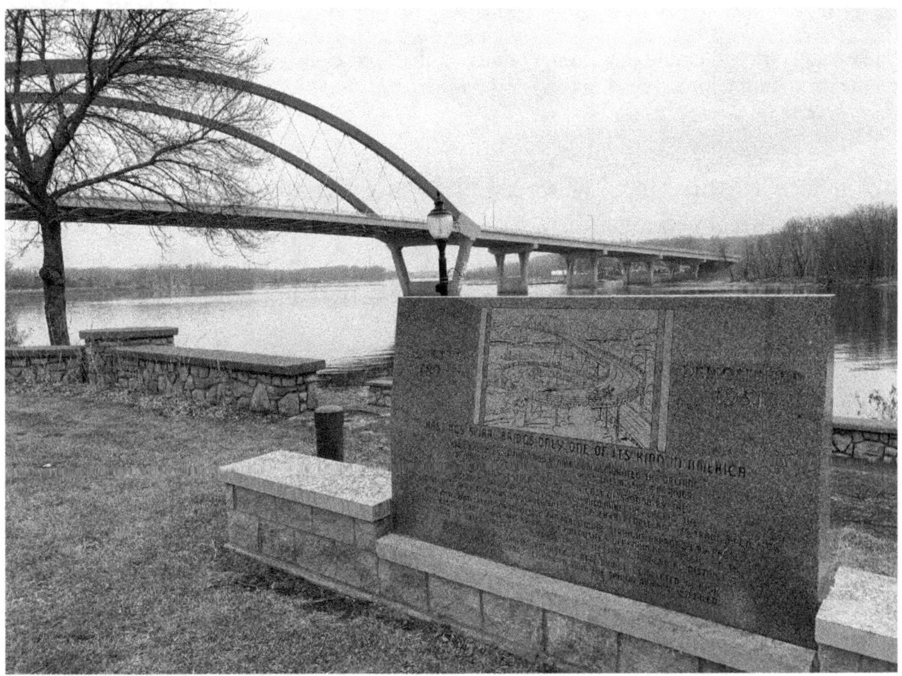

This monument near the location of the south abutment of the Spiral Bridge along the riverwalk in Hastings commemorates the Spiral Bridge as the "only one of its kind in America." *Photo by Steve Gardiner.*

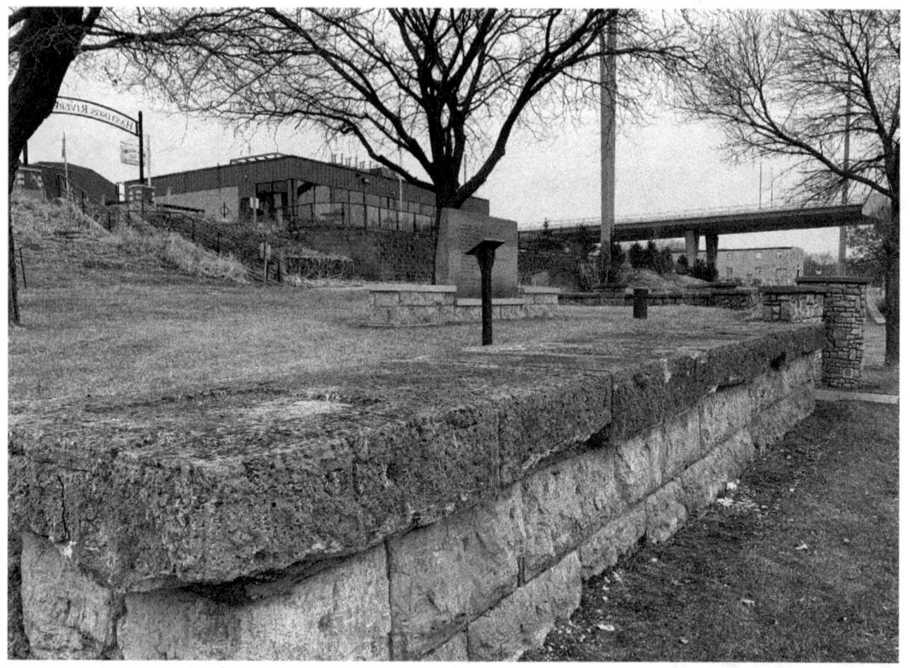

This stonework is the only remaining footing of the Spiral Bridge. The indention in the top of the stone in the foreground marks where one of the metal legs of the bridge was placed. *Photo by Steve Gardiner.*

bill nearly to this effect was passed by the Senate and House, but was vetoed by the governor after a lobbying effort to do so by several Hastings businessmen at the Capitol. Dakota County's famous, if not dizzying, landmark was razed in 1951," according to the Dakota County Historical Society (DCHS) website.

The Spiral Bridge had lasted fifty-six years. After the veto, the Spiral Bridge was dismantled and hauled away, but a replica of the bridge is on display at the Little Log House Pioneer Village, about ten miles south of Hastings just a short distance east of Highway 61 on 220 Street East.

Hastings High Bridge

In many ways, it is amazing that the Spiral Bridge lasted until 1951, but at that point, in spite of the protests of local citizens, the bridge faded into history as the Hastings High Bridge replaced it at a cost of $356,000.

As the High Bridge went into place, it gave off a majestic feel. The channel span of 514 feet and the two additional center spans featured a continuous arch-shaped Warren through truss. The full length, 1,832 feet, of the bridge carried Highway 61, also known as the Great River Road, across the Mississippi River and Second Street. Thus, it passes over the downtown area, a concern that led to the unique design of the Spiral Bridge.

By the 1990s and early 2000s, the Twin Cities were expanding, and Hastings had reached a point where it was considered part of the Minneapolis/St. Paul metro area and traffic on the bridge had increased. The bridge was the busiest two-lane highway bridge in the state, seeing more than thirty-two thousand vehicles per day, according to the U.S. Department of Transportation.

With the collapse of the I-35W bridge in Minneapolis in 2007, extensive inspections of all bridges in the state were conducted, and the Hastings High Bridge presented some problems. The inspection revealed a lot of rust and a shift in the structure that could shear bolts.

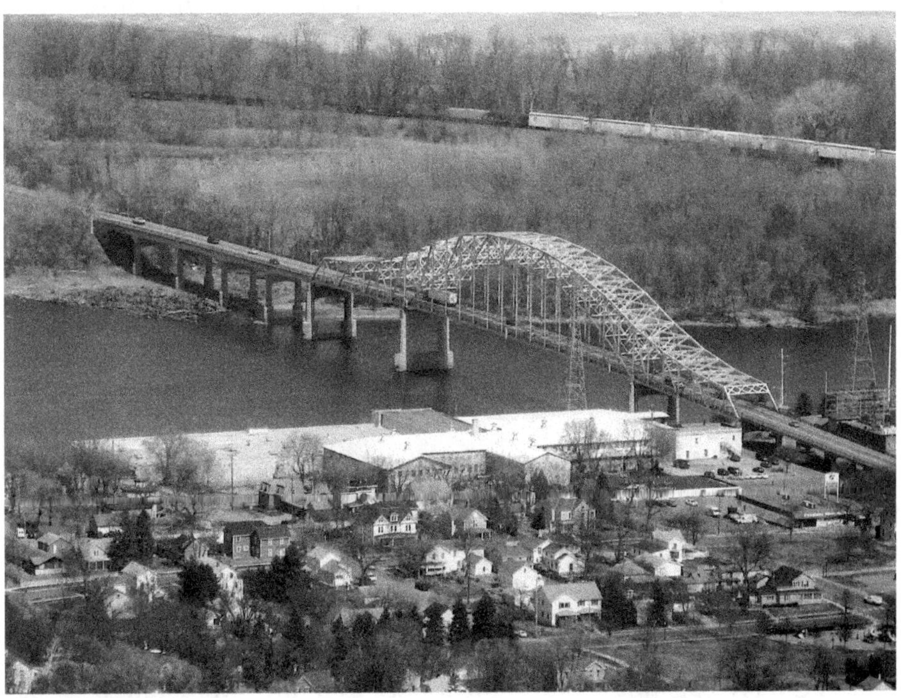

The Hastings High Bridge, a steel through truss bridge, was built in 1951 to replace the aging Spiral Bridge. The High Bridge lasted until 2013, when the current bridge was opened. This photo shows the High Bridge circa 1990. *Courtesy of Dakota County Historical Society*.

The Hastings High Bridge was designed by Sverdrup & Parcel, the same company that designed the I-35W bridge, according to an August 8, 2007 article in the *Hastings Star Gazette*.

"It's one of the things we generally put our faith in, the safety of our bridges and roads," Hastings City Council member Danna Elling Schultz said in the article.

But the incident with the I-35W bridge destroyed much of that faith and increased everyone's concern. The *Star Gazette* reported that city officials had been calling for replacement of the bridge for several years and that pressure to rebuild it grew stronger.

In 2008, the Minnesota Department of Transportation made some repairs to extend the life of the bridge. In order to reduce the load on the bridge, MnDOT restricted it to one lane of traffic. Traffic lights allowed cars to take turns crossing the bridge, causing extensive delays.

But the repairs were only temporary. The High Bridge was scheduled to be torn down in 2019, but with heightened safety concerns following the collapse of the I-35W bridge, MnDOT decided to shorten that timeline, and construction of a new bridge began in 2010. The new arch bridge was finished in 2013, and the High Bridge was dismantled.

HASTINGS BRIDGE

The importance of a bridge as part of a community's identity was clear to Paul Hicks, who was mayor of Hastings from 2006 to 2014.

"True to Hastings' distinctive local character, the new Hastings Bridge stands out from the skyline with its terra cotta–colored arches," wrote Hicks in the March 13, 2013 issue of *MINNPOST*. "It is the longest free-standing arch rib in North America."

MnDOT wanted a bridge that would require minimal maintenance for more than one hundred years, and they hired Lunda Construction Company, at a cost of $130 million, to replace the aging Hastings High Bridge. The plan called for not only a replacement of the bridge but also an upgrade to the civic amenities surrounding the bridge.

"Each investment that Minnesota makes to enhance its public transportation system is an investment back into our communities," Hicks noted. "The new bridge was designed with safety and innovation in mind and includes features that will benefit the community and visitors alike."

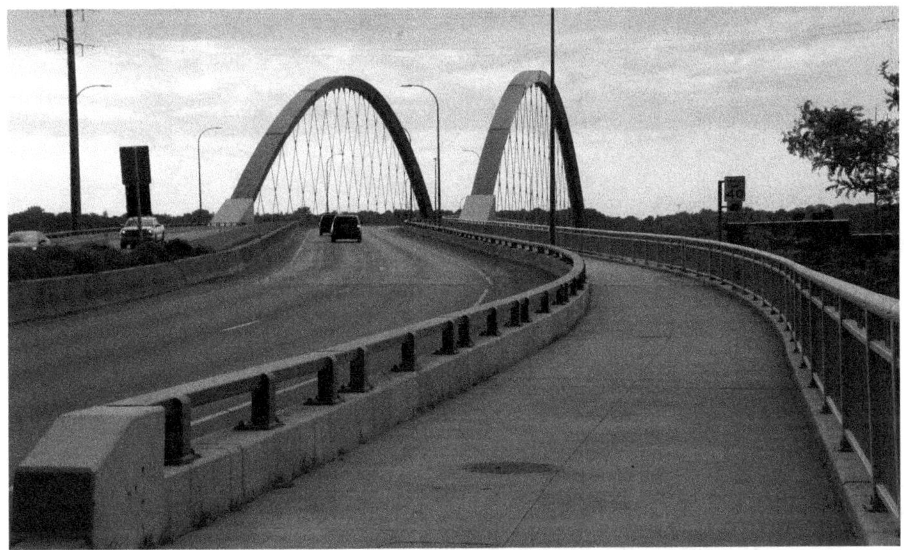

The Hastings Bridge carries two lanes of traffic in each direction across the Mississippi River and features a biking/walking lane. It is a tied-arch bridge, and the cables coming down from the arches support the main span of the bridge. *Photo by Steve Gardiner.*

Some of those improvements included the four lanes of traffic, a twelve-foot-wide pedestrian/bike path on the east side of the bridge, an anti-icing system for the bridge roadway, a public art display on the south abutment wall, a scenic overlook near Levee Park and additional parking under the bridge.

Construction of the 1,938-foot-long bridge with a 545-foot tied arch main span took three years and featured an event watched by thousands of onlookers when construction crews floated the main span of the bridge on the river and lifted it into place.

"Public infrastructure is vital to the economy's health," Hicks said. "We can grow state and regional jobs, move people, goods and services, and seek long-term economic benefits. The benefits from this new bridge will reach far beyond the immediate community."

The Hastings Bridge does not move but has two arches that support the bridge deck with cables from the arches to the deck, a system called tied-arch. The center span of the bridge is sixty-four feet above the water, high enough that even commercial river traffic can easily pass below.

The new bridge was constructed just upstream from the Hastings High Bridge. When the new bridge was complete, the High Bridge was removed and traffic was directed onto the new bridge.

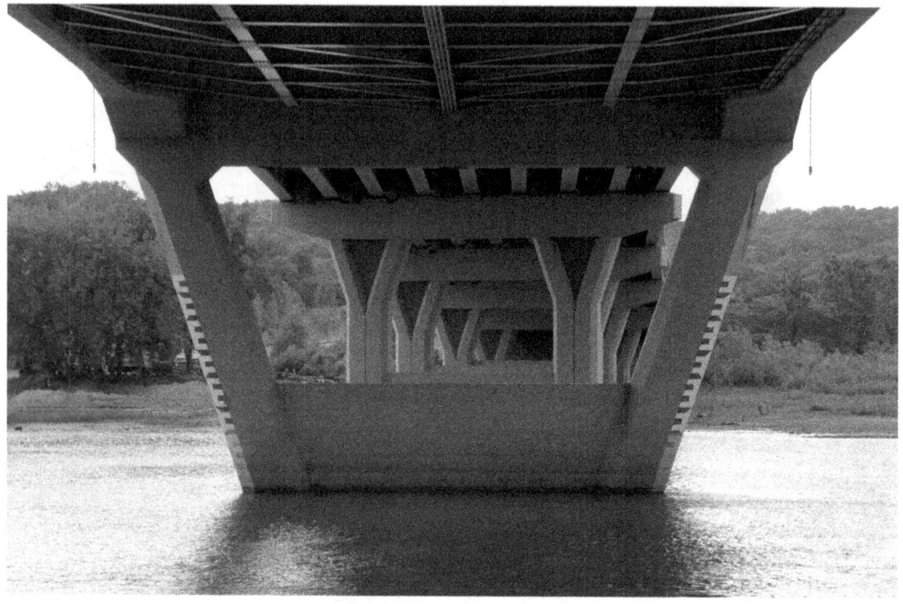

This photo shows the substructure of the Hastings Bridge. *Photo by Steve Gardiner.*

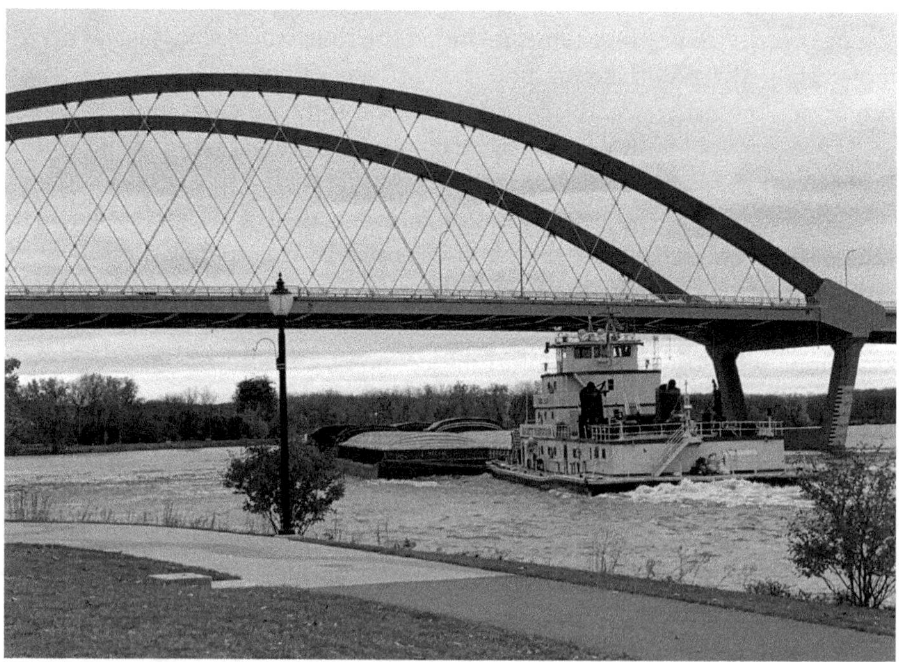

A tow with a fleet of barges passes beneath the Hastings Bridge on October 27, 2019. *Photo by Steve Gardiner.*

The Hastings Bridge provided a challenge for the footings because on the south side in Hastings, the bedrock is shallow, but on the north side, the main span foundation and the approach piers had to be driven in 180 feet, according to an article in the July/August 2013 issue of *Deep Foundations* magazine.

HASTINGS RAILROAD BRIDGE

The Hastings Railroad Bridge, however, does move up and down. There are four vertical-lift bridges on the Mississippi, and one of them is the railroad bridge near downtown Hastings. The bridge, used by the Canadian Pacific Railroad and the Amtrak Empire Builder, has a center section that lifts by moving up two vertical towers, one on each side. Warren through trusses support both the stationary and movable sections of the bridge, which was built in 1981 to cross a navigation channel slightly more than 300 feet wide. The length of the longest span is 324 feet with a total length of 1,755 feet.

The original bridge at this location was designed by engineer James Warren, the creator of the Warren truss used on many bridges throughout the region. It was a swing bridge that was built by the Minnesota and

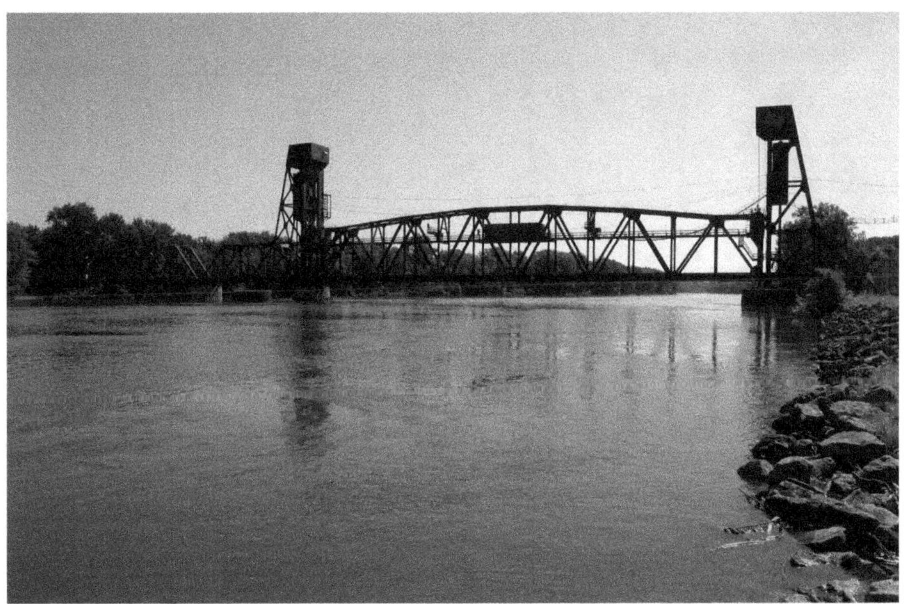

The vertical-lift railroad bridge at Hastings is seen here on June 27, 2018. It supports one track of the Canadian Pacific Railway and has a clearance of sixty feet when the lift span is raised. *Photo by Steve Gardiner.*

Pacific Railroad as part of a line from St. Paul to Winona. In late 1871, the Chicago, Milwaukee and St. Paul Railway bought the line, including the Hastings Railroad Bridge, and extended the line across the Mississippi River at La Crosse, Wisconsin, then to Milwaukee and eventually to Chicago, connecting a direct line between the Twin Cities and Chicago.

VERMILLION RIVER BRIDGE

Visitors to Vermillion Falls Park in Hastings can see both the 35-foot-high Vermillion Falls and Ardent Mills, the first operating mill in Minnesota, which originally used the river for power. In addition, visitors can use several walking trails, including one that crosses the Vermillion River Bridge, a girder bridge open only to pedestrians. Its longest span is 60 feet with a total length of 140 feet.

The bridge offers excellent views from eighty feet above the Vermillion River Gorge in both directions, but it is perhaps more famous for another highlight—it has become a popular place for couples to attach "locks of love" like those on the Pont des Arts bridge in Paris.

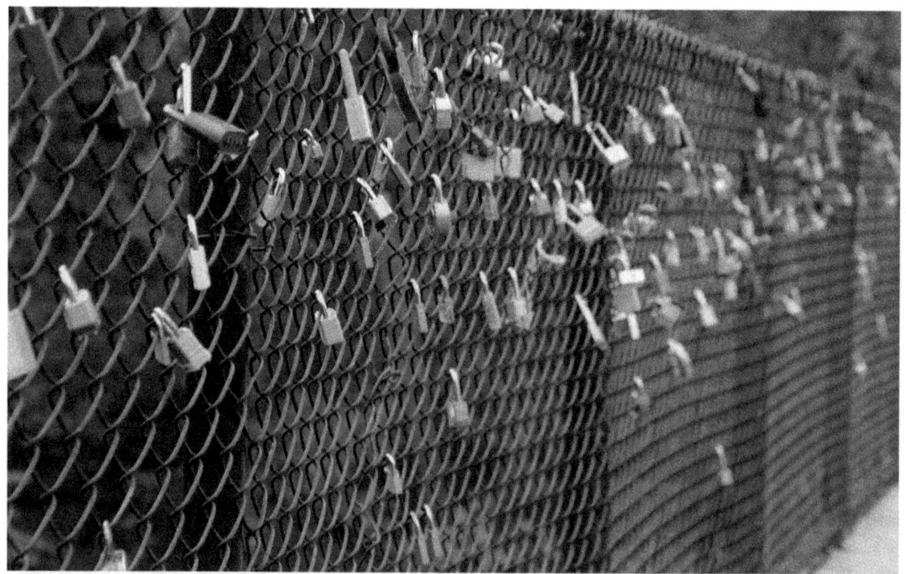

The Vermillion Falls Trail Bridge is a girder bridge on a walking trail over the Vermillion River in Hastings. The bridge has become a popular place for pedestrians visiting Vermillion Falls Park to leave locks of love. *Photo by Steve Gardiner.*

"It's not a program that we started," said Chris Jenkins, parks and recreation director for the City of Hastings, in the March 11, 2020 issue of the *Red Wing Republican Eagle.* "It is entirely just people who have gone out there and done it on their own. It's totally fine by us."

Jenkins noted that there could be one problem—if the locks become too heavy for the fence.

"Then we are going to have to go out and either move it so it is not there, or clip locks. I hope we don't have to do that."

POINT DOUGLAS DRAWBRIDGE

In 1805, Lieutenant Zebulon Pike was exploring the upper Mississippi River. He camped at what is now Prescott, Wisconsin, before continuing up the Mississippi to establish Fort Snelling at the confluence of the Mississippi and Minnesota Rivers. At Prescott, he noted that Point Douglas stretched into the Mississippi River and narrowed the distance across the river, thus making it a good place to command the river if needed, according to a September 9, 2020 article in the *Stanley Republican.*

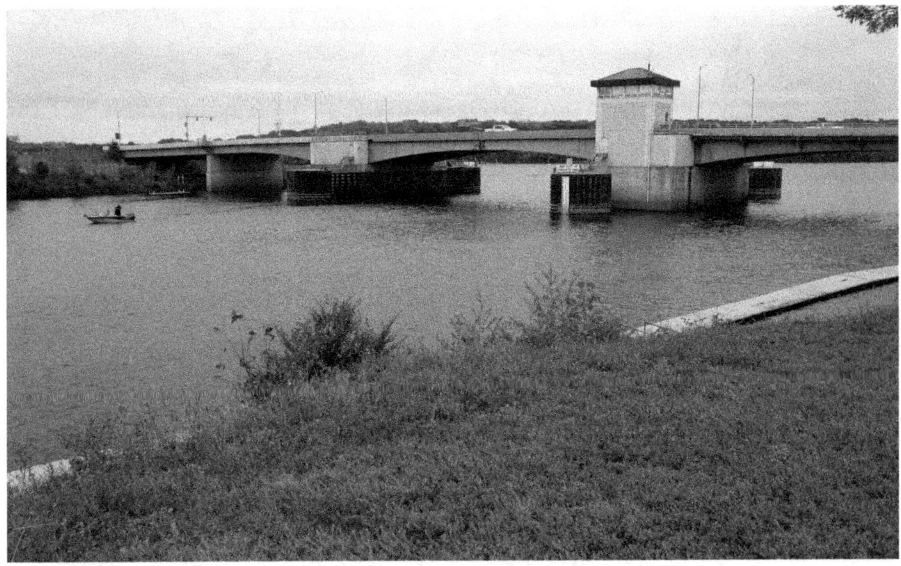

The Point Douglas Drawbridge, also called the Prescott Drawbridge, connects Point Douglas Park in Minnesota with Prescott, Wisconsin. It has two sections or bascules that separate at the point where the white pickup is crossing and lift up to allow boats to pass through. The deck of the bridge is a steel grate. *Photo by Steve Gardiner.*

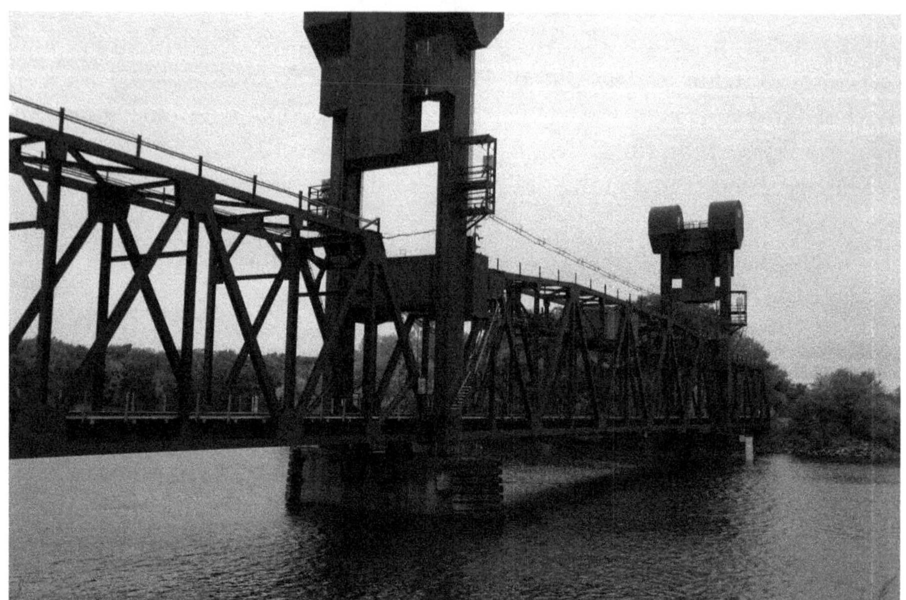

The BNSF Railroad St. Croix Bridge, shown from the Wisconsin side, is just downstream from the Point Douglas Drawbridge and spans the St. Croix River. Handling as many as forty trains per day, it is a heavy-duty steel truss bridge. Large counterweights help lift the center span when boat traffic needs to pass through. This bridge, built in 1984, replaced an earlier swing bridge constructed by the CB&Q Railroad. *Photo by Steve Gardiner.*

That same feature of Point Douglas made it a logical place to set up a rope ferry, which was replaced by an aerial lift bridge in 1923. The lift span was 174 feet long with approach spans of 172 and 192 feet. All three were through truss spans. The bridge served until 1990, when the current bridge was constructed in a year and a half by Lunda Construction of Black River Falls.

Officials studied several bridge designs and decided that a drawbridge would be the best plan. Hazelet and Erdahl, Inc. of Chicago designed the drawbridge, which cost $12 million to build. While some drawbridges use weights to counterbalance the section of the bridge that lifts upward, the Point Douglas Drawbridge, sometimes called the Prescott Drawbridge, is primarily raised by a large gear powered by hydraulics. The bridge, on U.S. Highway 10 across the St. Croix River, is a steel girder bridge. On the sections of the bridge that lift, the roadway surface is a steel grate.

Just downstream from the Point Douglas Drawbridge stands the BNSF Prescott Lift Bridge, built in 1984 to replace a swing bridge. It is currently used by the BNSF Railroad and has a main span of 250 feet.

WATERFORD HISTORIC BRIDGE

Located just off Canada Avenue near Waterford north of Northfield, the Waterford Historic Bridge crosses the Cannon River. It was constructed in 1909 by the Hennepin Bridge Company and listed in the National Register of Historic Places in 2010, about the same time it was closed to vehicle traffic and replaced by a concrete bridge just upstream. The concrete bridge gives easy access to good views of the Waterford Historic Bridge.

The 140-foot span is a Camelback through truss, which means the upper chord of the truss is polygonal with exactly five slopes. Not many bridges in Minnesota feature this type of truss.

Several times the bridge has shown signs of deterioration and erosion, but discussions of removing it were stopped by concerned citizens and organizations that raised money for rehabilitation. Funds from the National Trust for Historic Preservation and the Twin Cities Partners in Preservation helped with the work.

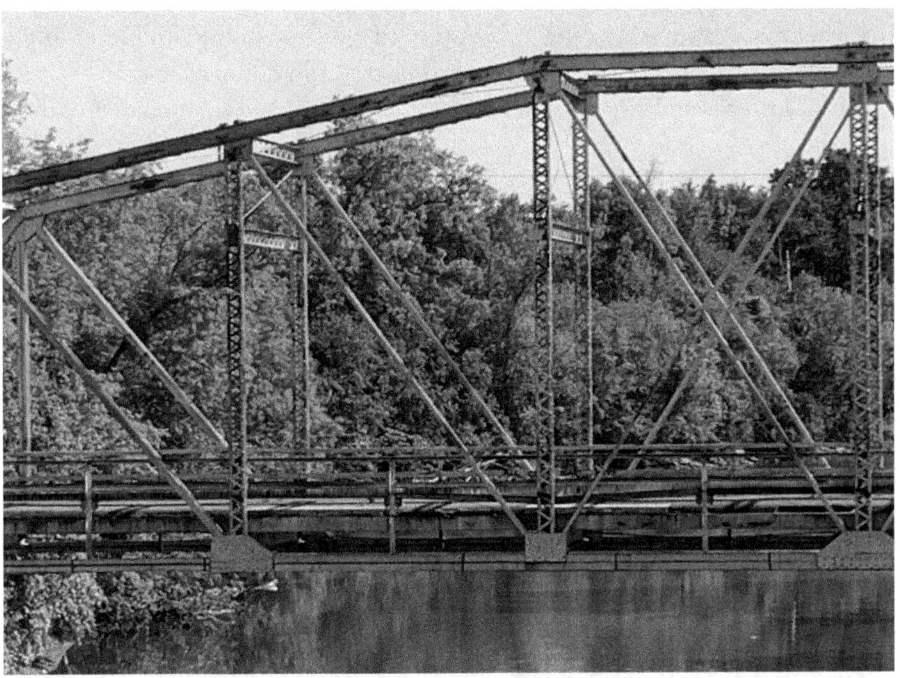

The Waterford Bridge is a classic example of a through truss bridge. *Photo by Steve Gardiner.*

Cannon Falls Third Street Bridge

The Third Street Bridge in Cannon Falls was completed in 1910 and rehabilitated in 2002 and 2021. It is owned by the City of Cannon Falls and was listed in the National Register of Historic Places in 1989.

The nomination form with the National Register of Historic Places notes, "The Third Street Bridge is a steel, single-span, riveted Pennsylvania through truss bridge. It carries Third Street north over the Cannon River. Its overall length is 184.3 feet, and its overall width is 17.7 feet."

The form specifies that the Third Street Bridge is eligible for inclusion in the National Register because it was built by A.Y. Bayne of Minneapolis and the Loweth and Wolff engineering firm of St. Paul and because it represents an unusual type of truss span.

"The Pennsylvania truss (often called a 'petit truss' in turn-of-the-century texts) has the distinctive aspects of subdivided panels and polygonal upper chord," the report states. "This type of truss could span a greater distance than the simpler Pratt and Warren trusses. As a bridge with riveted panel intersections, it represents the application of this technology to increasingly longer spans replacing the previous standard of pin connections."

The Third Street Bridge is still in use for traffic with a load limit of five tons.

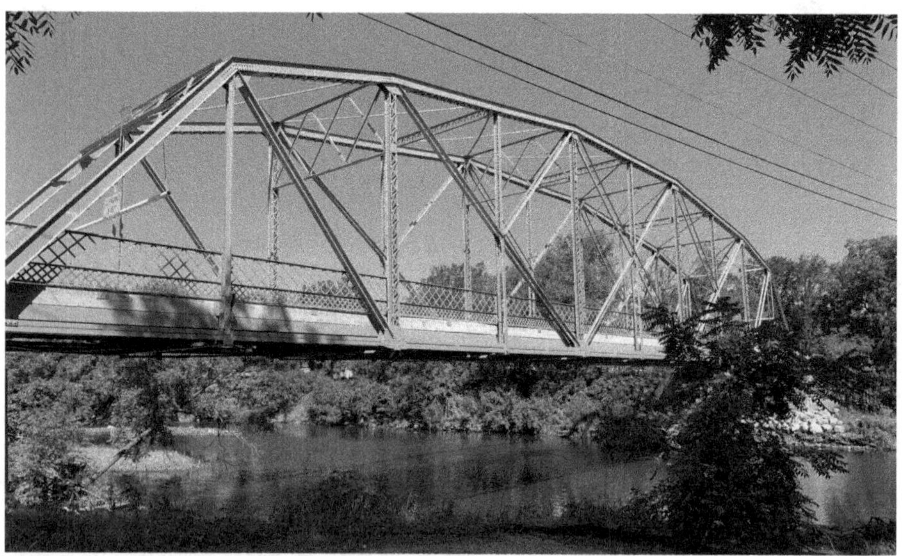

The Third Street Bridge in downtown Cannon Falls is a riveted Pennsylvania through truss bridge built in 1910. It is a steel single-span bridge that is 185 feet long across the Cannon River. *Photo by Steve Gardiner.*

Chapter 3

RED WING

A Bridge with Presidential Pride

The dedication of a bridge across the Mississippi River is a major milestone in the history of any community, and perhaps no dedication was bigger than the one that happened on October 18, 1960, in Red Wing.

The news that General Dwight D. Eisenhower, then serving as the thirty-fourth president of the United States, would be in town to cut the ribbon on the bridge had everyone talking. For months, Red Wing was astir not only with the excitement of having a new bridge but also with the anticipation of a presidential visit. Reaching the point of having Ike come to town had been an interesting adventure.

The Ferry

A century before Eisenhower appeared in Red Wing, there was a need to cross the Great River to connect Minnesota and Wisconsin. If early Red Wing residents wanted to visit Wisconsin, they had to board a small boat or skiff and find a way across the river, a difficult and sometimes dangerous prospect. However, when they realized that a better connection between the two states would mean increased business for Red Wing companies, they proposed a ferryboat between the two shores.

Frank Ives, commenting in the June 5, 1863 issue of the *Goodhue County Republican*, said, "The trade of the Trimbelle valley belongs to Red Wing, and we shall have it. No better investment can be made than to take stock in the ferry."

An October 20, 1863 article in the same paper noted that more than "three-fourths of the trade which now goes to Prescott will, if proper measures are taken to secure it, come to Red Wing, and our city will thus become the best market on the river between St. Paul and Dubuque."

Not long after, Captain Edward Speck started a service using an old flatboat with a paddle wheel on each side. The wheels were connected to a tramway on which two horses plodded all day long to power the wheels. The boat was steered by a long oar in the stern.

"The carrying capacity of the ferry was not large—about three teams—and the four-mile trip was a slow and tedious one," reported the *Daily Republican Eagle* on October 17, 1960. "Two round trips were made each day. The charge was one dollar a trip."

The Red Wing ferry took passengers out to the island, where they traveled a rough, often muddy road across the island to a second ferry across the narrower Wisconsin channel.

On March 5, 1866, the Red Wing council approved the purchase of 1,800 feet of cable for the ferry, and with a steam engine added to the boat, the connection between the two states improved greatly.

The ferry was improved, but that did not stop citizens from wanting an even better route across the Mississippi River. Over the years, several movements were formed to demand a bridge. One by one, those movements died out, but in 1872, the city finally received congressional approval to construct a bridge across the river.

In 1879, a bridge was built across the Wisconsin channel, eliminating the ferry there but leaving the main channel with the steam ferry and no bridge.

RED WING HIGH BRIDGE

The decision to build or not build a bridge can often be contentious, as can be the choice of location for any bridge that is approved. Many factors play into these decisions. Who will pay for the bridge? Who will maintain the bridge? How would the community be affected, for good or bad, by building the bridge?

Gus Freeman of Red Wing told the *Daily Republican Eagle* that "there was quite an agitation about the bridge—the heavy taxpayers didn't want it, but the people were getting sick of the ferry boat."

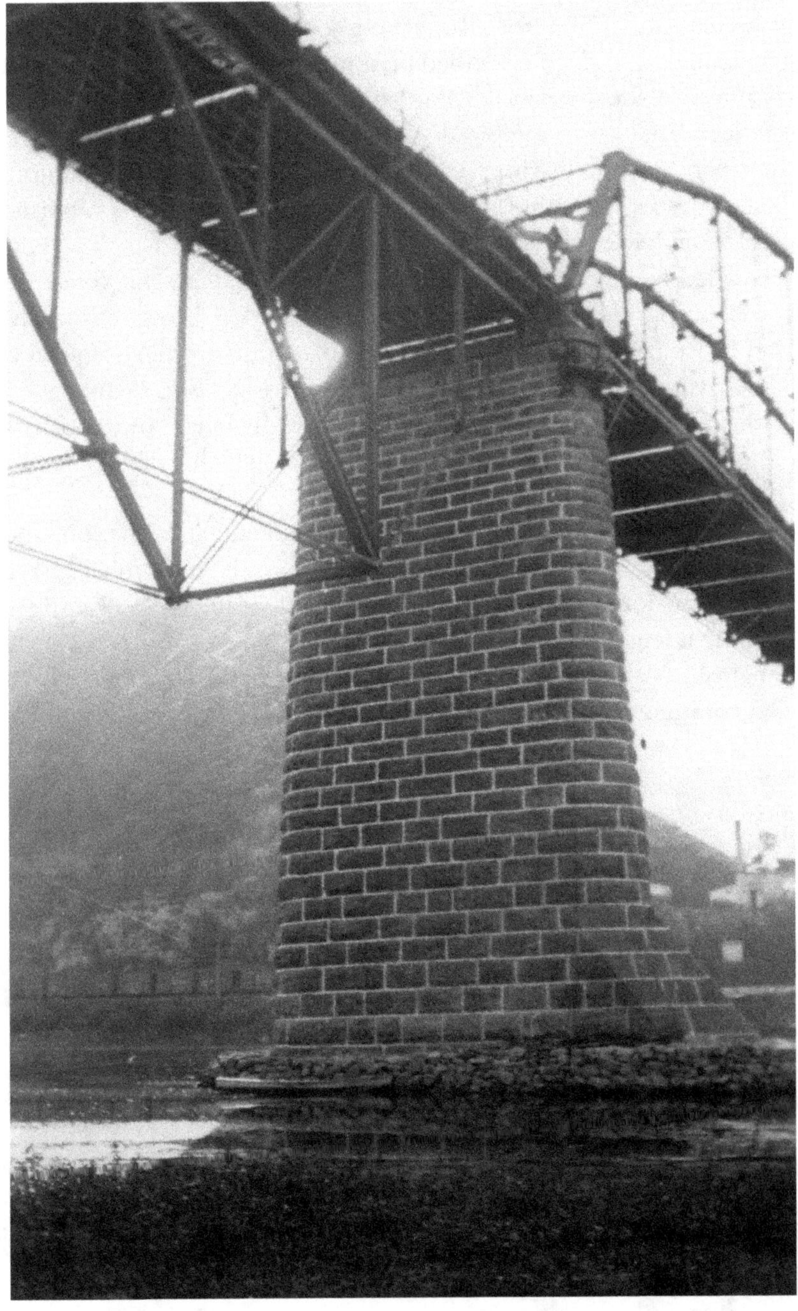

This is the abutment on the Red Wing High Bridge. *Courtesy of the Goodhue County Historical Society.*

On January 6, 1893, the Red Wing council engaged in a lengthy discussion about a bridge and ended up appointing a committee to examine the possibility. A few weeks later, the committee, along with the mayor, an engineer and a few citizens, visited Winona to see its new wagon bridge.

"They were delighted with what they saw and learned and came home stronger advocates of the bridge proposition than ever before," reported the *Daily Republican Eagle*.

They called for an election on February 8 and tallied the votes—1,353 in favor, 286 opposed. There was celebration in Red Wing that night and again on February 17, when a large group of people from Wisconsin came across the river to express their appreciation for what Red Wing had done. Soon, contracts were written, designs were put in place and construction work started on the Red Wing High Bridge, which was dedicated on May 1, 1895.

As a young boy, Carl Olson of Red Wing took advantage of the construction phase by carrying buckets of water to the workers. "They would give me a nickel or a dime for lugging water and most of the time they were thirsty, so I made quite a few nickels," he said.

A lengthy article in the *Daily Republican Eagle* on October 17, 1960, included comments from area residents who attended the dedication when

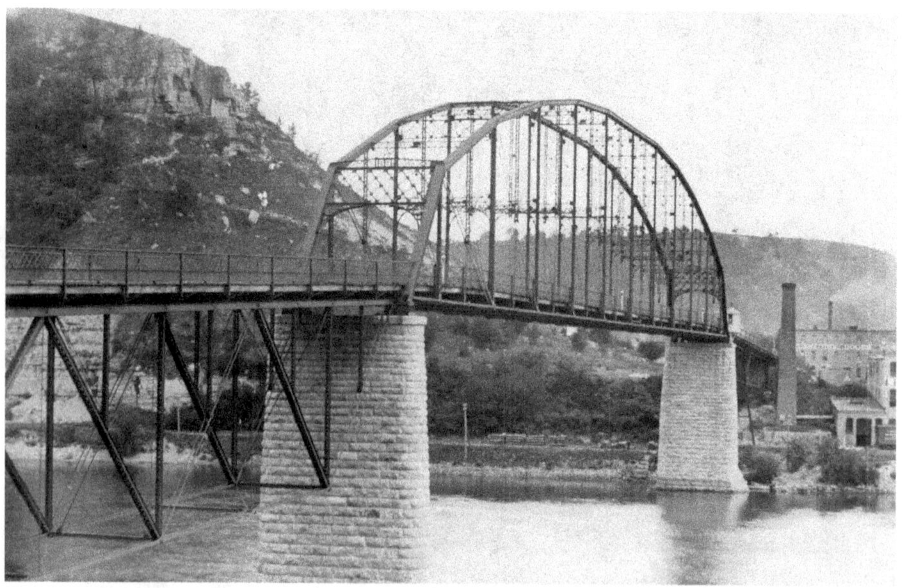

The Red Wing High Bridge showing the through truss center span with Barn Bluff/He Mni Can in the background. *Courtesy of the Goodhue County Historical Society.*

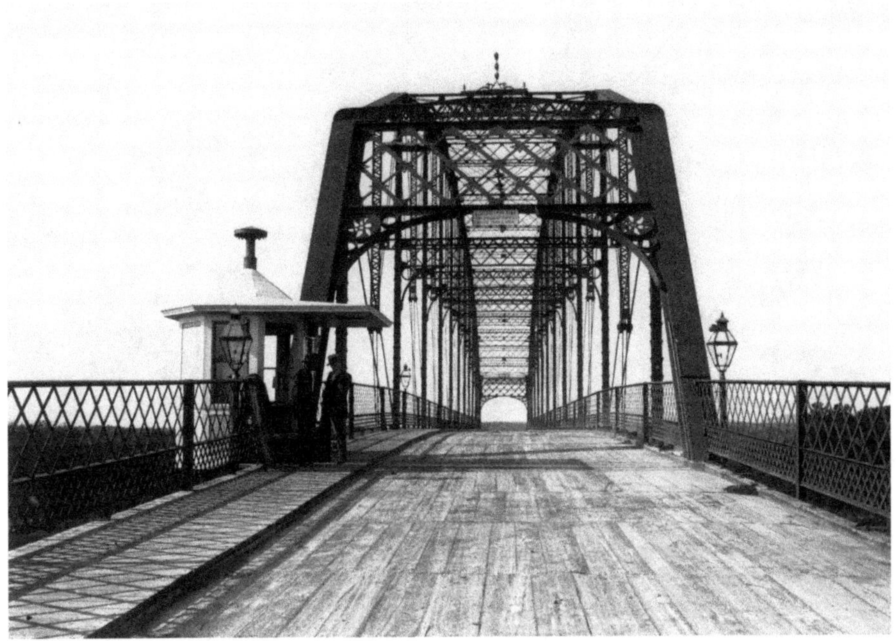

The High Bridge showing the wooden deck planking, the ornate lighting on each end of the bridge and two men standing near the tollhouse. *Courtesy of the Goodhue County Historical Society.*

they were children. Several recalled traveling on horseback or by buggy to Red Wing from neighboring towns or farms. John Sander from Welch spoke for many when he talked about the thrill of walking out onto the bridge and looking out over the Mississippi River.

One highlight of the dedication day was when a young daredevil dove off the bridge into the river, a moment anticipated by those in attendance. "I waited for the time when he made the plunge growing more excited by the moment," said Maggie Wiebusch of Millville, "and when it arrived, I sort of peeked through my fingers, almost afraid to look."

The ceremony included speeches and a band, but for most people, the excitement of the day was to join the crowd happily walking on the bridge from end to end.

The Red Wing High Bridge, sometimes referred to as the Wagon Bridge, was a spectacular bridge with a main through truss span supported by two towering masonry piers. Approach spans at both ends were built on deck trusses.

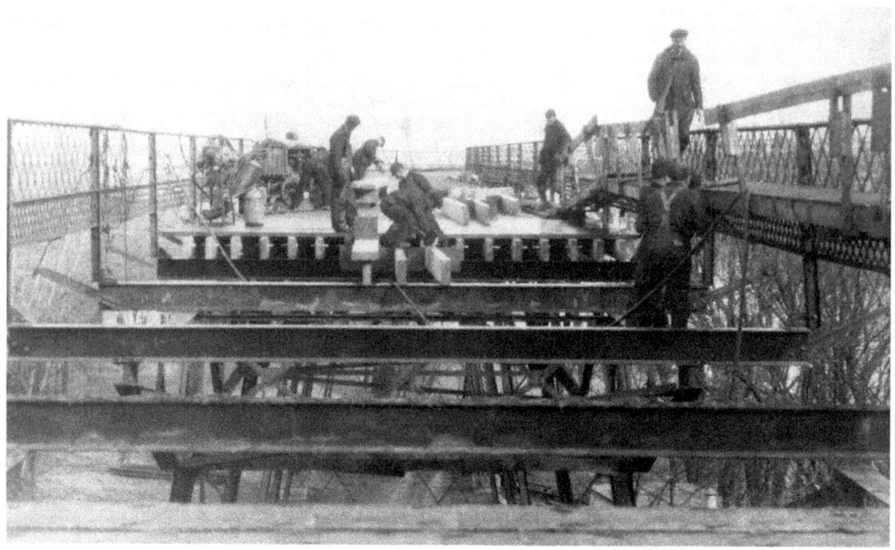

Work crews repair the planking on the deck of the 1895 High Bridge in Red Wing, circa 1930. *Courtesy of the Goodhue County Historical Society.*

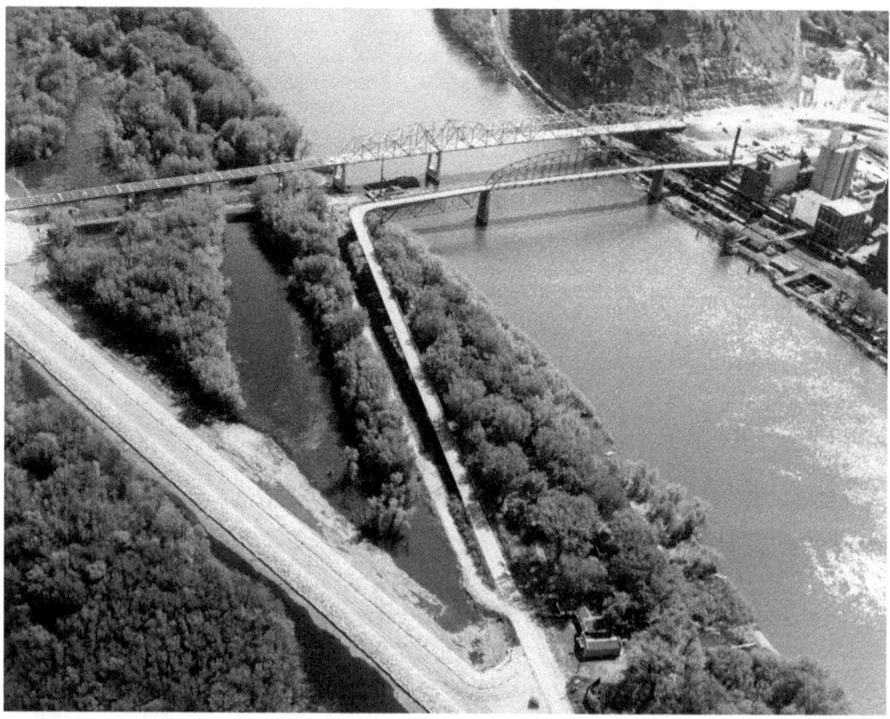

Aerial view of the Red Wing High Bridge and the Eisenhower Memorial Bridge at Red Wing, circa 1960. *Courtesy of the Goodhue County Historical Society.*

In addition to bonds sold to the public, the High Bridge helped pay for itself. It had a tollhouse on the Red Wing end for the first twenty-two years, and in that time, it earned more than enough to pay for the bridge and the salaries of the toll collectors, according to the *Daily Republican Eagle*.

The High Bridge was the pride of Red Wing and the region. It served well when the traffic was walkers, horses and wagons, but as motor vehicle traffic increased and the sharp turn at the end of the bridge on the Wisconsin end became more dangerous, cries for a new bridge were heard again in Red Wing.

An article from the *St. Paul Pioneer Press* in 1954 called the bridge a "death trap," noting that since 1937, there had been 149 accidents, 71 fatalities and 59 serious injuries. In a caption of a photo showing the sharp turn, it was reported that when a driver meets a truck, "that's when religion and mathematics come in for rapid play."

More action was needed, and it was soon set in motion.

EISENHOWER MEMORIAL BRIDGE

Construction of a new Red Wing bridge began in 1958. It was built alongside the High Bridge because shutting down the bridge would mean a detour to either Hastings or Wabasha, nearly thirty miles in either direction, for people to cross the river.

In the planning stages, it was called the Interstate Bridge, but by the time construction was complete, it was renamed the Hiawatha Bridge in honor of both the Hiawatha Valley which it spanned and the legendary Onondaga chief immortalized in the poem by Henry Wadsworth Longfellow.

The design chosen had three main spans, two cantilevers holding a central span supported by a Warren through truss and six approach spans with a total length of 1,631 feet. Work progressed well on the approach and cantilever spans, and by December 1959, pieces for the center span were placed on a barge anchored to the Wisconsin side and assembled. The 378-ton steel center span was then floated out into the river and hoisted into place to close the 288-foot gap between the two cantilever spans as a massive crowd watched from the end of the bridge and from Levee Park, according to a December 16, 1959 article in the *Daily Republican Eagle*.

With the center span locked in place by four large pins, work continued on the bridge, including building a deck that was thirty feet wide and made of seven inches of concrete resting on steel frames. Similar work was

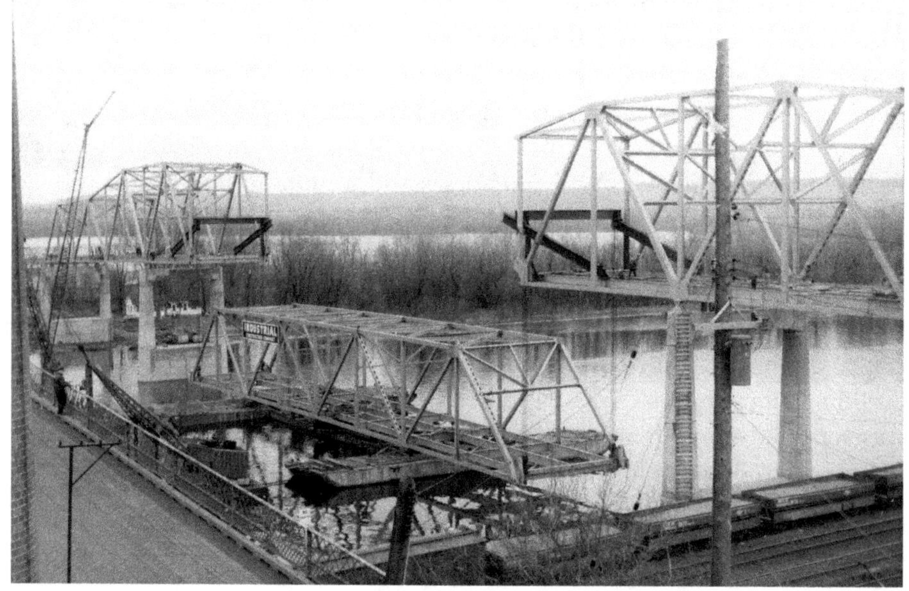

Above: Construction of the new Eisenhower Memorial Bridge in 1959. *Courtesy of the Goodhue County Historical Society.*

Opposite, top: The Eisenhower Memorial Bridge takes form next to the High Bridge in Red Wing in 1960. *Courtesy of the Goodhue County Historical Society.*

Opposite, bottom: President Dwight D. Eisenhower cuts the ribbon at the dedication of the Eisenhower Memorial Bridge in 1960. With Eisenhower are, *from left*: Halsy Hall, Hubert Humphrey, Governor Orville Freeman and Jane Freeman. *Courtesy of the Goodhue County Historical Society.*

completed on the back channel bridge finishing the connection to Hagar City, Wisconsin. In addition, the raised causeway road between the two bridges needed to be resurfaced.

ON OCTOBER 18, 1960, twenty thousand people showed up well ahead of time so they would not miss any of the festivities involved in having a president come to town. Two jets landed at Wold-Chamberlain Airport, now known as Minneapolis–St. Paul International Airport. The first jet contained forty reporters, according to the *Daily Republican Eagle*. Eisenhower landed on the second jet at about 8:25 a.m. He gave a brief speech at the airport and then flew by helicopter to Red Wing in time for the bridge dedication at 10:25 a.m.

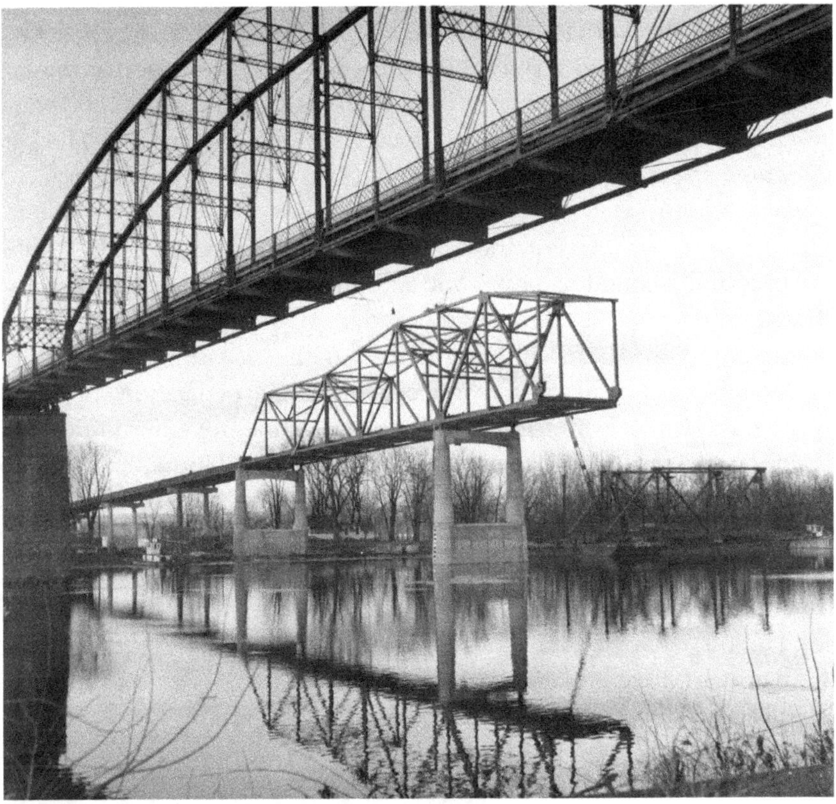

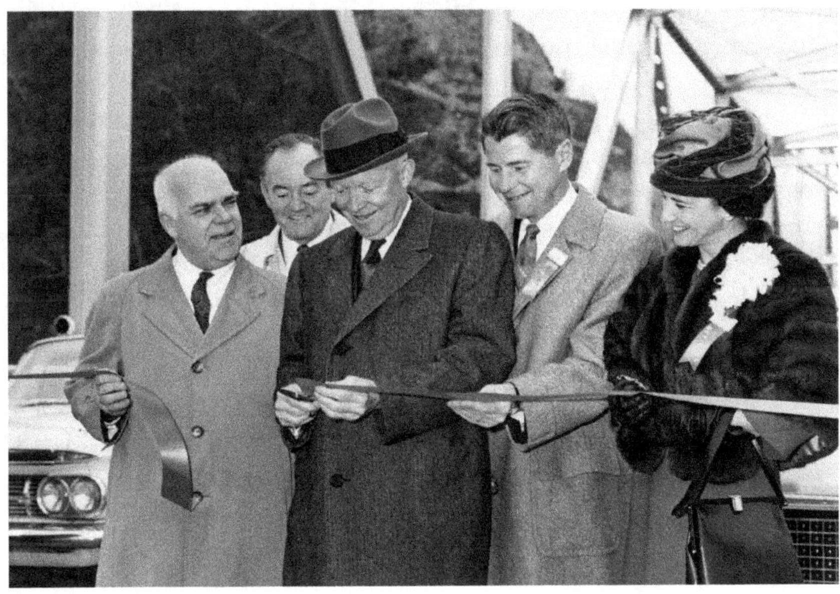

Speaking at the corner of Main and Broad in Red Wing in front of numerous "I Like Ike" posters, Eisenhower said, "The dedication of this great new bridge across the Mississippi is another effective example of Federal-State partnership in meeting both local and national needs. Hiawatha Bridge, now spanning the Father of Waters, is a part of the Federal-State highway program."

That program was part of the Federal Aid Highway Act of 1956, which would eventually build forty-one thousand miles of interstate highways.

Having served as supreme commander of Allied Forces in Europe during World War II, Eisenhower had seen the devastation of war and was promoting peace at every chance. During the dedication, he praised Hiawatha as a leader who tried to bring several tribes together in peace.

Eisenhower, nearing the end of his time in the White House, closed his Red Wing speech by saying, "I pray that this structure bridging a river between two commonwealths of our nation and its name may ever symbolize the purpose of forging and sustaining indestructible bonds between free people."

He ended his speech, boarded the helicopter and flew back to the Twin Cities. He still had a busy day ahead of him. Next stop was Abilene, Kansas, his hometown, where he would spend the afternoon at the dedication of the Dwight D. Eisenhower Presidential Library & Museum.

WITH THE HIAWATHA BRIDGE open to traffic in November 1960, work crews still had many finishing touches to complete. In May, they also began the long process of dismantling the High Bridge. On December 8, 1961, they planned to pull down the center span, but the first attempt snapped the cable connecting it to a steam barge, according to the *Daily Republican Eagle* in the next day's edition. Workmen cut into the framework with torches and then attached two cables to the span. The first was tied to the steam barge, and a second was hooked to a caterpillar on shore. On the next pull, the truss span dropped into the Mississippi River. It was winched ashore and cut into pieces. The remainder of the old bridge soon followed.

Another change soon took place. Not long after President Eisenhower's visit to Red Wing, the state legislature passed a law known as Minnesota Statutes Transportation 161.14. Subdivision 16 of that law read, "The bridge over the Mississippi River at the city of Red Wing, being part of Legislative Route No. 161, is hereby named and designated the 'Eisenhower Memorial Bridge.'"

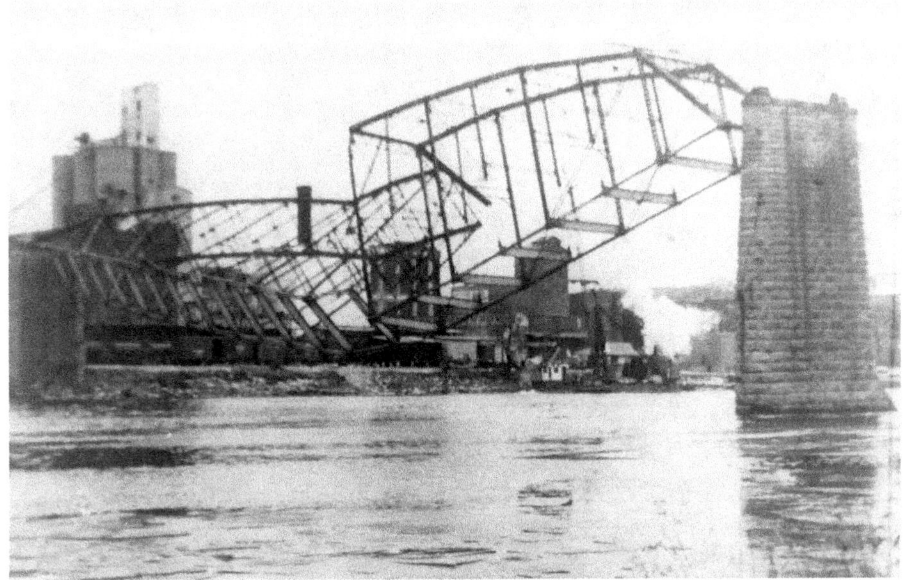

The destruction of the old High Bridge in Red Wing, circa 1960. *Courtesy of the Goodhue County Historical Society.*

RED WING WAS PROUD of its new bridge, and with the dangerous turn eliminated on the Wisconsin end, traffic increased, almost doubling that of the High Bridge.

Safety is always a concern for bridges, and when a Greenwich, Connecticut bridge with similar hangar assemblies collapsed in the summer of 1983, crews did an extensive inspection in Red Wing but found everything to be fine, according to an August 2 article in the *Daily Republican Eagle*. Then, when the I-35W bridge fell in Minneapolis in 2007, everything changed for every bridge in the country. Talks about building another bridge in Red Wing started sooner than expected.

EISENHOWER BRIDGE OF VALOR

Chad Hanson sat at his desk in 2009 and began working on a new Red Wing bridge, a project that would not be finished until November 21, 2019. As a principal project manager for the Minnesota Department of Transportation, Hanson, who has worked for MnDOT for more than twenty years, was the point man for a massive organizational venture.

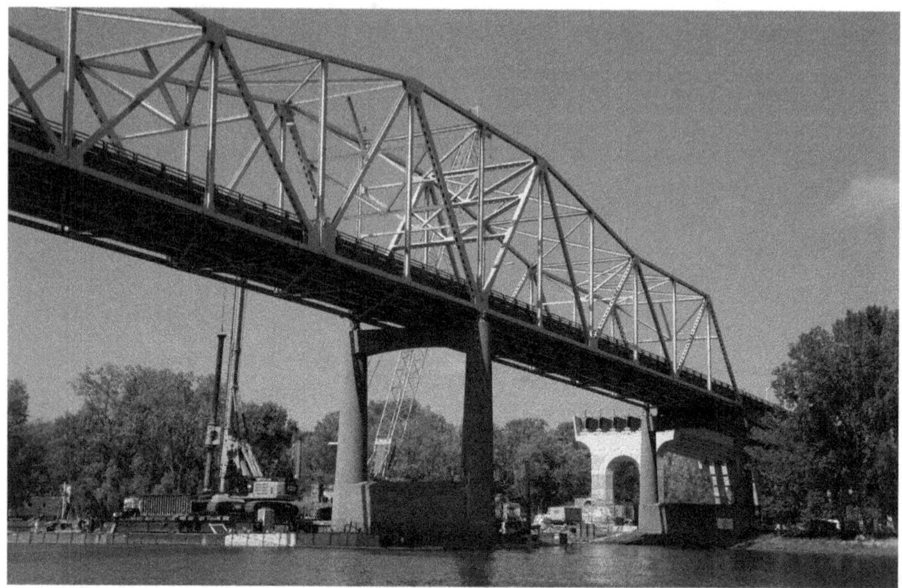

Work crews, in the shadow of the Eisenhower Memorial Bridge, construct piers for what would become the center span of the Eisenhower Bridge of Valor. Approach piers can be seen behind the Eisenhower Bridge in the lower right of the photo. *Photo by Steve Gardiner.*

"I worked to bring the different teams together," Hanson told the *Red Wing Republican Eagle* in an April 24, 2021 article. "I managed the overall scope of the project, the schedule, and the budget. I had to look at the environmental piece, the alternatives analysis, public involvement, and stakeholder involvement. I had to bring everything together."

Doing this required numerous meetings with the City of Red Wing, the Wisconsin Department of Transportation, the Federal Highway Administration and many others to learn about each group's concerns and needs. Conducting all the environmental studies and getting approvals required three years of work.

"It's kind of a learning process, because you don't know how the project is going to turn out until you get to the end," Hanson said. "You have to take a look at all the different steps along the way."

One of the forces that moved the Red Wing project along was a result of the collapse of the I-35W bridge in 2007, two years before Hanson began work on what was to become the Eisenhower Bridge of Valor.

"The state legislature set aside a certain amount of funding for all the bridges in the state that were considered fracture critical," Hanson said. "This is one that was identified in that program."

Fracture critical is the term used to describe a bridge on which a failure of a component under tension would result in the collapse of the bridge or the inability to continue using the bridge. Hanson said that any bridge in that category had to be evaluated to see if it could be repaired or if it needed to be replaced.

The Red Wing bridge needed to be replaced, so Hanson and his team had to evaluate how to handle thirteen thousand cars each day being directed into downtown Red Wing at the junction of three major highways. They also had to consider how to replace the bridge while maintaining traffic, since the nearest bridge upstream is in Hastings and the nearest bridge downstream is in Wabasha, both requiring long detours for traffic.

Hanson's job did not include designing the bridge, but he brought together the people who did. "There were dozens of people involved in the design of the bridge, and there were countless consultants who helped," he said.

At any one time, Hanson might be handling up to fifteen projects. While all those projects are interesting, it's the Eisenhower Bridge of Valor that has been his biggest accomplishment.

"Looking back on it, it's pretty remarkable," Hanson said. "All the people that helped support the project and provided input into it. It was definitely a team effort."

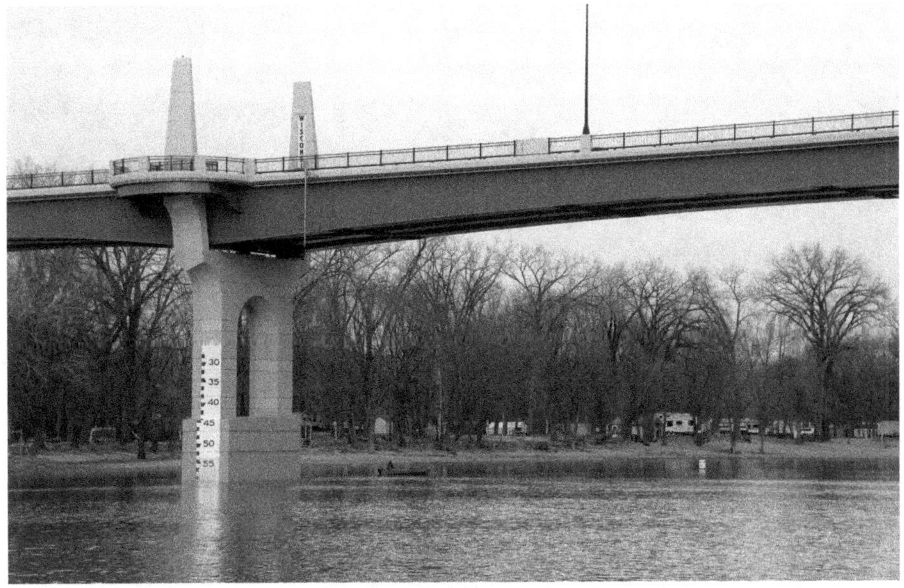

With the Eisenhower Bridge removed, the new Eisenhower Bridge of Valor is seen from Levee Park. *Photo by Steve Gardiner.*

ON NOVEMBER 6, 2020, Red Wing city engineer Jay Owens led a tour for Red Wing Chamber of Commerce staff and community members on the new bridge. Because of the careful process of designing the bridge, Owens said he expects the bridge will have a one-hundred-year life expectancy, based partly on the strength of the support system.

"The main piers, where you see the spires sticking up above the bridge, are on what are called drilled shafts," Owens told the group. "They are large shafts drilled all the way down until they got to bedrock, and then they drilled five feet into bedrock."

On the Minnesota side, the two main shafts are 12 feet in diameter and were drilled 60 feet deep. On the Wisconsin side, there are four shafts that are 9 feet in diameter, and they were drilled down 120 feet to reach bedrock.

The spans of the bridge are supported by three steel tub girders that are sixty-five feet above normal river level, leaving enough room for tows and barges to pass underneath. Using the steel tub girders also allowed the designers to eliminate the truss system used on the previous bridge.

The bridge, at the location where Highways 58, 61 and 63 meet in Red Wing, opened to traffic on November 21, 2019. The 1,640-foot bridge

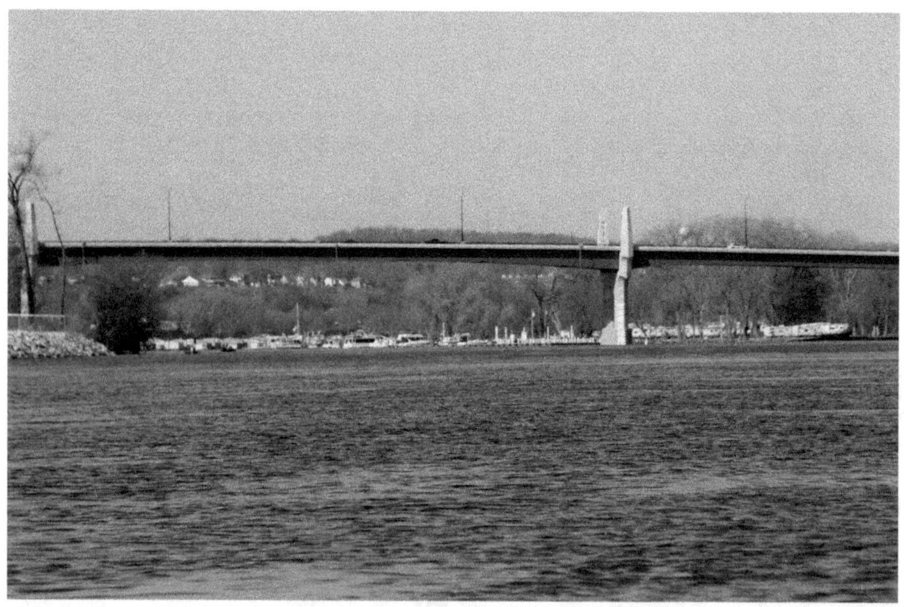

The Eisenhower Bridge of Valor seen from downstream in the middle of the Mississippi River with the boats of the Trenton Island Yacht Club in the background. *Photo by Steve Gardiner.*

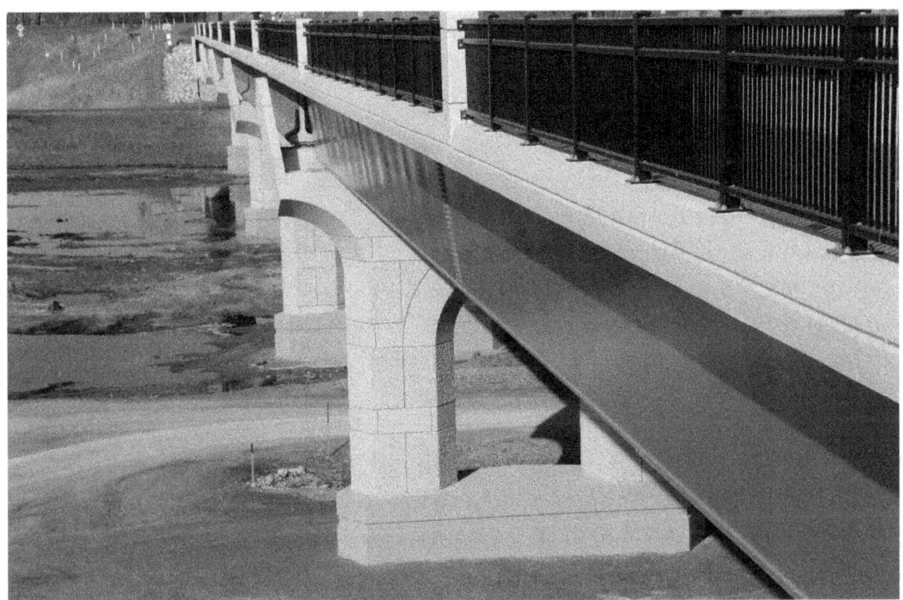

This photo gives a view of the steel tub girders and the concrete piers of the Eisenhower Bridge of Valor, which is 1,631 feet long. *Photo by Steve Gardiner.*

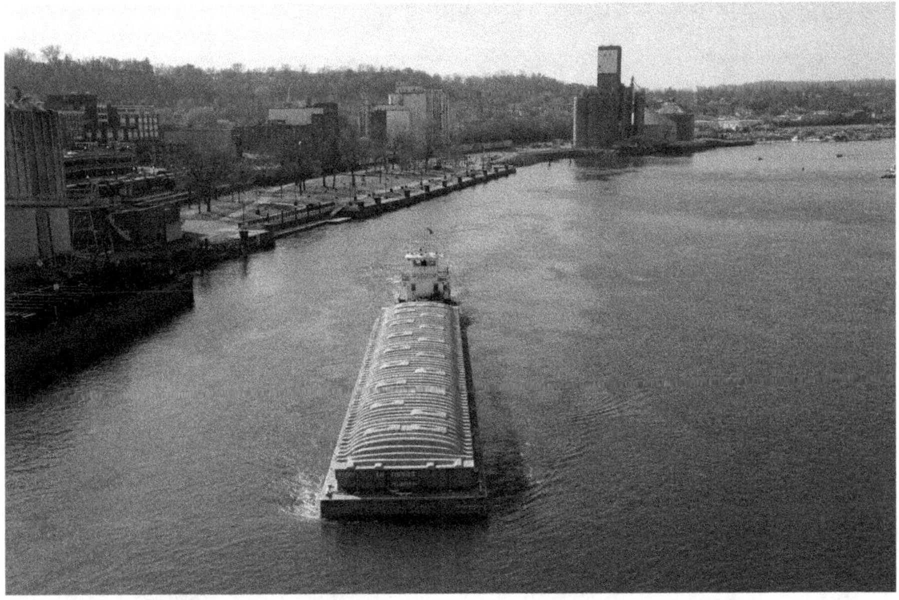

A tow with a single barge makes its way under the Eisenhower Bridge of Valor on November 5, 2020. *Photo by Steve Gardiner.*

carries two lanes of traffic on Highway 63 across the Mississippi River and has a 12-foot biking/walking lane. It features four spires, two marked for Minnesota and two marked for Wisconsin, and was built at a cost of $63.4 million, according to the City of Red Wing.

"The Highway 63 bridge at Red Wing serves as a vital link for communities and commerce in this region," Mike Dougherty, Minnesota Department of Transportation District 6 director of public engagement and communications, told the *Republican Eagle*. "Having a safe, reliable crossing for all who use this bridge will serve this region for generations and allow businesses and communities to grow and prosper."

With the new bridge in place, demolition of the old bridge began. On February 6, 2020, the center span was slowly lowered onto barges in the river and hauled to the Wisconsin shore. Material from the old bridge was taken to a pit in Wisconsin for recycling, with some pieces going to the Goodhue County Historical Center. Piers and abutments were removed, and on June 30, 2020, crews used explosives to remove Pier 2 to two feet below mud line, according to the City of Red Wing website. Before long, the removal of the Eisenhower Memorial Bridge was complete.

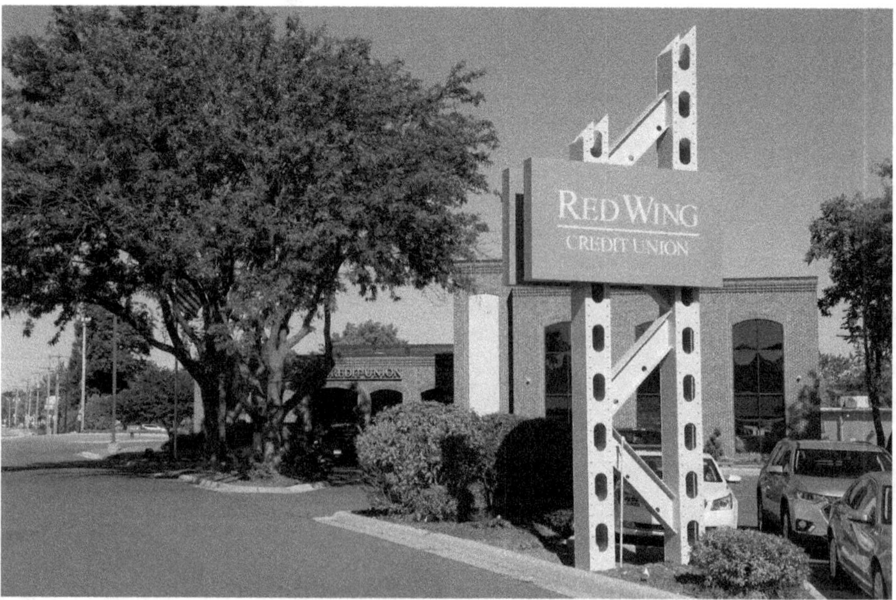

A piece of the Eisenhower Memorial Bridge lives on as the support for the sign in front of the Red Wing Credit Union. *Photo by Steve Gardiner.*

When he saw the bridge pieces being hauled away, Aaron DeJong, president and CEO of the Red Wing Credit Union, had an idea. He wanted to get a piece of the old bridge and use it to support a new sign in front of the credit union. He visited the recycling site and chose a piece for the sign and several smaller pieces to be used as planters near the front doors of the building. Work crews used a crane to set a twenty-four-foot beam five feet into the ground and built a six-foot-by-nine-foot base around it to support the sign.

"The bridge has been around since 1960," DeJong said in the September 12, 2020 edition of the *Red Wing Republican Eagle*. "The credit union has been around since 1954. It's always been part of our history, and we even used a silhouette of it [the bridge] in our logo for many years. We have a connection to it, and it is a symbol of Red Wing, so to be able to preserve a little bit of that history was important."

BUILDING A NEW BRIDGE is a difficult process, but so is naming that bridge. As the construction process unfolded, many Red Wing citizens were involved in discussions about a name. Through several meetings, they considered many

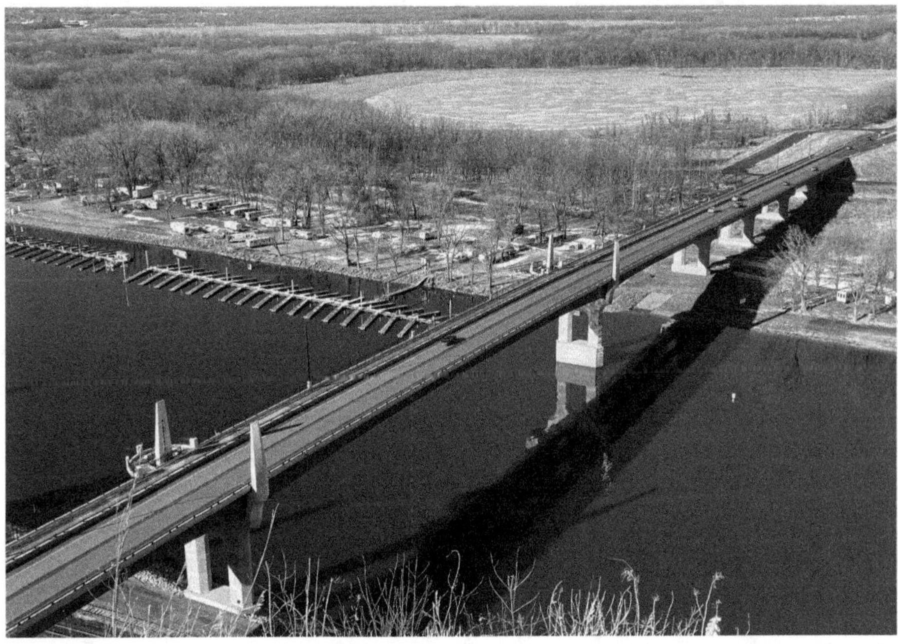

The Eisenhower Bridge of Valor as seen from the top of Barn Bluff/He Mni Can on November 25, 2022. *Photo by Steve Gardiner.*

names but settled on Eisenhower Bridge of Valor, which would continue the legacy of President Eisenhower and expand it to honor veterans from all wars, law enforcement, firefighters and families of those heroes.

In May 2019, the Minnesota House and Senate passed the Transportation Omnibus Bill, which reworded Statute 161.14, Subdivision 16 to read, "The bridge over the Mississippi River at the city of Red Wing, being part of Legislative Route No. 161, is designated as the 'Eisenhower Bridge of Valor.'" On June 11, Governor Tim Walz signed that bill into law.

CANNON BOTTOMS ROAD BRIDGE

As settlers moved into the Minnesota Territory in the 1840s, they needed roads to help them through the region. In 1849, Congress provided $40,000 to build what was called a military road from Mendota to Wabasha along the western bank of the Mississippi River, allowing passage anytime that Lake Pepin was frozen. In the late 1850s, Goodhue County took control of the road, and it became part of the state highway system.

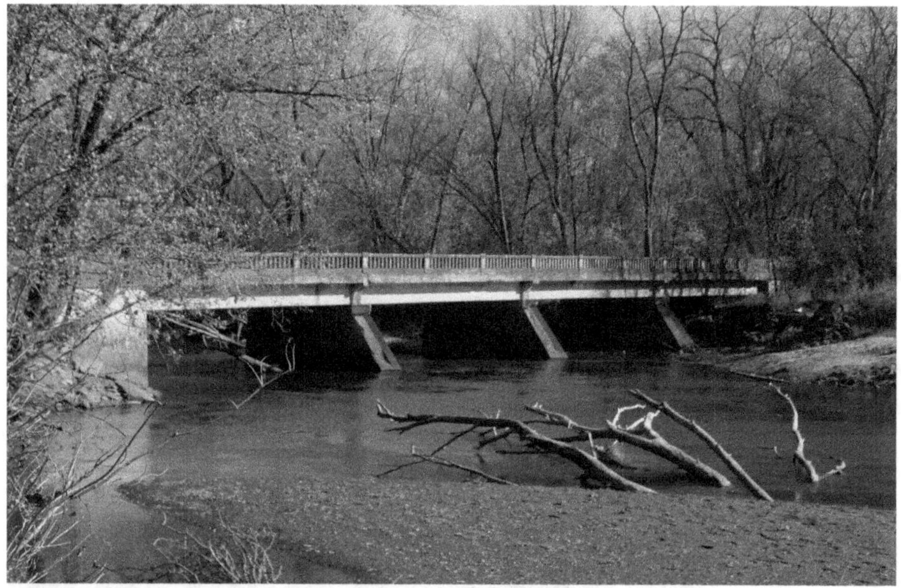

In the 1840s, immigrants to Minnesota Territory had a difficult time traveling. In 1849, Congress provided funds to build what were called Military Roads, and one of them, from Mendota to Wabasha, included this abandoned bridge on Old Cannon Bottom Road near Red Wing. *Photo by Steve Gardiner.*

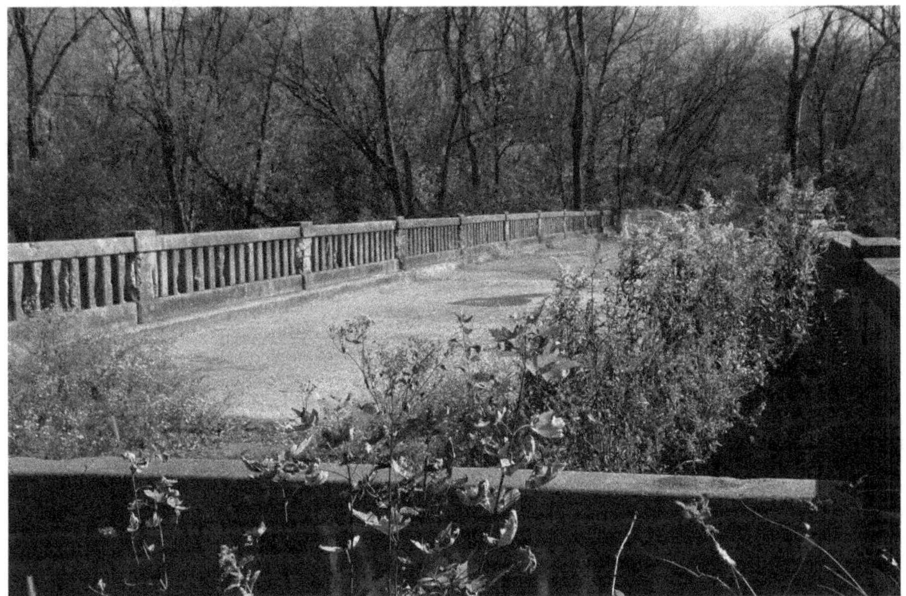

This is a view of the deck and concrete railings of the Cannon Bottoms Road Bridge. *Photo by Steve Gardiner.*

In the early 1900s, Goodhue County built three bridges on this road. Two were iron bridges over small branches of the Cannon River, and the third, built in 1921, is a concrete bridge over the main channel.

In 1931, the state built a new section of highway along what is now Highway 61 and the old military road became known as Cannon Bottoms Road.

The city removed the two iron bridges in 2012, but the concrete bridge, closed to traffic, still exists. It is a T-beam bridge that is 194 feet long and 21 feet wide featuring an open concrete railing on both sides of the bridge.

HAY CREEK BIKE BRIDGE

Walkers and cyclists can cross this bridge on the Hay Creek Trail just off Pioneer Road in Red Wing. There are several similar bridges along the trail, which begins near the Pottery Museum in Red Wing and goes to Hay Creek, a distance of about six miles. It can also be accessed from several points along the trail.

A short city trail connects the Hay Creek Trail with the Cannon Valley Trail, which goes almost twenty miles to Cannon Falls. Future plans include

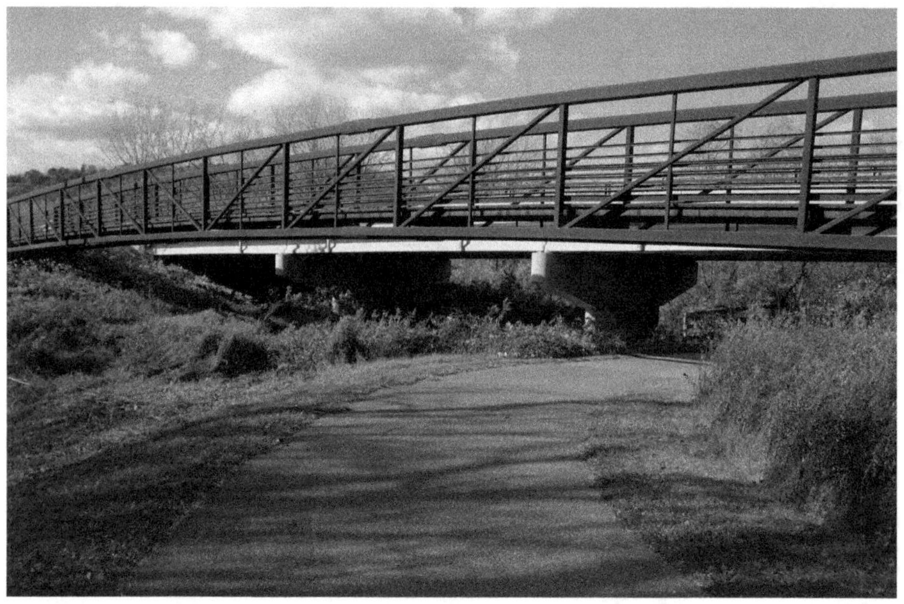

Cyclists use this bridge on the Hay Creek Trail just off Pioneer Road in Red Wing. *Photo by Steve Gardiner.*

incorporating the Hay Creek Trail into the Goodhue Pioneer Trail, which would connect Red Wing, Goodhue, Zumbrota, Mazeppa, Bellechester and Pine Island, where riders could join the Douglas State Trail into Rochester.

RED WING RIVERVIEW SKYWAY

Under discussion for more than ten years, this pedestrian/bicycle bridge developed as part of the Old West Main and Upper Harbor Renewal Project with the City of Red Wing. The bridge connects neighborhoods and West End District businesses with Bay Point Park and the Upper Harbor.

"The bridge is a really important step in starting a renewal of the whole Upper Harbor area," said Jay Owens, city engineer, in an October 18, 2021 article in the *Republican Eagle*. "The project involved some complicated design issues and challenging work with the railroad, but everything came together, and the staff worked hard as a team to get the funding. Now we're grateful that two important areas of Red Wing are connected, and we're excited to see lots of people using the skyway."

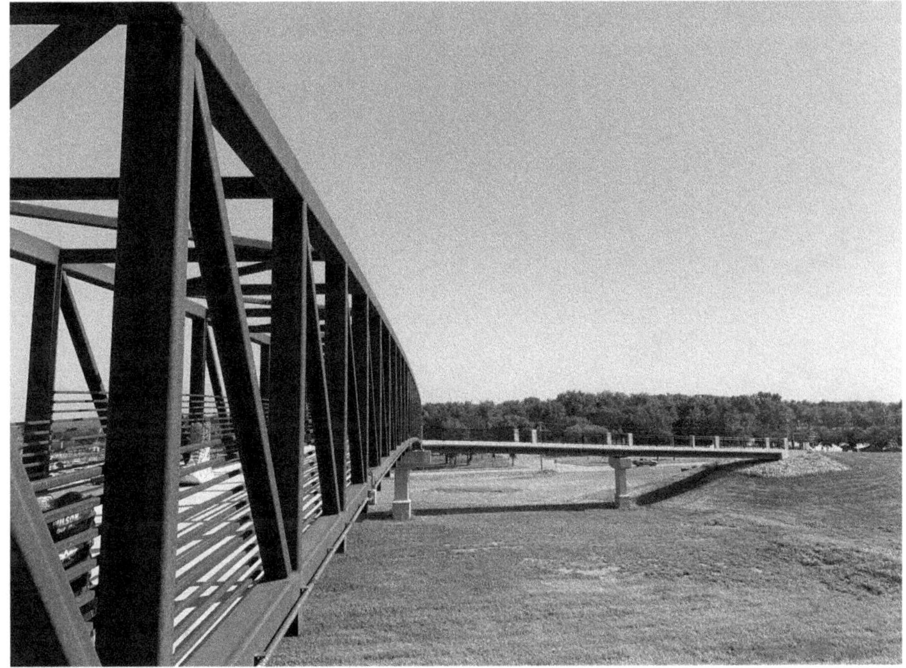

The Red Wing Riverview Skyway opened in October 2021. *Photo by Steve Gardiner.*

Plans for the bridge were submitted to the Minnesota Department of Transportation in June 2020 and approved the following month. The skyway opened in October 2021.

Chapter 4

ROCHESTER

A Bridge over the Zumbro

"The most exciting accident that has ever occurred in Rochester took place last Saturday morning," reported the *Rochester Post* on December 1, 1866.

"The frame for the covering of the new railroad bridge across the Zumbro was in place but had not yet been securely fastened. As the train from the east, which gets in about nine o'clock in the morning, was crossing the bridge, at a little faster rate than usual, a rope hanging from one of the beams caught against the forward car. This brought the whole frame tumbling upon the cars."

Seven carpenters were working on the roof of the bridge. When the accident happened, they and all the timbers they had been putting in place tumbled off the bridge and into the water. The article went on to describe the injuries to each man. Fortunately, none was killed, and no passengers on the train were hurt, largely due to the efforts of the brakeman, Peter Smith, who held on to his brake even though he was "jammed through the car window by a huge timber with the wheel of the brake still in his hands."

The story, written in the journalistic style of the day, illustrates the dangers and challenges faced by early bridge builders. There was a lot of learning to be done in the art of bridge design and construction, and many bridges in the area suffered problems.

An August 3, 1949 article in the *Rochester Post Bulletin* explained that the Zumbro River had been a barrier between Rochester and other areas of the state in the early days of the city. To cross that barrier, locals built a log bridge in 1856. It consisted of three stringers thirty feet long with poles across the stringers with hay and sod on top of the poles. It lasted ten years until a spring flood washed it out. A similar log bridge was built and survived until 1876, when another flood carried it away.

When an iron bridge crossed the Zumbro, W.H. Seward wanted his delivery wagon loaded with furniture to be the first across it. Driven by Oliver Berg, the wagon was so quick on the scene that Berg had to wait at the end of the bridge for the final plank to be placed before he could exit the bridge, according to the *Rochester Post* on November 23, 1877.

It was never easy building bridges, and even though Rochester did not have to span the Mississippi River as other communities did, they had plenty of work to do to cross the tributary rivers in the area.

One source of help and inspiration came through the Good Roads Project. The Minnesota version of this organization held a two-day convention in St. Paul in January 1893, and four hundred delegates attended, according to the MnDOT website. They planned to provide information and resources to help communities build solid roads and bridges, stating that a good road "is like a good chain; no better, no stronger than its weakest link."

In 1898, the Minnesota Good Roads Movement convinced voters to approve a state tax for county bridge construction. The funds would be handled by a state highway commission. By 1918, the Good Roads work

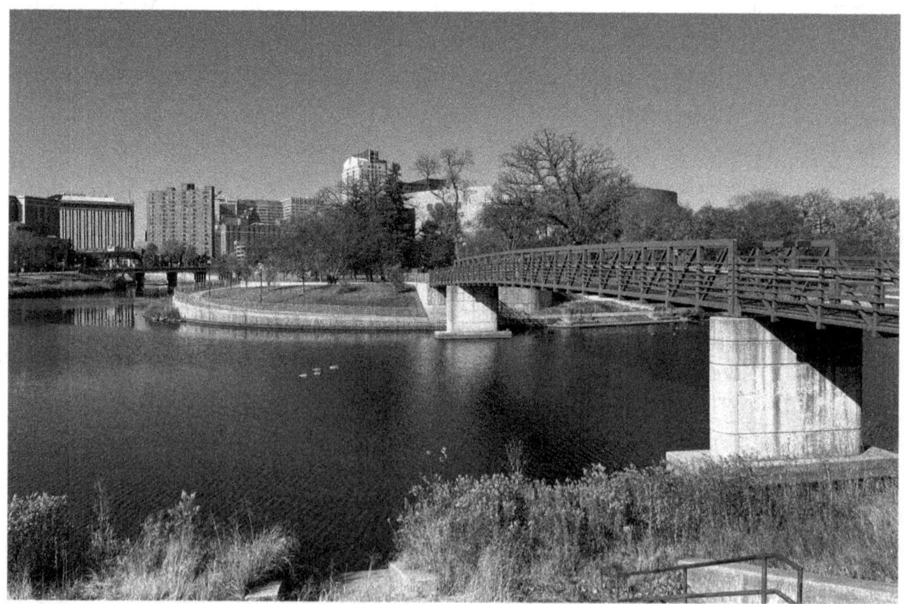

This bridge takes walkers and bikers to Mayo Park in Rochester. *Photo by Steve Gardiner.*

had spread outside the Twin Cities, and the Olmsted County Good Roads association promised citizens that it would "put the bridges of Olmsted County in first-class shape and on a permanent basis," reported the *Rochester Daily Post and Record* on January 21.

The importance of a new bridge to a community is made clear in an article in the *Rochester Post* dated August 5, 1898. The unnamed writer, sharing the emotions of the city, stated, "There it stands, a handsome structure, the new steel Fifth Street Bridge, spanning the tree embowered Zumbro. The sight of the new bridge is not novel to many, to others it is a revelation, to visitors it will be a surprise, to the city it will always be a mark of civic pride."

THIRD AVENUE BRIDGE

No one walking in the area of Second Avenue and Second Street SE could ignore the noise. In fact, residents lined the banks of the Zumbro River to watch as crews with the L.M. Feller Construction Company used a pile driver to sink fifty-foot steel shafts into the sand and mud in the river bottom.

The crew set each piling in place and then built a guide tower around it. The 3,800-pound hammer would slide inside the guide tower and strike a faller cap placed over the top of the piling. It took the crew an hour to drive each piling down to bedrock, according to an October 18, 1949 article in the *Rochester Post Bulletin*. They had thirty-eight shafts to drive in place.

The Third Avenue Bridge, sometimes called the Mayo Park Bridge, was designed by Richard Wheeler of Minneapolis and cost $250,000. Construction of the bridge required altering the course of the Zumbro River 60 feet south where retaining walls were built, wrote the *Rochester Post Bulletin* on November 7, 1950, one day before the official opening of the 220-foot-long, 44-foot-wide bridge.

Mayor Claude McQuillan, City Engineer Ralph Monson and other officials held a brief ceremony at four o'clock in the afternoon, after which city officials drove the first cars across the reinforced concrete bridge. Crushed gravel approaches to the bridge were paved the following spring.

The city was proud of that bridge, and it served well, in spite of two major floods that damaged other bridges and property. By late 1991, the U.S. Army Corps of Engineers had plans for the $140 million Rochester Flood Control Project, a nine-mile improvement plan designed to prevent the type of damage caused by the 1978 flood. The project included deepening and widening the Zumbro River channel. In addition to replacing the Third

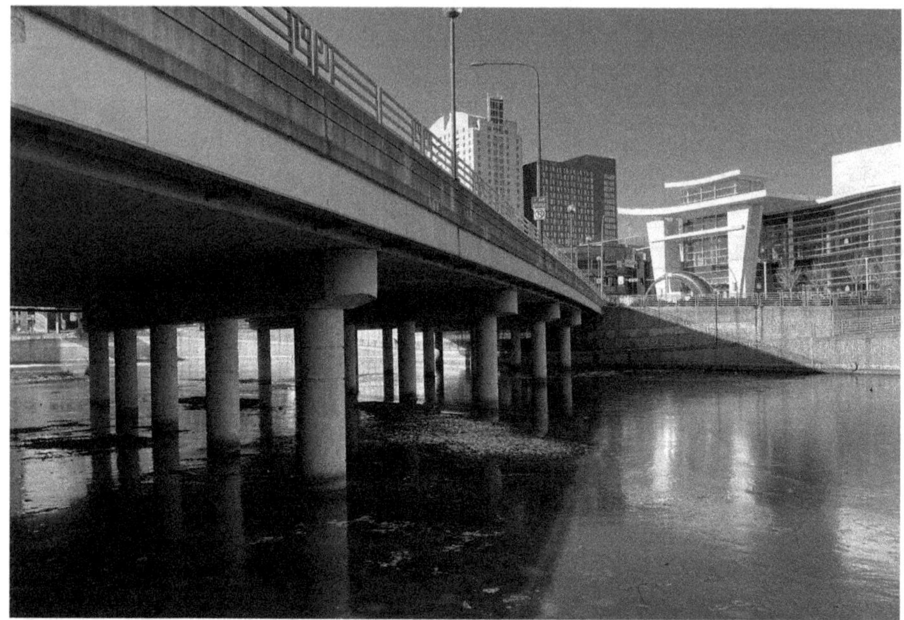

The Third Avenue Bridge, on November 22, 2022, with the Mayo Civic Center in the background. *Photo by Steve Gardiner.*

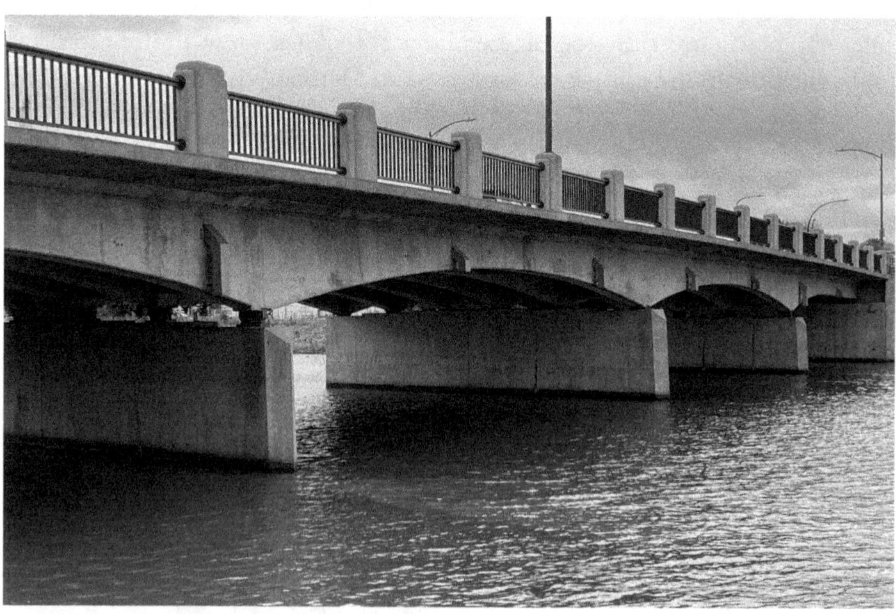

Built in 1956, the Seventh Street NE Bridge carries traffic over the Zumbro River in downtown Rochester. It is a concrete girder bridge with an ornamental railing. *Photo by Steve Gardiner.*

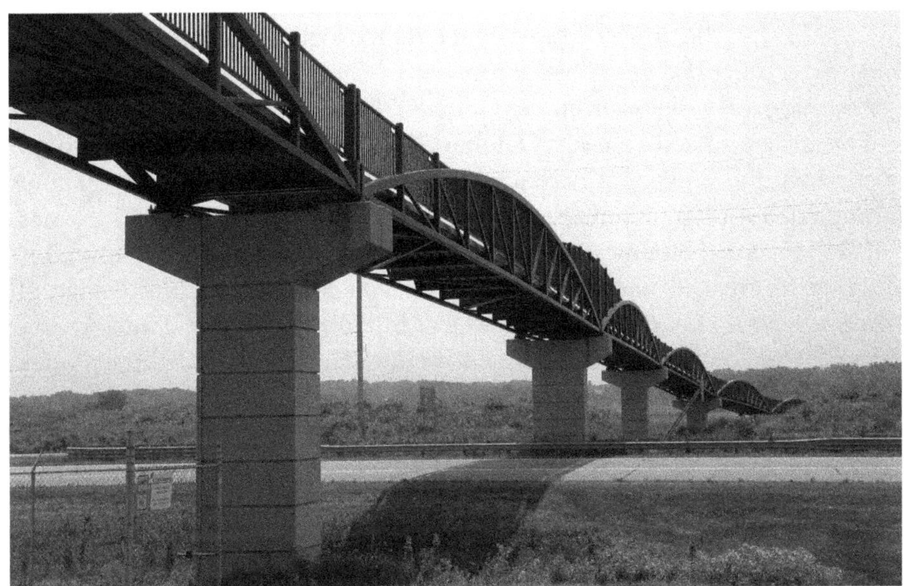

The Arianna Celeste Macnamara Memorial Bridge is named in honor of a seven-year-old girl who died of injuries she suffered while riding her bike on Highway 14 with her family. The bridge allows bikers and walkers to safely cross some of the busiest streets in Rochester. *Photo by Steve Gardiner.*

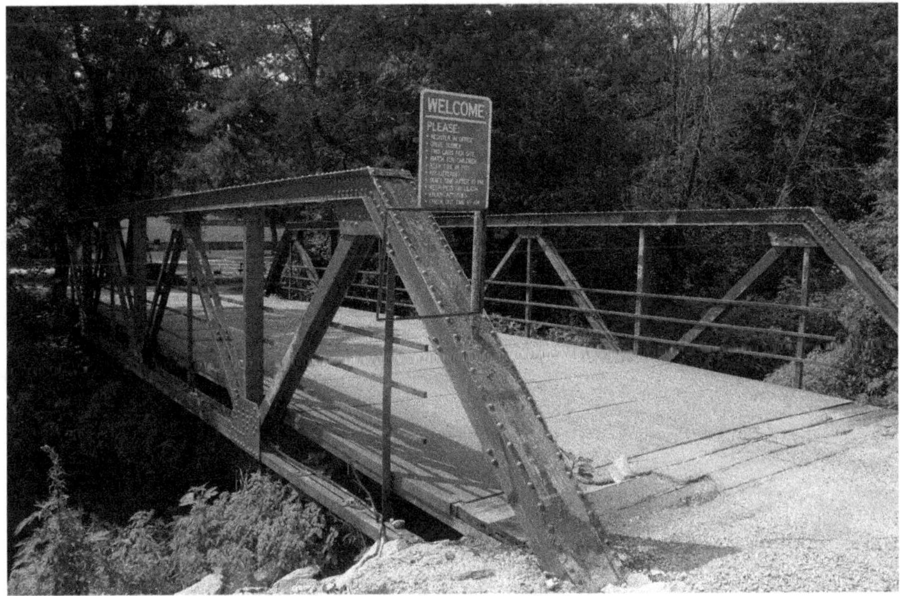

The Ferguson's Willow Creek Campground Bridge is a Warren pony truss bridge located just off U.S. Highway 63 near the Rochester Airport. *Photo by Steve Gardiner.*

Avenue Bridge, the project constructed a railroad bridge, a pedestrian bridge and hiking and biking paths, according to the December 1991 issue of *Crosscurrents*, a newsletter from the Corps of Engineers.

The bridge closed in early October 1992, and the replacement bridge opened with a dedication ceremony on November 8, 1993. The opening prompted a bridge naming contest, and officials received 130 entries. Suggestions for the names of several prominent citizens were submitted in addition to creative names such as Civic Freedom Bridge, the Bridge of Hope and New Horizon Bridge, as well as retaining the name Third Avenue Bridge. The Rochester City Council used a scoring system to tally votes, explained the *Rochester Post Bulletin* on November 25, 1993, and in the end, the bridge remained the Third Avenue Bridge.

SILVER CREEK ROAD BRIDGE

This steel and concrete bridge was closed to traffic in 1988 but is used frequently by walkers and cyclists. It is located near the Quarry Hill Nature Center and is sometimes called the Quarry Hill Bridge.

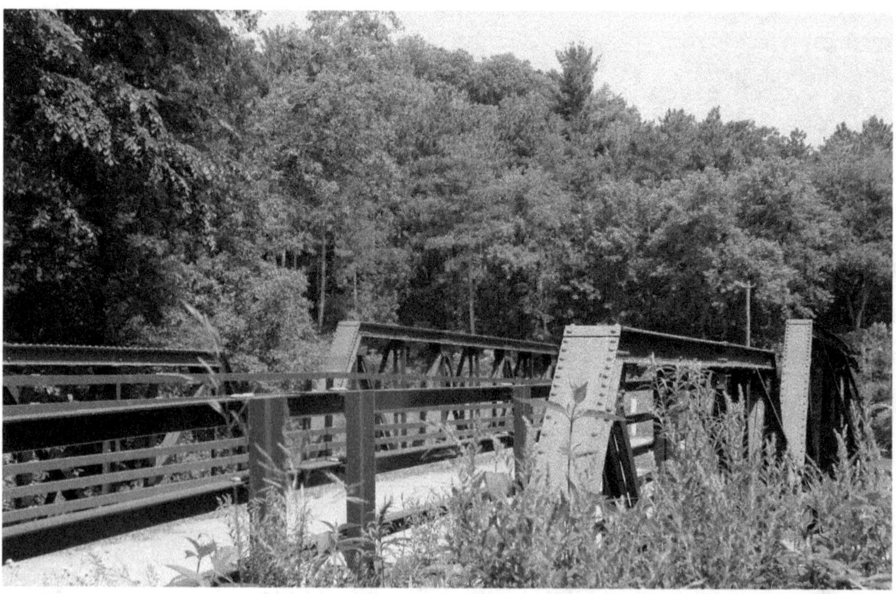

The Silver Creek Bridge near the Quarry Hill Nature Center in Rochester is a two-span pony truss bridge. The first span was built in the 1920s, and the second span was added in the 1930s. It is now closed to traffic and is part of the City of Rochester Bike Trail. *Photo by Steve Gardiner.*

The bridge, painted dark green, is a pony truss bridge in two sections, one higher than the other. One section was built in the mid-1920s and the other section in the mid-1930s. The total length is 109 feet, and the width is 18 feet. It was constructed to connect the state hospital with farms that supplied crops and livestock as food for the hospital.

According to a November 24, 2014 article in the *Rochester Post Bulletin*, the bridge was showing its age, and the Rochester City Council voted to repair, rather than replace, the bridge using funds from a Department of Natural Resources legacy grant. Work crews removed and repaired several parts of the bridge, especially on the substructure of the bridge, completing the project in 2015.

Silver Lake Bridges

According to the Department of Natural Resources, there are four counties in Minnesota that do not have a natural lake; Olmsted County is one of them. In the 1930s, local residents decided to create Silver Lake.

"Silver Lake is actually a reservoir that was created by first hand-digging a basin to hold water and then constructing a dam from 1935–1936 to back-up river water," according to the City of Rochester website. "It was built for half a million dollars during the 1930's Great Depression as a work relief project, providing work for over 400 unemployed men."

The original lake was seventeen acres, including an island. In 1936, workers built three stone-faced closed-spandrel pedestrian bridges to connect walking paths to an island in the lake. The park was dedicated on June 25, 1937.

Frank's Ford Bridge

This bridge, now closed to traffic, used to carry County Road 121 over the South Fork of the Zumbro River about two miles from the city of Oronoco.

It is a steel pin-connected Pratt through truss bridge built in 1985 by Horace E. Horton and the Chicago Bridge and Iron Company. The bridge is 146 feet long with a main span of 72 feet and a timber deck 16 feet wide.

"In 1908 the bridge was washed downstream in a flood, then repaired and elevated, with all work being done by the original builder, Chicago Bridge &

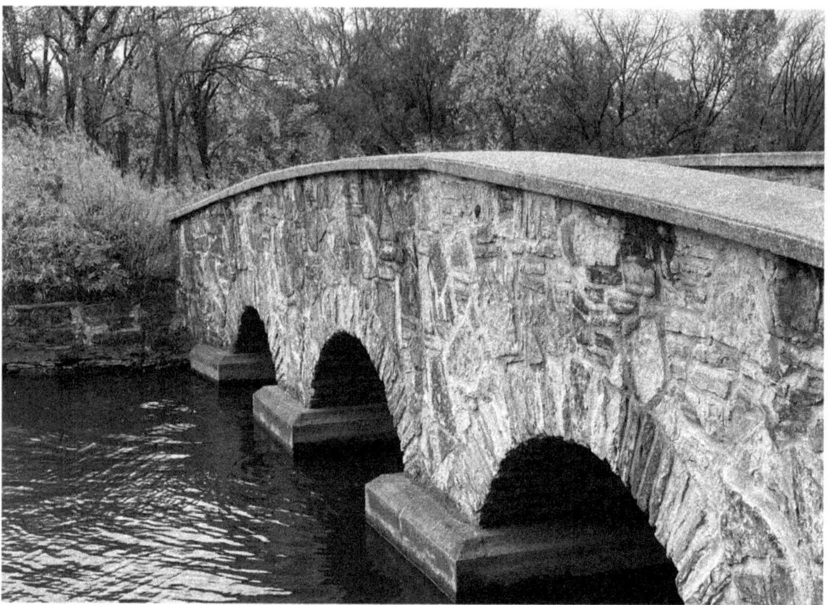

This is one of three similar arch bridges that connect several footpaths throughout Silver Lake Park in Rochester. *Photo by Steve Gardiner.*

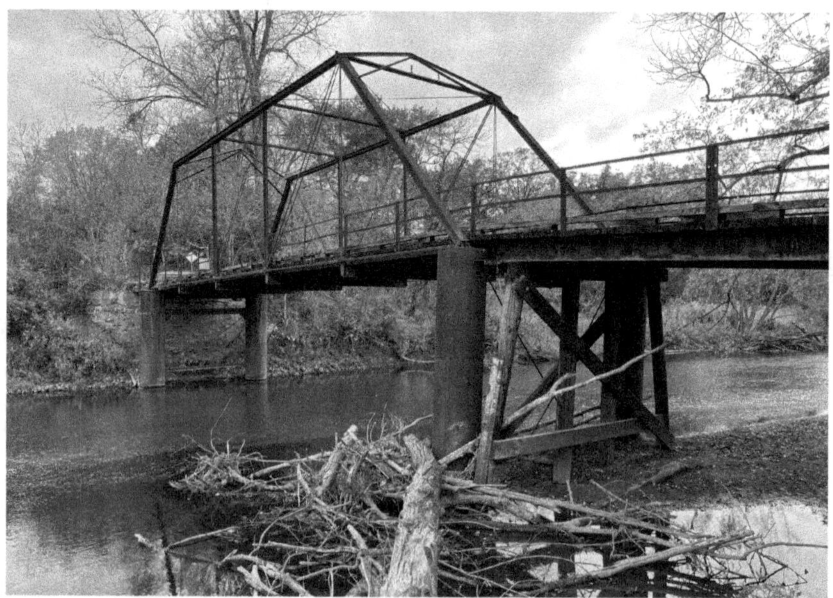

Frank's Ford Bridge is a Pratt through truss bridge with a wooden deck over the Zumbro River north of Rochester. It was constructed in 1895 by Horace E. Horton and the Chicago Bridge and Iron Company and is now closed to vehicle traffic. *Photo by Steve Gardiner.*

Iron. The main span has been connected to the original stone abutments by two timber-pile spans of more recent construction," according to the nomination form for the National Register of Historic Places completed on May 30, 1980.

In their Historic Bridge Report, MnDOT recommends that Frank's Ford Bridge, because of its abandonment and deterioration, is a candidate for relocation and rehabilitation.

ORONOCO BRIDGE

Crossing the Middle Fork of the Zumbro River was a challenge for early Oronoco residents, so in 1866, they built a wooden arch bridge. The gorge was prone to flooding, and the bridge was washed away in May 1876. Soon after, an iron Warren through truss bridge, built by Horace E. Horton, replaced it. That bridge served well until 1918, when improved techniques of building with reinforced concrete inspired the city to build an open-spandrel arch bridge in the same location.

The longest span on the concrete arch bridge is 208 feet, and the full length of the bridge is 295 feet. The original width was 20 feet. By 1987, the city needed a wider bridge and proposed a renovation. Because the bridge has historical significance, Olmsted County worked with the Minnesota Historical Society to develop a plan, according to a March 18, 1987 article in the *Post Bulletin*. Construction workers saved the original arch and reused it, replacing the deck with a new version that is 40 feet wide.

In 1937, the Federal Works Progress Administration constructed a concrete dam just upstream from the bridge that created the 230-acre Lake Shady, giving residents a popular recreation area. By the 1970s, sediment carried into the lake had restricted recreational use, according to the Minnesota Pollution Control Agency website.

Flooding continued to be a problem, and in September 2010, the swollen Zumbro River damaged part of the dam and washed out the entire approach at the north end of the Oronoco bridge, shutting down County Road 18. It took time, but the damage to the bridge was repaired. The dam, however, needed too much work, so other solutions had to be considered.

Local officials launched the Oronoco Dam Removal and Zumbro River Restoration Project, and in the winter of 2016–17, the dam was removed. Soon after, the river was restored to a more natural flow and several recreational amenities were added to the former lakebed.

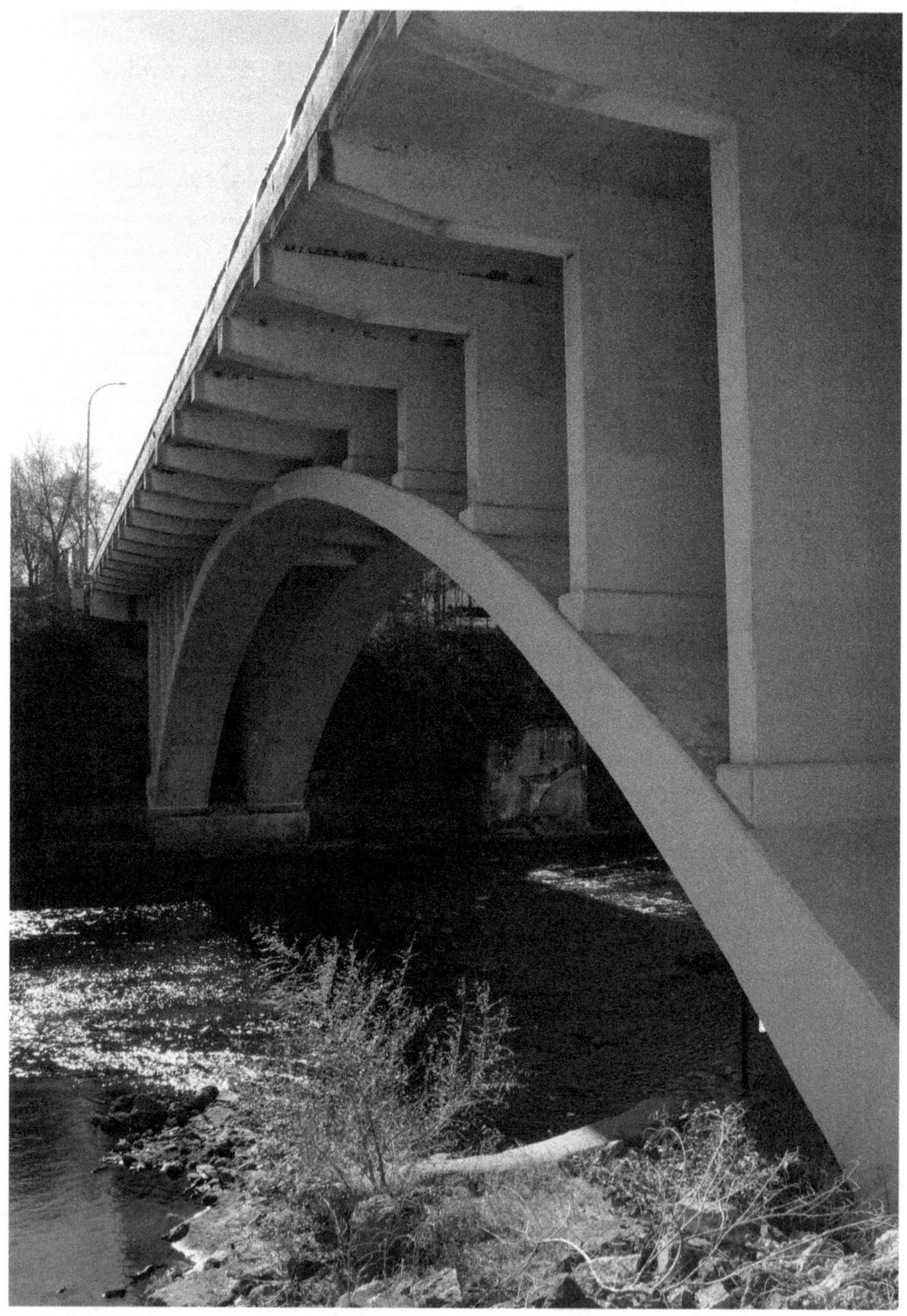

The substructure of the Oronoco Bridge shows the concrete arches and supports that keep the bridge, built in 1918 and rehabilitated in 1987, working strong today. The arch spans 208 feet, which is longer than most similar bridges. *Photo by Steve Gardiner.*

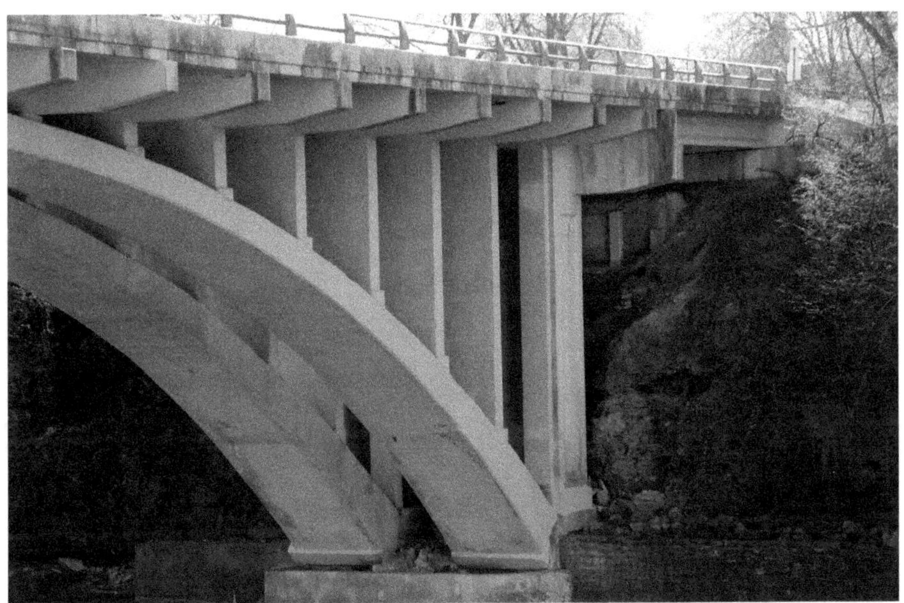

This is a view of the south abutment of the Oronoco Bridge on the southern edge of downtown Oronoco. The bridge carries County Road 18 across the Middle Fork of the Zumbro River. *Photo by Steve Gardiner.*

Terry Lee, water resources manager for Olmsted County Environmental Resources, told the *Post Bulletin* on December 22, 2016, that "the dam removal and river restoration will benefit the bridge. It will be a more stable stream, and water will be diverted away from the pilings, avoiding the kind of damage that was done in the last flood."

The restoration program included adding ten rock arch cascades in the river easily seen from the bridge.

WHITE BRIDGE

Built across the Minnesota River in 1885, White Bridge served the North Mankato community until the bridge was moved to Lake Zumbro in 1918, the same year the Oronoco concrete arch bridge was built. White Bridge, four miles east of Oronoco, was a popular place to visit, especially the Fisherman's Inn on the west side of the lake.

County officials had looked at the five-hundred-foot through truss bridge several times and considered replacing it because it was getting old and had a six-ton weight limit, according to a September 8, 1972 article in the *Post*

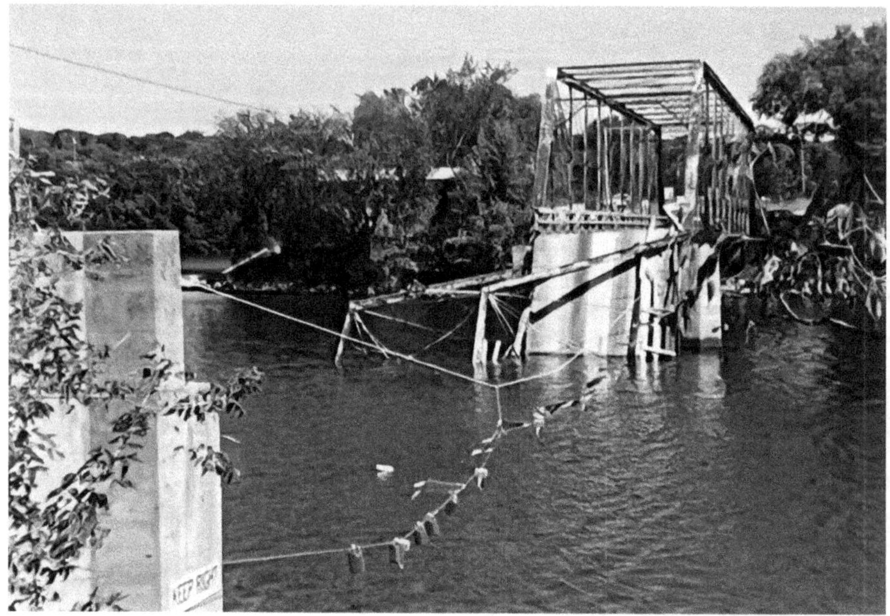

The remains of the White Bridge stand shortly after the bridge was knocked down by a car in 1972. *Courtesy of the Oronoco Area History Center.*

Bulletin. Unfortunately, the decision about the bridge was made for them. On that date, a car "hit a guard rail, skidded 50 feet along the rail then struck a beam," according to the *Post Bulletin*. Both the car and two hundred feet of bridge fell into the water.

Bill Hess from Pine Island, who was working at the Fisherman's Inn, helped pull the driver, Vernon Jahnke, twenty-three, from the lake. Jahnke was taken to St. Mary's Hospital and treated for injuries. Sheriff's deputies showed up to direct cars and boats away from the fallen span.

In November, an old army "Bailey Bridge" was installed as a temporary solution. Four years later, the Sandy Point Bridge, a half mile upstream, opened, and the remains of the White Bridge were removed in 1977.

Zumbrota Covered Bridge

The bridge in Zumbrota is the only covered bridge left in Minnesota, and it has been listed in the National Register of Historic Places.

The bridge was constructed in 1869 using a Town lattice truss design, a support system patented by Ithiel Town in 1820. It is 150 feet long and 15 feet wide and was built across the Zumbro River to help farmers get their crops to markets in Red Wing.

Two years later, in 1871, the bridge was covered with wooden sides and a roof with cedar shingles. The covering was designed to protect the bridge from harsh weather and extend the useful time of the structure.

In 1932, the Minnesota Highway Department built a steel bridge to handle the increased traffic coming through the area. The covered bridge was moved to the Goodhue County Fairgrounds, where it served several purposes as a fair exhibit area, a storage building and a beer hall.

Then, in 1964, the Zumbrota Covered Bridge Society purchased land near the Zumbro River and created Covered Bridge Park. They moved the bridge there and placed it on the ground, not over the river. It stayed there more than thirty years until, in 1997, Minnowa Construction from Harmony placed it on a steel framework across the Zumbro River in a spot one block west of its original location, according to a February 1, 1997 article in the *Red Wing Republican Eagle*.

Because the bridge had sat on the ground for several years, some of the bottom had deteriorated, so when the bridge was placed over the river, a

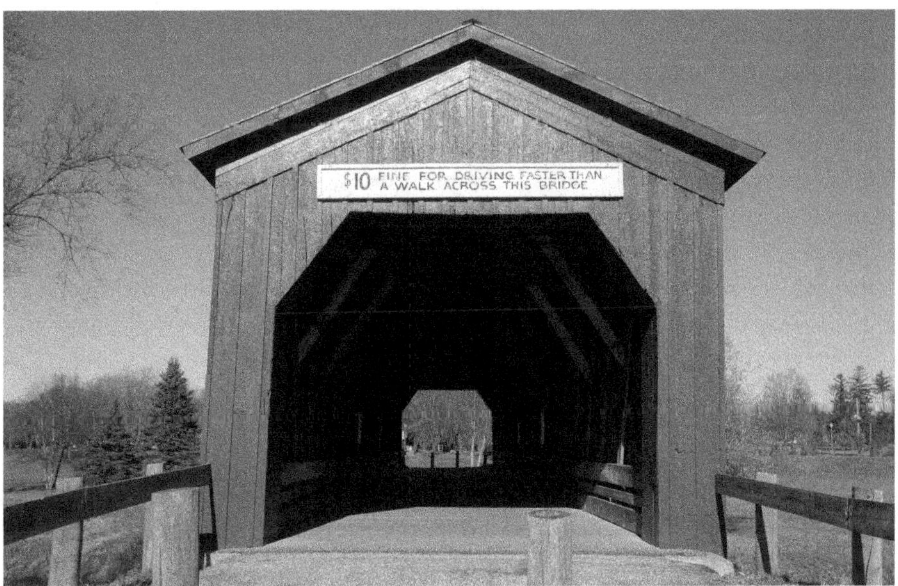

The wooden floor of the Zumbrota Covered Bridge caused problems for farmers who traveled to town in the winter. The roof kept snow off the deck, so horses couldn't pull sleighs across the bridge. The roof of the covered bridge partially collapsed under heavy snow in February 2019. *Photo by Steve Gardiner.*

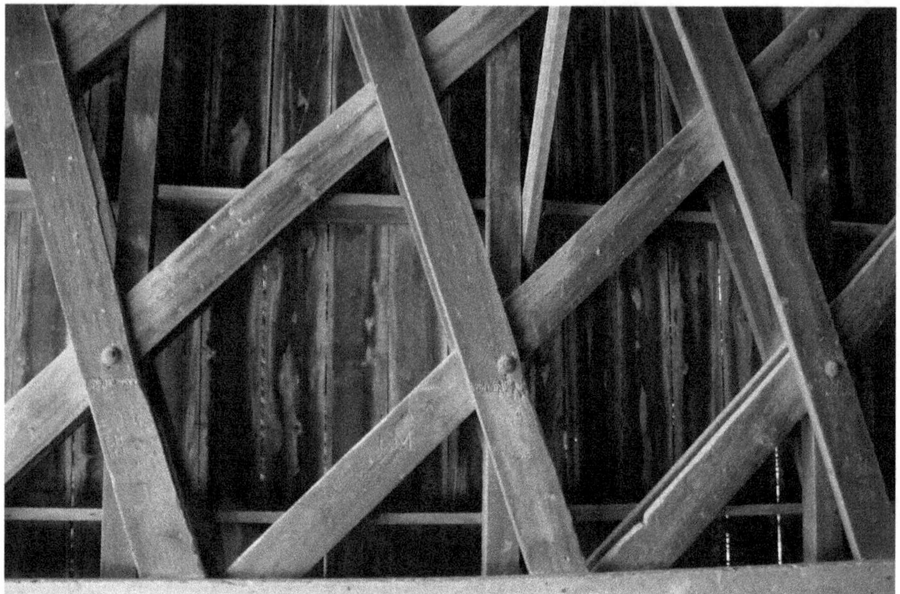

The trusses that support the Zumbrota Covered Bridge are Town lattice trusses, a style popular on covered bridges in New England. *Photo by Steve Gardiner.*

concrete center post and steel support beams were added. It is easily visible to motorists on Highway 58.

The bridge no longer handles vehicles but is reserved for pedestrians and bicyclists using the trails in the park and those walking from the community swimming pool to downtown. It is the site of the Covered Bridge Festival, which is held each year on the third weekend in June.

In February 2019, heavy snows collapsed the roof of the bridge. The gabled roof fell flat against the trusses beneath, and reconstruction of the roof was completed in November 2019.

Walnut Street Bridge

The Walnut Street Bridge crosses the North Branch of the Zumbro River in Mazeppa. It is a Pratt through truss bridge with a total length of 172 feet with a vertical clearance of 12.8 feet. It functioned as the main bridge in Mazeppa until 1922, when a new dam, which included a road, was built on the river.

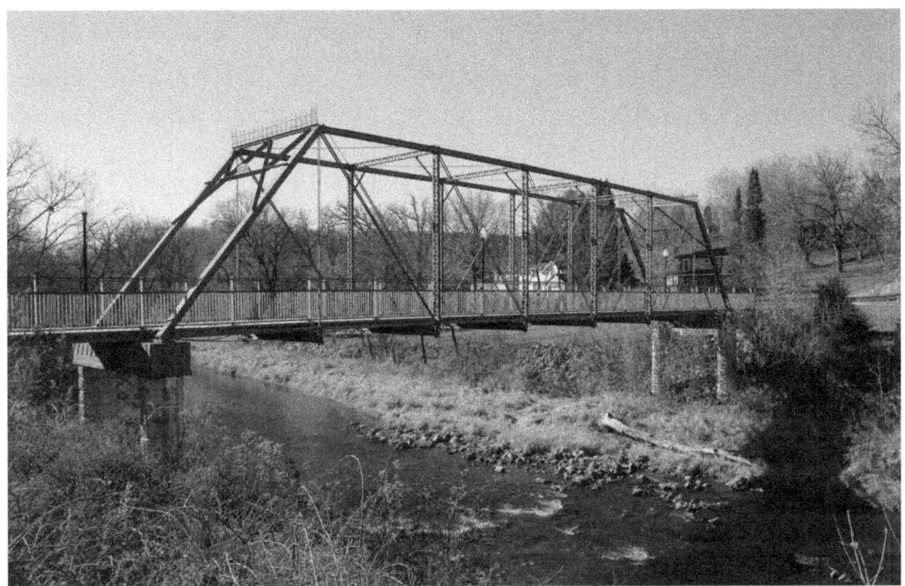

The Walnut Street Bridge in Mazeppa is a Pratt through truss bridge built in 1904. *Photo by Steve Gardiner.*

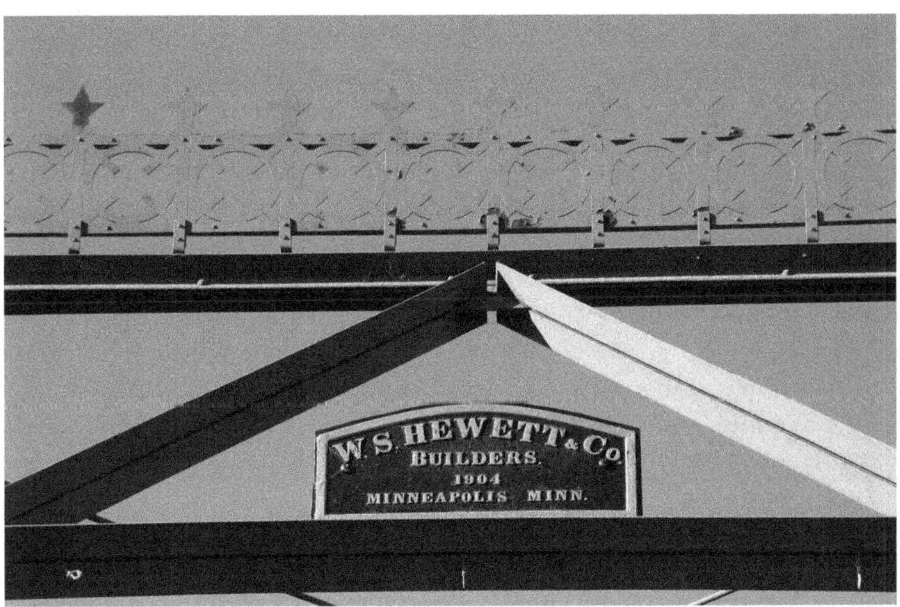

Many bridges have signs—like this one on the Walnut Street Bridge in Mazeppa—that indicate the builder and construction dates of the bridge. Above the sign is an example of decorative ironwork that was often used on older bridges. *Photo by Steve Gardiner.*

In 1980, the bridge was closed to vehicle traffic and served as a pedestrian bridge until 1995, when it was closed after a state engineer ruled it unsafe. Town residents wanted to save the bridge, so they found money from the state and other sources to repair it.

"That's part of the city's heritage," said city administrator Duane Hofschulte in the *Rochester Post Bulletin* on February 2, 2001. "This day and age, everything seems to be being knocked down and disappearing and years later you go, 'Why didn't we save that?'"

The rehabilitation was completed in 2002, and the bridge was reopened to pedestrian traffic and remains so today. The improvements earned the city an award from the Preservation Alliance of Minnesota. The bridge was listed in the National Register of Historic Places on January 15, 2003.

"The Walnut Street Bridge is significant as an example of the work of William S. Hewett and the W.S. Hewett Company, an important Minnesota engineer and bridge building firm," explained MnDOT on its website. "It is also significant for its high artistic value, as expressed in its exceptional ornamentation."

ZUMBRO PARKWAY BRIDGE

Designed by J.M. Evans, engineer with the Wabasha County Highway Department, and erected by the Works Progress Administration in 1937, the Zumbro Parkway Bridge, just outside Zumbro Falls, carries County Road 68, a two-lane unpaved road, across a tributary of the Zumbro River. The fifty-nine-foot-long bridge features two twenty-five-foot concrete arches, which are one of its unique features. Each arch is made of corrugated iron segments that are bolted together, a process called multi-plate. Metal cylinders were often used for bridges and culverts, but a full pipe was often difficult to ship and handle at the worksite. Multi-plate segments could be shipped nested inside each other, and because workmen were handling only segments, the metal could be thicker and used for longer spans.

"The corrugate-metal vault supports earth fill, which, in turn, supports the roadway," MnDOT reported in its History Inventory Form of the bridge. "Ornamented with simulated cut-stone voussoirs of cast concrete, the multi-plate arches are anchored in place by stone masonry head walls and straight-back retaining walls that rise above the roadway to serve as parapet railings."

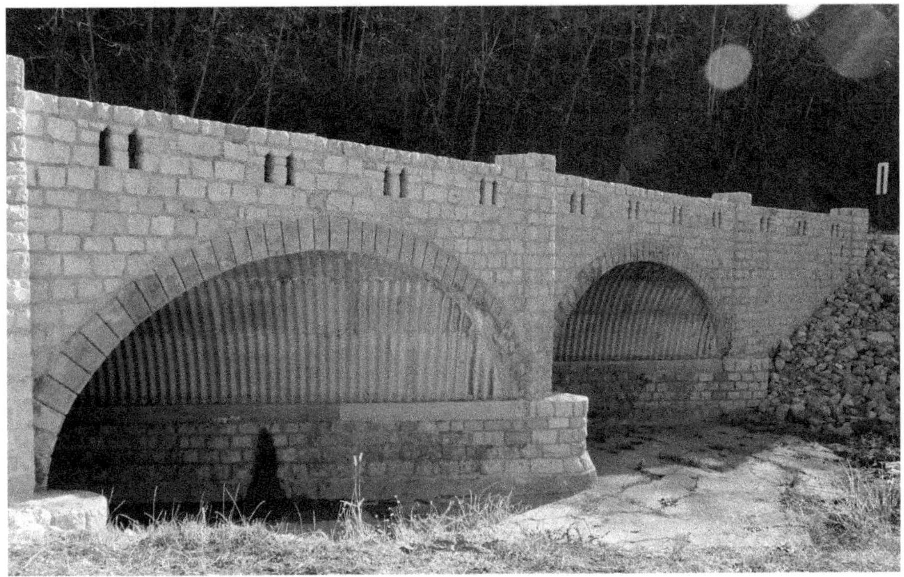

The Works Progress Administration built the Zumbro Parkway Bridge near Zumbro Falls in 1937. It is a double-arch, multi-plate bridge carrying County Road 68 over a tributary of the Zumbro River. *Photo by Steve Gardiner.*

MnDOT added that "the Zumbro Parkway Bridge is one of the finest examples of its type."

The bridge, owned by Wabasha County, has remained unaltered throughout its existence and was listed in the Register of Historic Places in 1989. The nomination form for the Zumbro Parkway Bridge states that the stone facing of the arches "took on the appearance of a stone arch bridge, which strongly appealed to the New Deal agenda of encouraging roadside beautification, local craft skills, and labor-intensive public works projects."

Chapter 5

WABASHA

A Bridge across the Channel

The Mississippi River presented a major challenge to any community developing along its banks. The town of Wabasha, occupied since 1826 and named in 1843, was no exception. By 1862, there were attempts to establish a ferry service between Wabasha and what is now the town of Nelson. The problem was reaching the Wisconsin shore because of the extensive backwaters.

The January 8, 1931 *Wabasha County Herald Standard* explained that "the poor road conditions through the Wisconsin bottoms made the operation of a ferry a most dubious business venture, with little profit in case of success and a much better chance for loss. The city, which had been operating the ferry, was on the verge of abandoning it because of its inability to get a satisfactory road through the bottoms when James G. Lawrence, president of the Wabasha Roller Mill Company, leased the ferry and at a great expense constructed a splendid new road to Nelson."

The Wabasha Roller Mill Company became the Big Jo Flour Mill in Wabasha, and adding Wisconsin grain to the mill was a boost to business, so Lawrence bought a cable ferry, called it the Big Jo Ferry and put it into service. On October 3, 1921, he gave the City of Wabasha permission to run the ferry, and on May 13, 1929, he gave the ferry to the city. The city made good money from running the ferry and in 1930 reported earning $14,049.28.

The success of the Big Jo Ferry in the late 1920s made it clear that traffic from Wabasha to Wisconsin was increasing. Other cities like Red Wing had had success building bridges across the Mississippi River, and many people in Wabasha were ready for their own bridge. In 1929, a group of citizens formed the Wabasha-Nelson Bridge Company and launched the process of designing and building a bridge.

Not everyone was pleased.

In the January 9, 1931 edition, the *Winona Republican Herald* called the Big Jo Ferry a "landmark in the state" and noted that "for the past 60 or 70 years, a ferry of some sort has been operated at Wabasha; at first a skiff, next a steamboat, after that cable ferries run by horses or steam power, and finally the gasoline engine."

The *Republican Herald* reported that ferries were able to handle horse and wagon traffic but stated that a "change came with the automobile and the increasing amount of travel which has severely taxed the capacities and efficiency of ferries. They do not meet the exigencies of a motor age, and like many another tried and true institution, will eventually have to go."

READS LANDING PONTOON BRIDGE

The early ferry connections seemed to keep most people happy in the 1860s and 1870s. However, by the 1880s, railroads were expanding their lines to include more markets, and the Milwaukee Road was running a line that crossed the Mississippi River at Prairie du Chien, Wisconsin, and continued up the west side of the river into the Twin Cities. They wanted to expand a line to Eau Claire, Wisconsin, and needed to make a connection somewhere upriver from Wabasha.

Several locations wanted the crossing to help local business, but the railroad chose Reads Landing, a site already booming from the many companies floating white pine logs down the Chippewa River and combining them with log rafts on the Mississippi.

Today, Reads Landing has a handful of buildings, but in the 1880s, because of the logging, "there were 27 hotels, 21 saloons, many businesses supporting the lumber trade, doctors, attorneys, and ladies of the evening in town," wrote Arlyn Colby in his book *The Chippewa Valley Line*.

Opponents complained that the location required long approaches on both sides, but the railroad argued that the channel at Reads Landing had not changed in twenty-five years, making it a good location. In March 1882, the Forty-Seventh Congress granted the Chippewa Valley and Superior Railway Company the rights to build the bridge at Reads Landing.

They chose to build a pontoon bridge with a center span that could be released and floated out of the way when river traffic needed to pass. It could then be moved back into place for rail traffic. Such a bridge was a complicated one to build and required some very creative engineering.

"Although the pontoon was 400 feet long, the river is nearly three miles wide including the sloughs on the east side, so long trestles formed the approaches," Colby explained. "The overall length of the bridge system was 2,795.5 feet. The east approach consisted of 64 timber pile trestle spans for a distance of 1,011 feet. In addition to this, there were a 105-foot span pony truss allowing passage of small watercraft and two iron span girders."

The pontoon bridge opened in July 1882, and not only was it a difficult bridge to build, but it required constant maintenance as well. Work crews monitored water levels in the river, using a system of jacks and blocks to raise and lower the pontoon so it matched the level of the tracks on the trestles.

"Three shifts of men each working eight hours a day manned the bridge," Colby wrote. "Besides the normal wear and tear, floods and ice damaged the bridge and trestle work frequently, even though the pontoon was protected by wooden ice breakers, huge wooden structures that projected out of the water to deflect ice. They had to be frequently rebuilt, so a pile-driver barge was always kept nearby."

Several major repairs and replacements were required to keep it in operation, including renovations in 1890 and 1932 and replacements of the pontoon span in 1891, 1907 and 1931. Those fixes were only a preview to what happened in 1951, when an ice sheet broke off Lake Pepin and washed out the pontoon span. Within days, the bridge cable broke and a second wave of floodwaters and ice broke thirty-two spans of trestle, some 480 feet of the east approach of the bridge, according to Colby.

The November 1, 1951 issue of the *Winona Republican Herald* reported that the damage was serious enough that Milwaukee proposed to shut down the Reads Landing Pontoon Bridge. The Interstate Commerce Commission accepted the proposal, and the bridge was taken out of service.

WABASHA-NELSON BRIDGE

The Big Jo Ferry, which had been running continuously in some form since the Civil War, made its final run at 11:45 p.m. on New Year's Eve 1930.

At 6:00 a.m. on New Year's Day 1931, the Wabasha-Nelson Bridge opened as a private toll bridge. The first day saw $60.35 in profit, and the first four days accounted for $282.30, making bridge proponents happy.

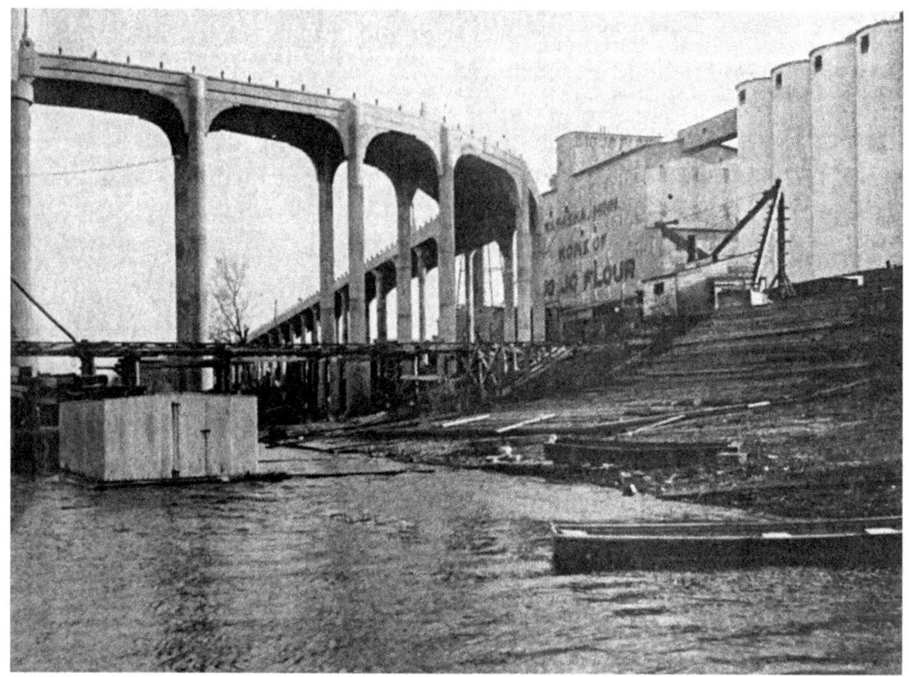

They were especially happy because many of them were stockholders. The Wabasha-Nelson Bridge Company had sold 4,750 shares of preferred stock at $100 per share as well as common stock to pay for the bridge in advance. Tolls, amounting to as much as $42,000 in 1946, kept the bridge running well, and in 1947, investors were again pleased when the company sold the bridge to the States of Minnesota and Wisconsin for $400,000, with each state paying half of the bill, according to the March 25, 1947 *Winona Republican Herald.* The sale, which included 2.4 miles of dike road between the east end of the bridge and Nelson, also brought one more bit of joy to area residents: the tollhouse was closed and the bridge was free.

"The celebration was on," the *Republican Herald* reported. "All business places in Wabasha closed, and a caravan of more than 25 cars started across the free bridge to spread the news in Nelson, Wis., just across the river. Nelson businessmen joined in the parade, and the celebrating crowd moved on to Alma. Alma businessmen joined in the celebration, informal in nature, and Pepin, Wis., joined hands. Then everybody went back to Wabasha where 'open house' prevailed until the 'wee hours' of today."

The Wabasha-Nelson Bridge, built by the Minneapolis Bridge Company and engineer Claude Allen Porter Turner, was a polygonal Warren through truss bridge. It had a total length of 2,365 feet with a 422-foot-high truss

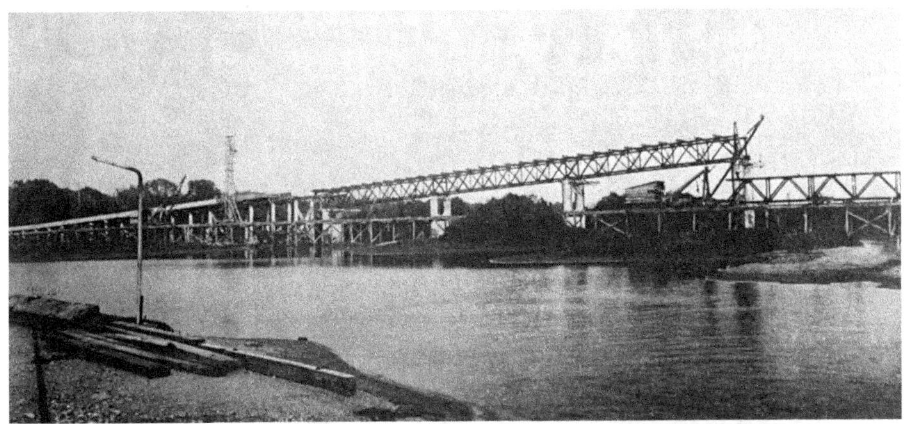

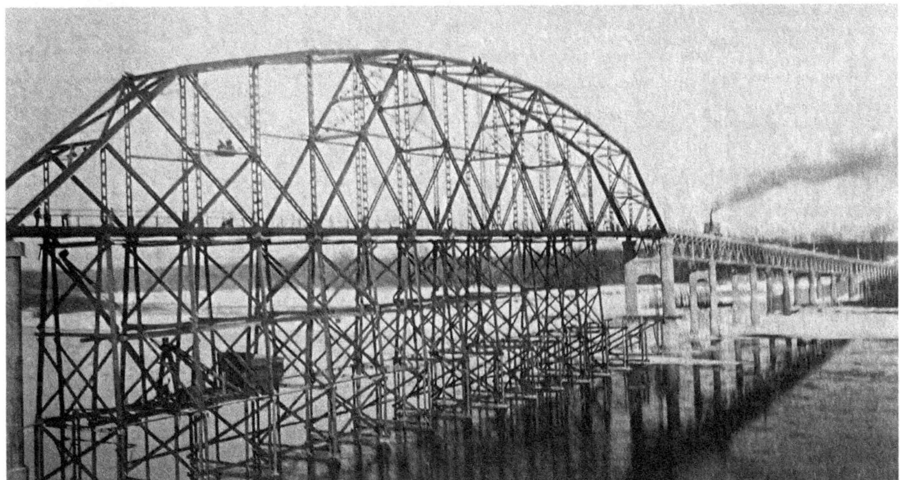

Opposite: This photo, circa 1929, shows the approach ramp on the Minnesota side during construction of the high truss bridge at Wabasha. It gives a good view of the piers supporting the ramp and the curve of the bridge in front of what were originally the Big Jo Flour buildings, later the home of International Multifoods. *Courtesy of the* Wabasha County Herald.

This page, top: Taken from an island upstream of the bridge, this photo, circa 1929, shows the early construction of the approach on the Wisconsin side. In front of the bridge is a service track with a crane that could be moved along the track as work developed. The crane is visible in the right center of the photo at the end of the last completed section. *Courtesy of the* Wabasha County Herald.

This page, bottom: Temporary structures called falsework support the center span of the Wabasha Bridge as the workers on the deck, in the middle of the trusses and on top of the trusses prepare the span for placement. This view is from Wabasha looking toward Nelson, Wisconsin. *Courtesy of the* Wabasha County Herald.

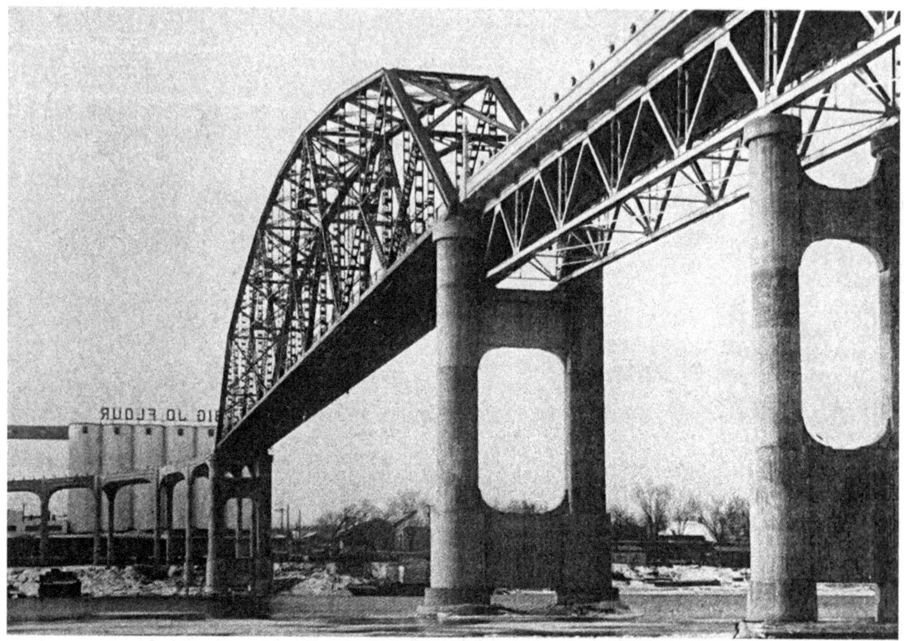

From the Wisconsin shore, the completed Wabasha Bridge stretches across the Mississippi River and then curves downstream in front of the Big Jo Flour buildings in Wabasha. The bridge opened to traffic on January 1, 1931. *Courtesy of the* Wabasha County Herald.

over the navigation channel. The steel and concrete bridge served well but, like most bridges of the time, suffered a few problems along the way.

In the spring of 1943, floodwaters washed out part of the approach dike between Wabasha and Nelson, closing the bridge until the water receded and the road could be repaired. In the summer of 1968, a pier collapsed and was replaced, closing the bridge for several days. Then the bridge was barricaded at both ends for several weeks in February and March 1969 when work crews discovered a one-fourth-inch crack in a gusset plate below the bridge deck, an eerie preview of a similar problem that caused the collapse of the I-35W bridge in Minneapolis thirty-eight years later.

The problems in 1968 and 1969 inspired change, and bills were introduced into the Minnesota legislature to authorize a new bridge at Wabasha. Damage wasn't the only reason to consider replacing it.

The Wabasha-Nelson Bridge featured two ninety-degree turns in order to direct traffic into downtown Wabasha, much like the Spiral Bridge in Hastings was designed to do for that city. That worked fine when traffic was wagons and a few small automobiles; they were able to negotiate the turns easily. However, when car traffic increased, accidents on the turns became more frequent. Then when commercial trucks became a major part of the region's economy, they had trouble with the sharp turns and often exceeded weight limits placed on the bridge by MnDOT.

In fact, in August 1987, MnDOT set up a weigh-in-motion scale, and during a forty-four-hour test period, they found that "228 trucks crossed the bridge. Sixty of these exceeded the single axle limit, some by very large margins. Nineteen of the vehicles exceeded the gross vehicle weight limit, and several were by very large margins. The posted limits are 5 tons per axle, 15 tons per single unit and 24 tons per combination unit," according to the *Wabasha County Herald* of September 30, 1987.

The bridge had simply outlasted its usefulness.

MICHAEL DUANE CLICKNER MEMORIAL BRIDGE

It took nearly two decades of discussing, planning and policy making, but in October 1986, Lunda Construction of Black River Falls, Wisconsin, began work to replace what was generally called the Old Wabasha-Nelson Bridge with the New Wabasha-Nelson Bridge.

The new bridge was built alongside the old bridge and was also a Warren through truss; thus, the two bridges looked more alike than other bridge replacements in the region. The steel trusses gave both bridges a sturdy, strong appearance.

The new bridge eliminated the two sharp turns. The Minnesota approach extended straight from the bridge over several streets before reaching ground level. That extension required removing old buildings from Main Street and a few houses and large trees from other streets.

By January 1987, crews were driving steel rod pilings into the riverbank and using seventy steel interlocking sheets to construct a cofferdam that would provide a fifty-foot-deep water-free chamber in the river to allow workers to complete the main channel work, noted the *Wabasha County Herald*.

In March 1988, residents were astounded to watch as steel beams 130 feet long and weighing sixty tons each were hauled into town, making the tight turns with some mechanical assistance.

"The task is eased considerably by a hydraulically driven motor attached to the rear sets of wheels, that when controlled by the truck driver, can turn on their own, swinging the beam around a corner as the truck moves forward," explained the *County Herald* in a March 2 issue.

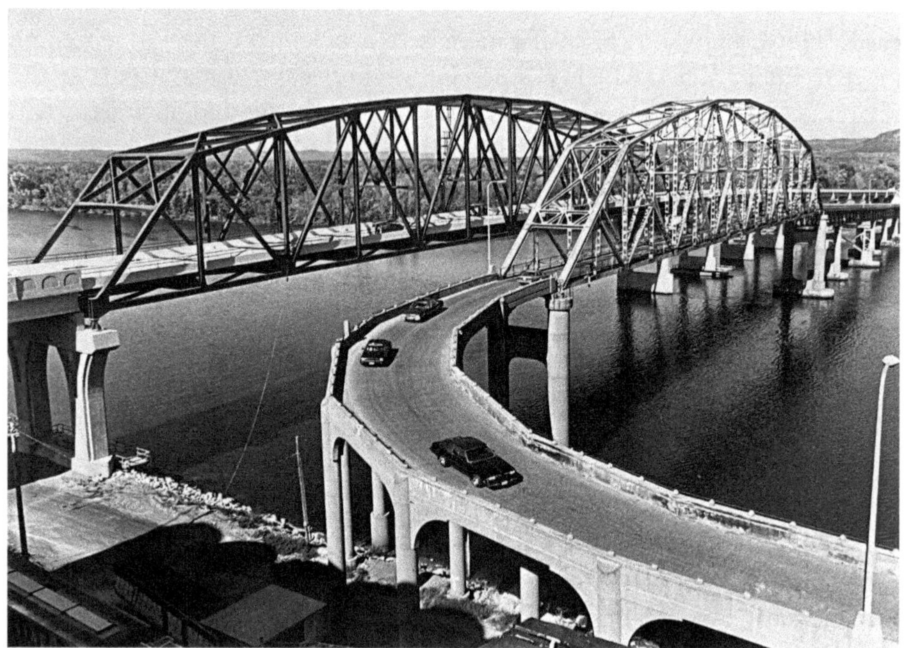

The new Wabasha-Nelson Bridge, *left*, stands beside the old Wabasha-Nelson Bridge before the old bridge was demolished. *Courtesy of the Wabasha County Historical Society*.

Another moving project occurred after crews spent three months assembling the 470-foot center span on the Wisconsin side of the river, according to the October 13, 1987 *Wabasha County Herald*. The next day, workers moved the span using two connected barges, which were winched downstream about 1,000 feet. Once crews had the span lined up with the concrete piers, they ballasted the barges with water to let them slowly sink down, setting the span in place. More water was added to the barges to lower them enough to let them clear the bottom of the span and move away from the bridge. Commercial and recreational uses of the river were shut down during the placement of the span.

With that major step complete, work—which would take another year to finish—resumed on the rest of the structure and concrete deck, as well as noise walls on the Wabasha approach to the bridge. The dedication and opening of the bridge to traffic was held at 11:00 a.m. on October 22, 1988, as Wabasha mayor Dan Losinski and Nelson Village president Elroy Averbeck cut the ribbon.

With the new bridge in place one hundred feet upstream, it remained for the crews to remove the old bridge, which had been closed the day the new

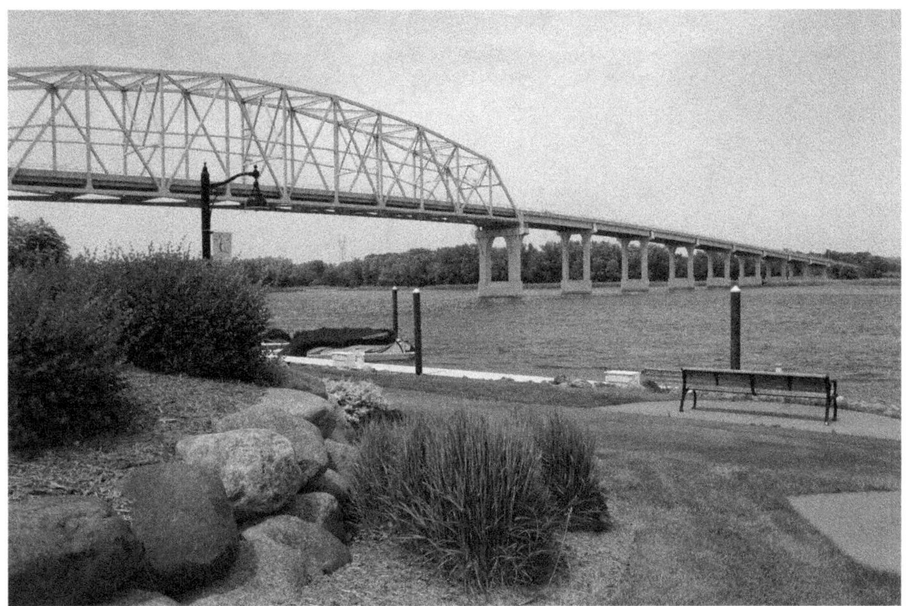

This view of the Wabasha-Nelson Bridge, which opened in 1988, is from the riverwalk in front of the National Eagle Center in Wabasha. Since 2014, the bridge has officially been known as the Michael Duane Clickner Memorial Bridge. *Photo by Steve Gardiner.*

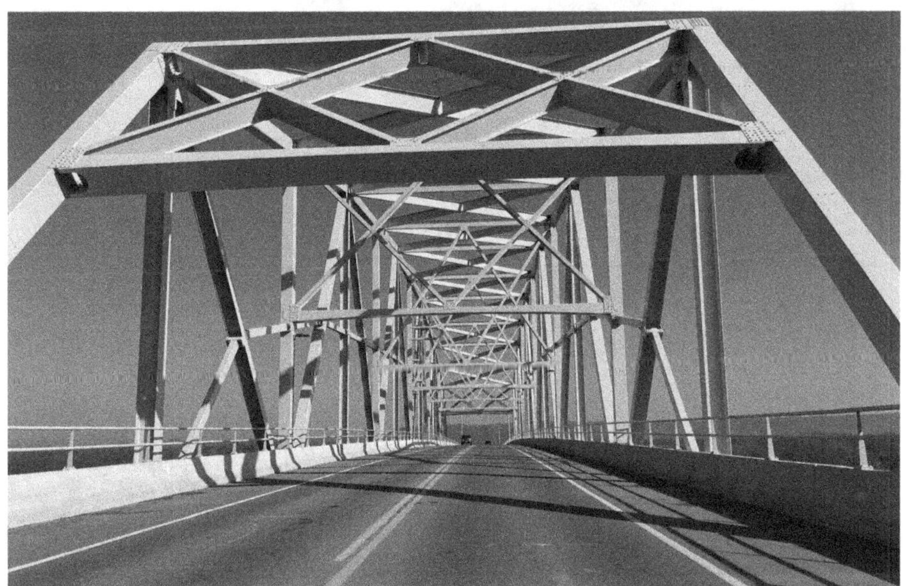

The Wabasha-Nelson Bridge is a through truss bridge with a main span of 470 feet and a total length of 2,462 feet. The clearance beneath the main span is 62 feet. *Photo by Steve Gardiner.*

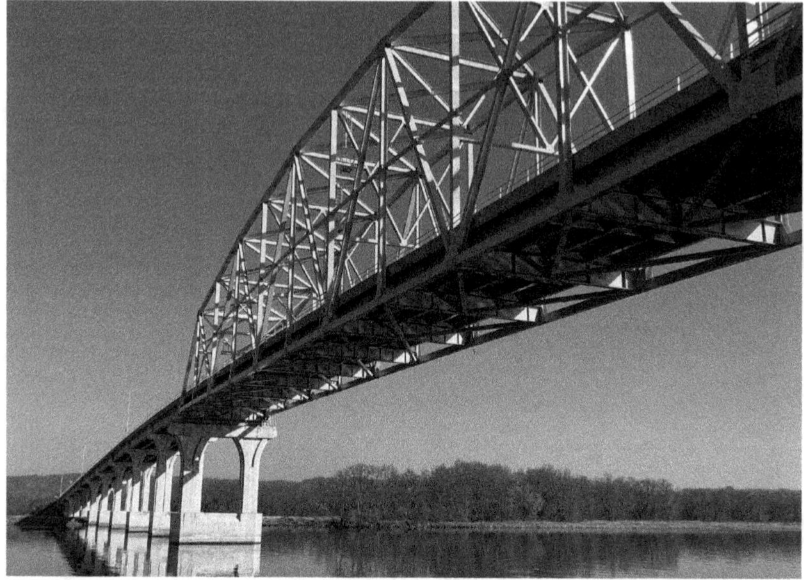

This view of the Wabasha-Nelson Bridge shows the multiple piers required for such a long bridge as it lowers into the Wisconsin side of the Mississippi River. *Photo by Steve Gardiner.*

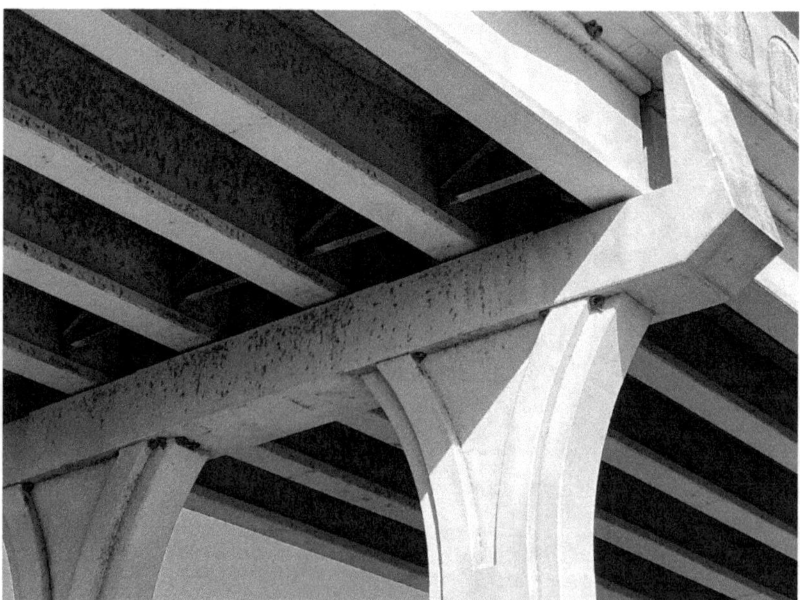

This is a close-up look at the point where one of the piers near Main Street in Wabasha joins the deck structure of the Wabasha-Nelson Bridge. *Photo by Steve Gardiner.*

bridge was dedicated. The demolition contract went to the same contractor that built the new bridge, Lunda Construction.

On January 3, 1990, cranes pulled the center span of the old bridge down into the river, reported the January 3, 1990 *Rochester Post Bulletin*. The span was then dismantled and removed from the river, and the piers were taken down. The new bridge remained standing by itself.

Eliminating the turns from the old bridge removed a dangerous problem, and it also allowed Wabasha to develop a riverwalk and, in 2007, build the National Eagle Center building.

In 2014, Governor Mark Dayton signed legislation renaming the New Wabasha-Nelson Bridge as the Michael Duane Clickner Memorial Bridge in honor of a Wabasha High School graduate who was killed on April 11, 1970, while serving in the army in Vietnam. Clickner was the only Wabasha resident killed during the war, reported the *Rochester Post Bulletin* of May 22, 2014.

ZUMBRO BOTTOMS IRON BRIDGE

This bridge, also called the Funk Ford Bridge, is in the Zumbro Bottoms Management Unit, part of the Richard J. Dorer Memorial Hardwood State Forest, which is a popular location for camping and horseback riding.

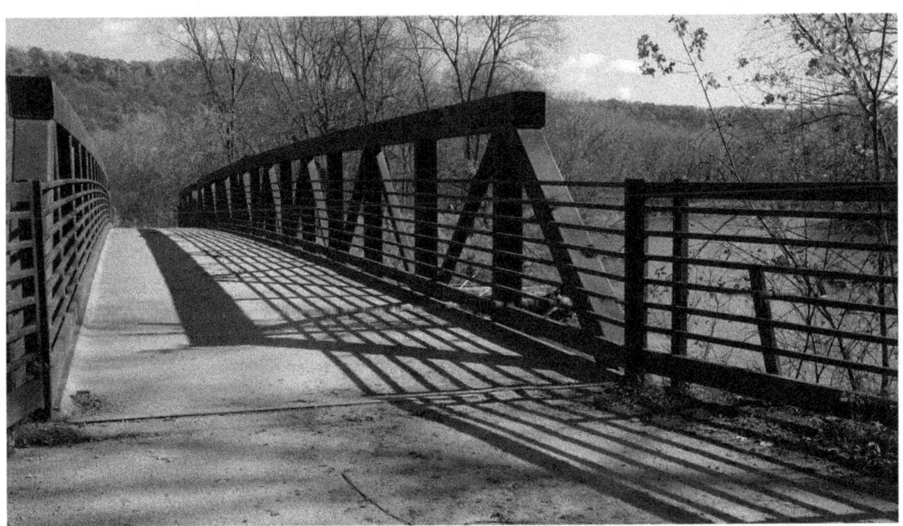

The Funk Ford Bridge in Zumbro Bottoms is an example of a pony truss bridge in which the trusses on the sides are shorter and don't connect over the top, as would happen in a through truss bridge. *Photo by Steve Gardiner.*

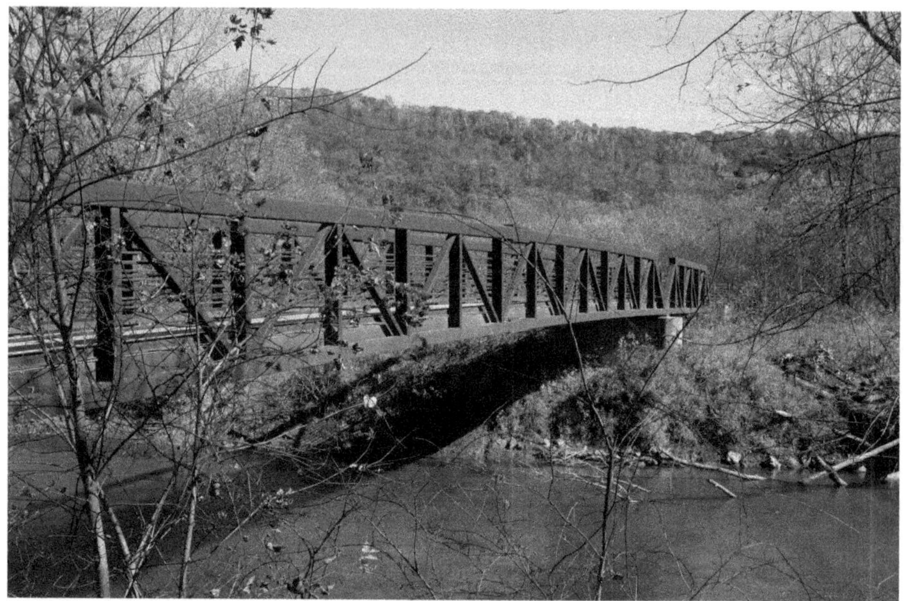

Funk Ford Bridge in Zumbro Bottoms is closed to vehicles but is used frequently by walkers and riders. *Photo by Steve Gardiner.*

Funk Ford Bridge used to carry 235th Avenue across the Zumbro River but has been closed to traffic. The bridge was built in 1910 and rehabilitated in 1930. The longest span is 128 feet, and the total length of the bridge is 190 feet.

Navigation Channel

All the bridges on the Mississippi River must be high enough that towboats, barges and cruise boats can pass under or have a lift or swing span to allow for river navigation to continue. The piers and abutments of these massive bridges can make navigating the river a challenge for pilots.

One other problem for river navigation is the constantly changing nature of the river and its bottom. The amount of water in the big river moves sediment in, filling low spots and reducing curves. So in addition to moving past bridges, commercial river traffic has to negotiate problems in the river bottom.

In the early days of navigation on the Mississippi River, boats were on their own to solve the problems presented by the ever-changing water. Then, as more and larger boats used the waterway, Congress authorized the four-and-a-half-foot river channel, giving the job to the army. They used wing dams, piles of brush and rock to direct the river flow into the center, where the current could scour the bottom and flush sediment farther downstream until it settled in slower-moving spaces between the thousands of wing dams they built. That worked for a while, but as even larger boats were built, a deeper channel was needed.

Congress increased the depth to six feet in 1906 and increased it again in 1930 to nine feet. The wing dams continued to help this process until the system of locks and dams was built in the early 1930s, raising the overall river level and submerging the wing dams into history.

Today, the U.S. Army Corps of Engineers is assigned the task of keeping a navigation channel open during the shipping season. They have a hydrographic crew that takes a survey boat out and makes passes through the river channel using sonar to record depths. The results of each survey are sent to a dredge boat. That crew uses the measurements to know where to dredge and how deep to go. Then the survey boat returns and measures the results to make sure the channel offers safe passage.

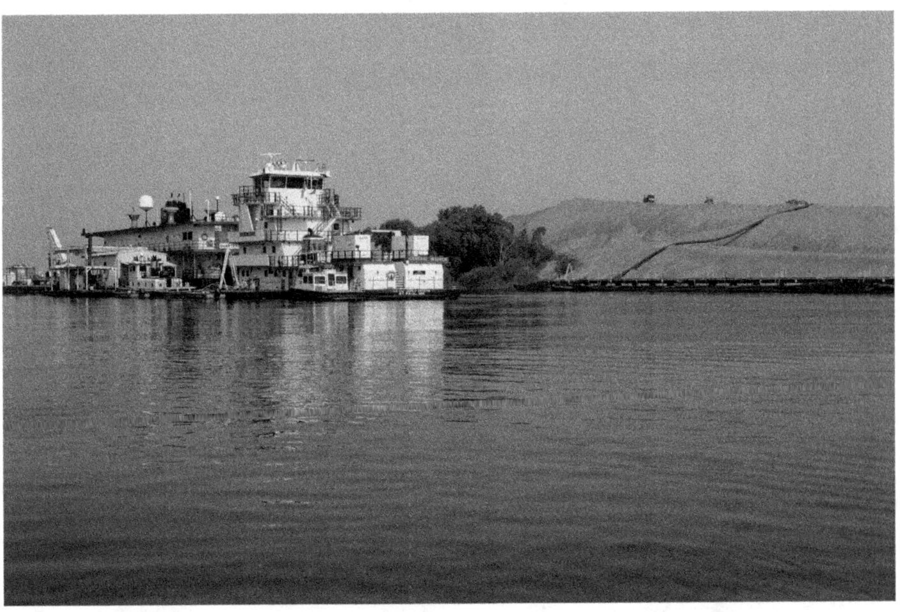

The U.S. Army Corps of Engineers runs a dredge boat to remove sediment from the bottom of the Mississippi River near Reads Landing and maintain a navigation channel. *Photo by Steve Gardiner.*

While they survey and dredge anywhere on the river, they have learned that there are certain problem spots that require more attention. One location that is dredged every year is at Reads Landing.

In an August 29, 2019 article in the *Republican Eagle*, Paul Machajewski, dredged materials manager for the U.S. Army Corps of Engineers, said the problem at Reads Landing is caused by the Chippewa River dumping sediment from Wisconsin into the Mississippi River.

"It's called the Nine-Foot Channel Project," Machajewski said, "but we dredge to twelve feet. We maintain the straightaways about 300 feet wide, but when you go around a corner, the barges need more room, so we will go 500 feet or wider on the bends, so they can get around the corner."

When the dredge boat is working at Reads Landing, the crew works around the clock with two twelve-person crews working twelve-hour shifts, Machajewski explained. He said that when they dredge at Reads Landing, they often remove as much as 60,000 cubic yards of sediment. "They do about 1,000 yards per hour, which is about 100 dump truck loads if you are trying to visualize that," he said.

The sediment dredged from the river bottom at Reads Landing ends up piled on an island across the river, forming a large sand dune. There are similar problem areas up and down the river.

Chapter 6

WINONA

A Bridge to Latsch Island

The city of Winona is located on a section of the Mississippi River that runs primarily east–west, meaning that river crossings happen in a north–south direction. Thus, Latsch Island at Winona splits the Mississippi River into what are called the North Channel on the Wisconsin side and the Main Channel on the Minnesota side. The island served as a convenient steppingstone in attempts to ferry, and later bridge, across the river.

Until the mid-1860s, getting across the river usually meant finding somebody who had a boat and was willing to make the crossing. Then in May 1865, Samuel D. Van Gorder set up a ferry service, capable of carrying four teams and wagons, that ran on a regular basis. By 1868, Van Gorder was busy enough that he built a road across Wisconsin bottomlands and a floating dock at the end of Walnut Street in Winona to improve his ferry service. He ran that ferry until 1880, when the City of Winona took over. In 1883, the city improved the road and in 1886 built a 1,500-foot wooden bridge across the North Channel. That bridge, leaving from a former stagecoach stop called the Old Stone House and crossing to Latsch Island, was finished in March 1887, connecting with what was by then a cable ferry.

In the meantime, railroad service had reached La Crosse, Wisconsin, downriver from Winona, but had no way to cross the river, so any goods intended for Winona had to be shipped by steamboat until the first railroad bridge in the region opened at Winona in 1871.

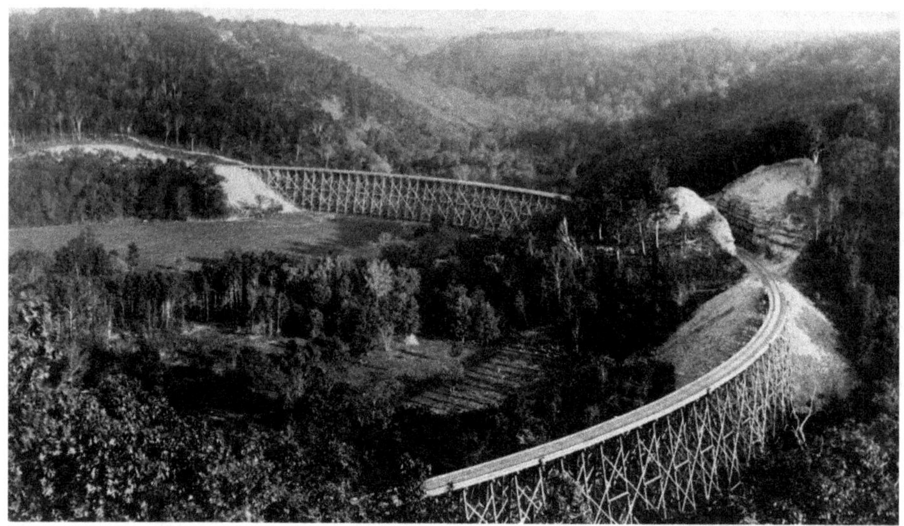

The Winona and Southwestern Railroad trestle between Rollingstone and Altura in about 1895. *Courtesy of the Winona County Historical Society.*

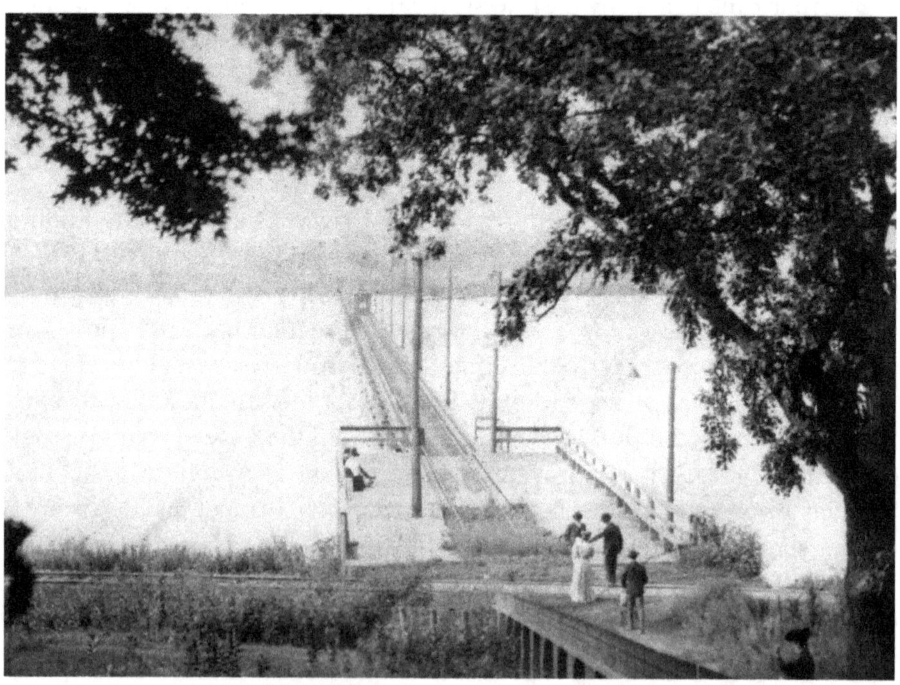

View of the Street Car Bridge across Lake World in about 1915. *Courtesy of the Winona County Historical Society.*

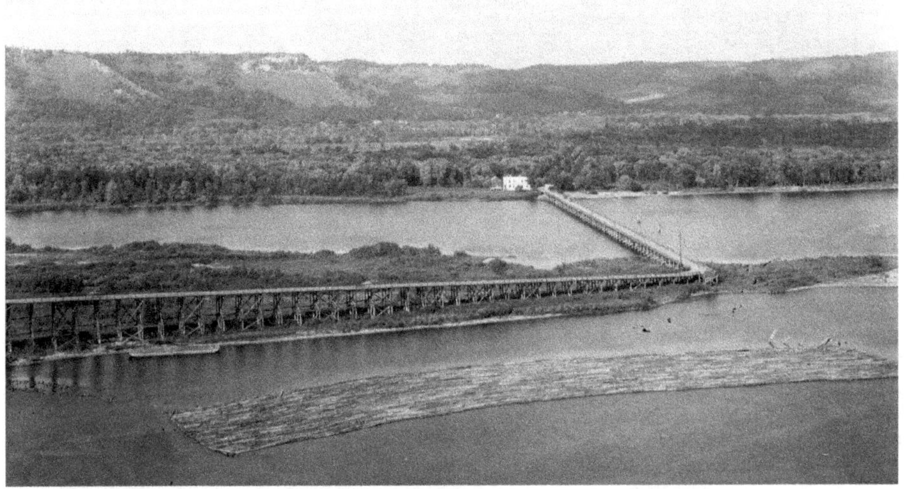

This photo shows the ferry bridge to Wisconsin by the Old Stone House in about 1900. *Courtesy of the Winona County Historical Society.*

The *Winona Daily Republican* reported that the new railroad bridge "is both imposing and symmetrical in its appearance, and it possesses all the strength and solidity that the most scientific combination of stone, iron, and wood, can impart to any structure of the kind."

The paper went on to note that the bridge created a path where a "great tide of commerce and travel" could pass through the city, adding that "Winona stands at the gateway of Minnesota—that through her portals must pass the great bulk of the commerce of the State."

That bridge built up everyone's hopes and then quickly dashed them.

WINONA SWING BRIDGE

That first railroad bridge, built by the Winona and St. Peter Railroad, had a swing span, and a large crowd gathered on Thursday, May 25, 1871, to watch the first train cross. The *Winona Daily Republican* reported that just after five o'clock in the afternoon, the locomotive Baltic pulling two passenger cars and a baggage car left the Winona depot, and as the train pulled onto the span, the crowd watched for any movement in the bridge, but "everything seemed as firm and substantial as the trestle work upon the shore."

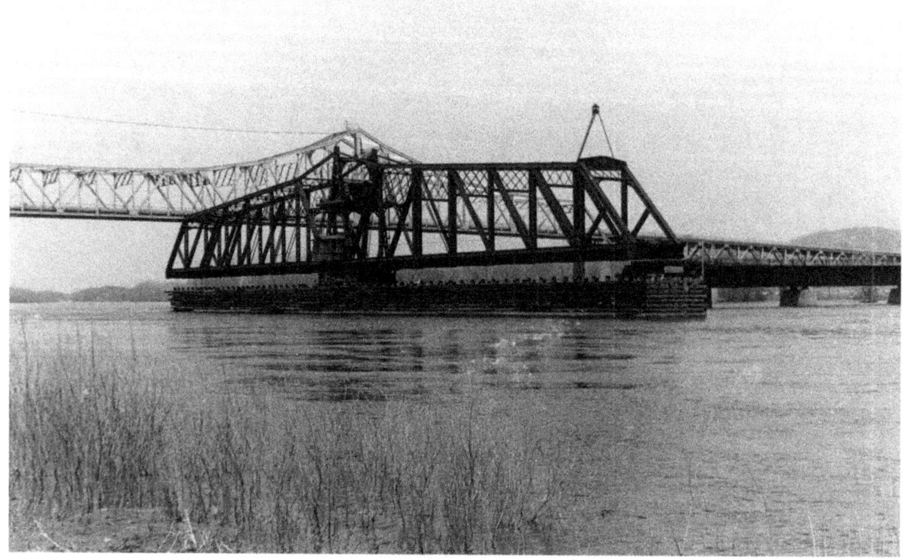

The Chicago Northwestern Railroad swing bridge from Winona to Wisconsin in the 1920s. *Courtesy of the Winona County Historical Society.*

The short train crossed into Wisconsin and then came back across the river to Winona, its passengers elated with their journey. With that test behind them, the railroad was eager to start running freight trains, and on Saturday, May 27, a train with fifty-four cars crossed from Wisconsin. As the train moved across, the swing span gave way.

News spread quickly through Winona, and many people went down to see the wreck.

"The river for a long distance was strewn with floating timbers and dotted with yawls and boats that had pushed out to rescue the unfortunate men who had gone down with the train, while men and women gathered around the boats as they came in with those whom they had snatched from a watery grave," wrote the *Republican* that evening.

Fortunately, no one was killed, but the bridge was severely damaged. With the need for traffic across the river, the railroad immediately began reconstruction. The original wooden swing span was replaced with a 363-foot iron span, and the bridge reopened the following year.

The January 20, 1872 edition of the *Rochester Post* reported that the second version of this bridge underwent significant testing before coming into use. Crews ran six platform cars loaded with iron onto the swing span, and the bridge passed the test.

"Under the weight of the railroad iron and two locomotives—110 tons in all—the deflection was only three-quarters of an inch, and it was the same with three locomotives and the iron—140 tons."

The Chicago and Northwestern bought out the Winona and St. Peter Railroad and continued to use the bridge at Winona. By 1895, both the bridge and the river were in constant use. Bridge tenders were required to turn in annual usage reports, and the 1895 numbers were high—4,428 boats, 1,324 barges and 1,655 rafts, according to the *Daily Republican* on November 15 of that year.

The bridge continued to undergo improvements, with the swing span being replaced in 1899 and the entire bridge being rebuilt on the same site in 1928, including a steel swing span. That version of the bridge was used until the bridge closed on December 24, 1977. After the closing, the swing span was removed, but the girder spans still stand just downstream from the Main Channel highway bridge.

WINONA BRIDGE RAILWAY

A second railroad bridge was built farther downstream on the east end of Winona by the Winona Bridge Railway Company, an entity that would encompass three railroads—Winona and Southwestern Railway; Chicago, Burlington and Northern; and the Green Bay, Winona and St. Paul—so that all three railroads could use the bridge.

On July 22, 1891, the *Daily Republican* reported that E. Gerber inspected the structure and said the bridge, a steel truss with a swing span, had been constructed in a "first class and very satisfactory manner," and it opened on August 1, 1891.

The bridge had heavy use, and seven years later, inspectors found that the pilings, ties and stringers were worn and needed replacing. Because of the height of the bridge, the pilings were longer than could be found in the region, and they had to be shipped in from Arkansas, according to the *Daily Republican* of November 28, 1898.

The repairs were made, and the bridge handled traffic until the 1970s, when loads became too heavy. At that time, the bridge was owned by the Burlington Northern, and it was abandoned. On December 17, 1989, a fire burned a section of the trestles, and the bridge was removed in 1990.

Winona High Wagon Bridge

In 1890, Congress authorized the City of Winona to build a bridge across the Main Channel of the Mississippi River. Like other bridges in the area at that time, it would be a toll bridge that would, officials hoped, pay for itself.

Also like other contemporary bridges, it featured two ninety-degree turns on the Minnesota end taking traffic from downtown Winona across the river to Latsch Island, where a road connected with the old ferry bridge into Wisconsin.

The Winona High Wagon Bridge opened on June 18, 1892, and within a handful of years, controversy about the toll was making news. Most voices wanted the toll removed, but on May 10, 1900, the *Daily Republican* reported that the Winona Retail Grocers' Association opposed making the bridge free. While a free bridge might entice more Wisconsin farmers to bring their produce to Winona grocery stores, the organization stated that "taxes at present are high enough, and the additional expense of operating the free bridge would increase the burden out of proportion to the benefits derived."

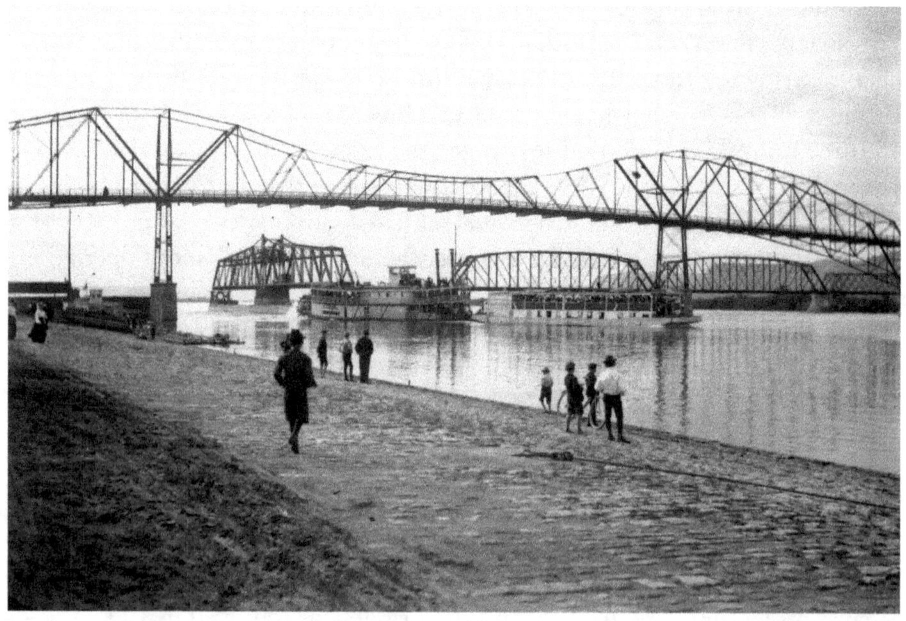

The High Wagon Bridge at Winona. *Courtesy of the Winona County Historical Society.*

By December 6, 1917, the *Republican Herald* stated that Winona was the only city on the Mississippi River in the region to still be charging a toll, as La Crosse dropped its toll the year before and Red Wing abandoned its toll the previous month. The paper called the toll an "unnatural barrier" to business and visitation between Winona and Wisconsin and warned that business that should come to Winona was heading to smaller markets in Wisconsin.

ALSO IN 1917, THE City of Winona built a replacement for the wooden ferry bridge across the North Channel on what was called Old Duke Road. The John A. Latsch Wagon Bridge, sometimes called the Historic Wagon Bridge, featured twelve 75-foot concrete arches with open spandrels. The 1,229-foot concrete bridge connected directly to the approach trestles of the High Bridge, making a complete crossing of the Mississippi River and channels.

"The new structure from Latsch Island to the Wisconsin side of the Mississippi River has greatly improved traveling over the river and is appreciated by the Wisconsin farmers," reported the *Republican Herald*.

THE TWO RIGHT-ANGLE TURNS on the Winona end of the bridge proved to be a serious problem on October 2, 1919, when a carload of friends headed to Wisconsin for a few drinks. On the way back to Winona, the driver, John Barry, a Minneapolis real estate agent, crashed into the railing of the bridge. Berry told the *Republican Herald* six days after the accident that he had become confused by lights on the street in Winona and misjudged the turn. The car ended up with the right front wheel suspended over nothing. Two passengers left the car through the right-side door and fell sixty-five feet onto concrete below, killing twenty-six-year-old Dennis Lynch and leaving twenty-four-year-old Percy Rollinger with permanent injuries.

IN 1920, THE MINNESOTA legislature created the State Trunk Highway System. Two years later, the Winona High Bridge and its approaches were incorporated into that system, meaning the City of Winona no longer needed to pay for the maintenance of the bridge. That opened the door for removal of the bridge toll on December 1, 1923, a development locals had been requesting for years.

As part of the turnover of the bridge, inspectors determined that there were $8,000 in repairs that needed to be paid for by the City of Winona before the state could assume responsibility, according to the November 21, 1923 edition of the *Republican Herald*. The city approved the expenses, and the bridge was repaired and the toll removed.

The same article noted that "the Wisconsin section of the bridge, as well as the dike road between the bridge and Bluff Siding have already been incorporated by the Wisconsin highway department into Trunk Highway No. 25."

ALL SEEMED WELL WITH the Winona High Bridge until August 9, 1935, when a section of the La Crosse bridge, similar in age and design, collapsed, killing two people. A warning had been sent.

OLD MAIN CHANNEL BRIDGE

With the bridge at La Crosse closed, much of the traffic was diverted to Winona, raising concern for the heavy use on the bridge. That inspired an August 16 editorial in the *Republican Herald* that stated, "The tragic mishap at La Crosse, the collapse of part of the bridge, dramatically awakens Winona to a latent problem in this community—construction of a new bridge across the Mississippi here."

The editorial noted the changing nature of transportation and the fact that the High Wagon Bridge had paid for itself many times over by bringing millions of dollars of business into the community.

With both communities in need of new bridges, another editorial on August 24 noted, "Seen in true perspective, efforts being made by Winona and by La Crosse to build new Mississippi River bridges are area undertakings rather than the ventures of the two individual cities chiefly concerned."

That call for cooperation would help in meeting the demand for connections between both cities and states. With the La Crosse bridge damaged, progress there was more urgent, and a replacement bridge was opened in September 1939. Progress happened in Winona as well.

On June 14, 1938, the *Republican Herald* reported that both the Senate and House of Representatives in Washington had authorized Minnesota and Wisconsin, jointly or separately, "to construct, maintain and operate a free highway bridge across the Mississippi River at Winona." Three days later, the bill was sent to President Roosevelt, who signed it into law.

Earlier legislation in both states and at the federal level had approved a trade of islands in the Mississippi River. Wisconsin agreed to give Latsch Island, a popular swimming spot for Winonans, to Minnesota in exchange for Barron Island, which held Pettibone Park, a favorite of the citizens of La Crosse, according to the September 4, 1918 *Winona Republican Herald*. The swap of islands later helped define the two sets of bridges.

Plans and designs for a new bridge at Winona were developed in 1939, and on November 11, the *Republican Herald* reported, "Under acts of legislatures of Wisconsin and Minnesota approved by Congress, the state boundaries at La Crosse and Winona were changed some years ago. All of the new La Crosse bridge is in Wisconsin, while all of the proposed Winona bridge will be in Minnesota."

This meant that each state would construct the approach on its side, and Minnesota would build the Winona bridge.

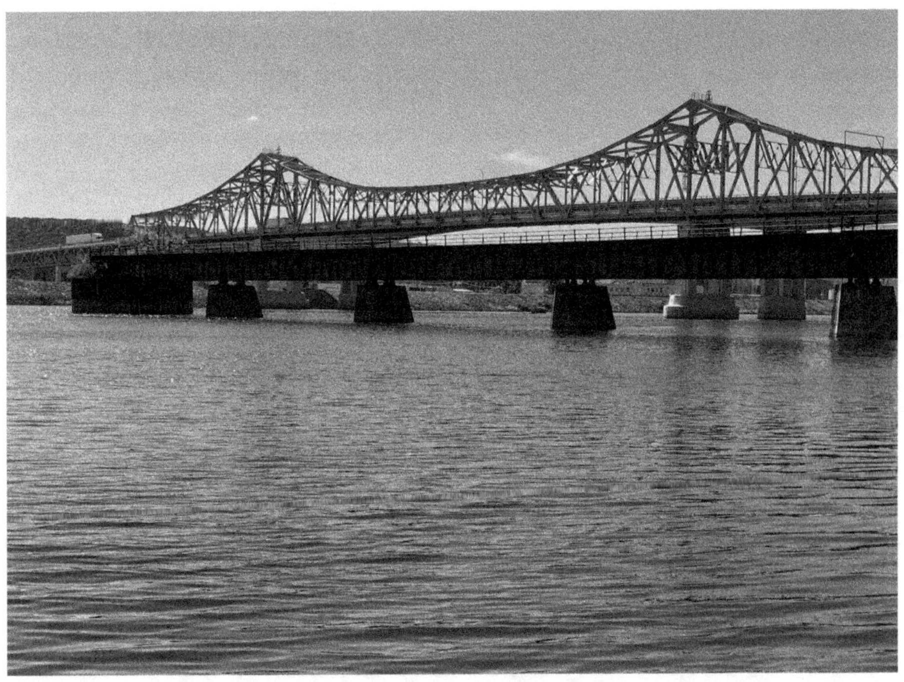

The remains of the old railroad bridge stand in front of the two current highway bridges at Winona. The original Main Channel Bridge is a cantilever bridge with a main span of fifty feet. The newer bridge, seen behind, is a concrete box girder bridge that opened in 2016. *Photo by Steve Gardiner.*

On May 19, 1940, a meeting in Winona heard concerns from navigation interests on the Mississippi River, a requirement of any bridge crossing a navigable river. By April of the following year, bids were out for construction of the new Winona bridge, which included the bridge over the main channel, a new bridge directly across the north channel and the connecting roadwork.

Work started soon after, and by May 29, 1941, the *Republican Herald* reported that crews were forming concrete abutments and piers and hoisting steel girders into place.

The Winona Main Channel Bridge, carrying Minnesota State Highway 43 across the Mississippi River to join with Wisconsin Highway 54, opened on November 21, 1942. It is a cantilever bridge with three spans. The 450-foot main span is a Warren through truss. The cantilever trusses give the upper chord a twin peaks look. The two approach spans are deck trusses, and the total length of the bridge is 2,288 feet.

WITH THE NEW BRIDGE in place, work crews tore down the High Wagon Bridge, and the steel was recycled in the war effort. The new North

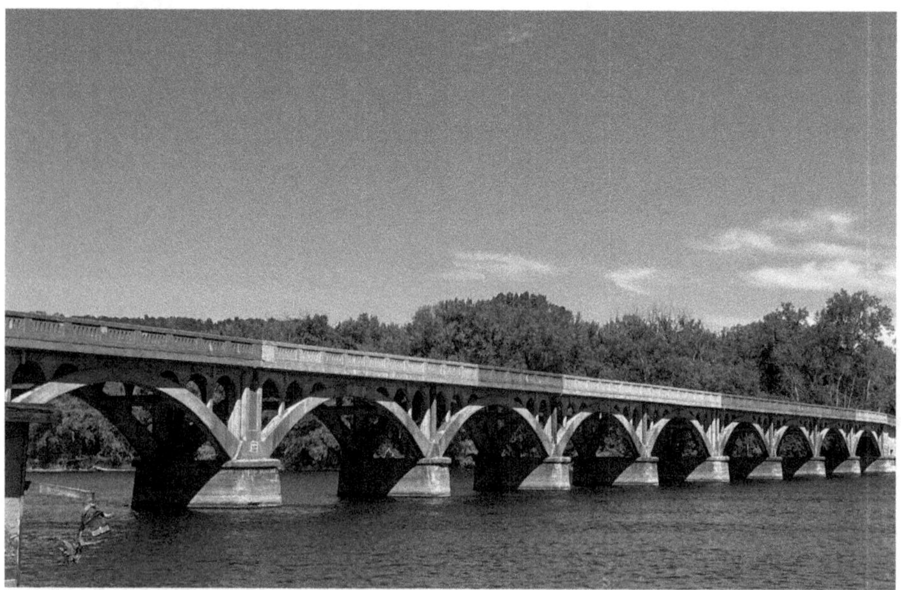

The John A. Latsch Bridge connects Latsch Island to Wisconsin. It was built in 1917 and replaced the original wooden bridge at the same location. It is a concrete arch bridge and had a concrete deck. *Photo by Steve Gardiner.*

Channel Bridge, which created a straight route across Latsch Island to Wisconsin, made the concrete arch Latsch Wagon Bridge unnecessary. With the approach to the High Wagon Bridge removed, the island end of the Latsch Bridge was several feet above ground. The expense to remove the Latsch Bridge and the lack of workers to do the job meant it was just abandoned for the time being.

After the war ended, the City of Winona gained control of the bridge and built a ramp on the Latsch Island end of the bridge so the bridge could again function. By 1996, the bridge, almost eighty years old, had deteriorated and was closed to traffic. The city considered removing the bridge, but citizens raised funds to pay for repairs, and the John A. Latsch Wagon Bridge reopened in 2004.

FOR SEVERAL DECADES, THE Old Main Channel Bridge was the pride of Winona. However, after the I-35W bridge collapsed in Minneapolis, bridges everywhere were examined more closely, and the Old Main Channel Bridge, having gusset plates similar to the ones on the I-35W bridge, was a concern. Inspectors found the plates were rusted and shut down the bridge on June 3, 2008, leaving travelers with a sixty-mile detour. The problem was fixed, and the bridge reopened on June 14, eleven days later.

The safety concerns made officials consider several proposals: rehabilitate the bridge; remove the bridge and build a new one; or build a second bridge alongside the first and then rehabilitate the first bridge using the two bridges to create two lanes of traffic in each direction. The latter idea seemed best, and on August 23, 2012, MnDOT announced plans to proceed.

NEW MAIN CHANNEL BRIDGE

Construction of the new bridge began in 2014, and the bridge opened on August 27, 2016. It is a concrete box girder bridge that is 2,295 feet long and 34 feet wide with two vehicle lanes and a bike/pedestrian path.

As soon as the New Main Channel Bridge opened, the Old Main Channel Bridge was shut down. All traffic was directed to the new bridge, and a full rehabilitation of the old bridge started, according to the *Rochester Post Bulletin* of August 27, 2016.

This process, which MnDOT said would extend the life of the bridge by fifty years, included removing and replacing the bridge deck, repairing the

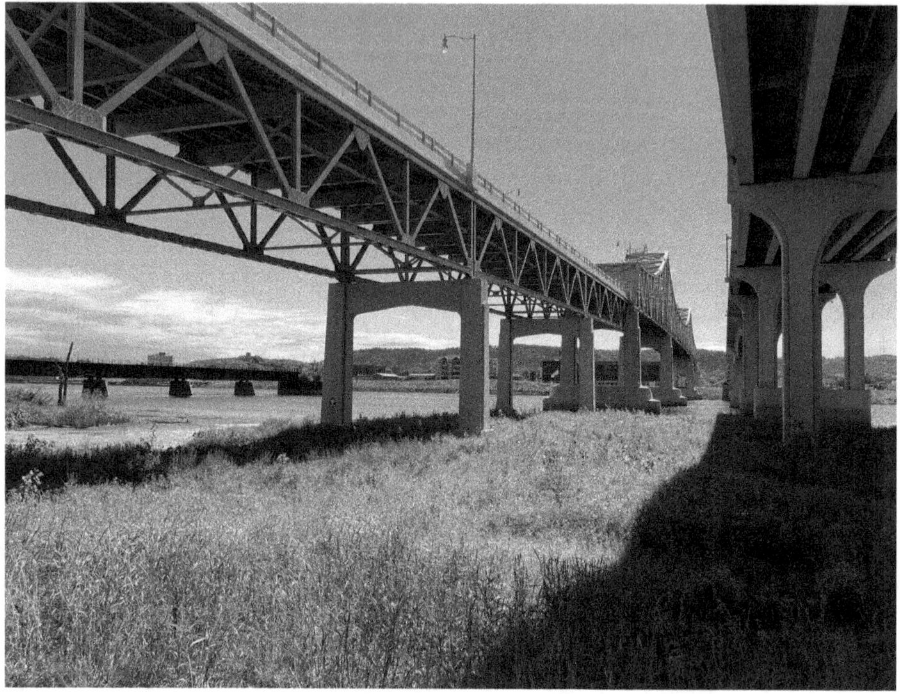

This view from Latsch Island shows the substructure of the cantilever bridge on the left and the concrete box girder bridge on the right. The old railroad bridge is to the far left. *Photo by Steve Gardiner.*

through truss sections, repairing floor beams and replacing the deck truss approach spans.

"The cantilevered through-truss main spans received extensive steel repairs and members were retrofitted for redundancy as required by state statute," MnDOT wrote on its website. Redundancy means that if one part of the bridge reached capacity or failed, the structural system of the bridge would allow other parts of the bridge to remain strong and provide support rather than allowing it to collapse.

With the New Main Channel Bridge opening in 2016 and the rehabilitation of the Old Main Channel Bridge completed three years later, the old bridge reopened on July 1, 2019. A ribbon-cutting ceremony on that day attracted a host of dignitaries, including Winona mayor Mark Peterson and Minnesota governor Tim Walz.

"Winona is a very historic river town," Peterson told the *Post Bulletin* at the opening ceremony. "The historic bridge ties in well with all the wonderful architecture we have here."

The bridge became even more famous when, in 2008, a photo marking 150 years of Minnesota statehood featured the river and the Old Main Channel Bridge.

"This bridge was on the sesquicentennial stamp of Minnesota," Walz said in the July 3, 2019 issue of the *Winona Post*. "When they picked one image that was going to commemorate our 150 years as a state, this bridge was the image that went on there. This is an iconic bridge that we're on. It symbolized the things that we did. It connects our two great states, and it also was an architectural wonder when it was done, and I think, for many of us, it's just plain beautiful to look at."

WITH BOTH BRIDGES OPENED, the city of Winona and its citizens realized a dream of more than a decade. Traffic was divided, with the old bridge carrying traffic from Winona to Wisconsin and the new bridge handling traffic headed from Wisconsin to Winona. The two bridges together form what is now called the Winona Main Channel Bridge.

WHITEWATER STATE PARK

Twenty-three miles west of Winona is a natural treasure, Whitewater State Park. In addition to excellent fishing and miles of beautiful hiking trails, the park is host to an interesting array of footbridges.

Heading south from the South Picnic Area, the trail along Trout Run Creek offers hikers a thick wooden beam bridge and one interesting wooden arch bridge.

Leaving from the North Picnic Area, one of the more popular hikes is to Chimney Rock, a vantage point offering views of the valley and park. The trail leaves from near the parking area and in a short distance arrives at a small lake. At the north end of the lake is the Whitewater State Park Recreational Dam and Footbridge. The Civilian Conservation Corps built the dam/bridge in 1935 at the north end of a man-made lake. It has two reinforced concrete abutments and a reinforced concrete pier. A twenty-foot-long span across the spillway of the lake and a twelve-foot span form the bridge, which has a total length of fifty-six feet. The railings are wood beams, and the eight-foot-wide deck is timber.

Beyond this dam/bridge, the Chimney Rock Trail continues a short distance before turning left to cross the Whitewater River. Here, hikers cross

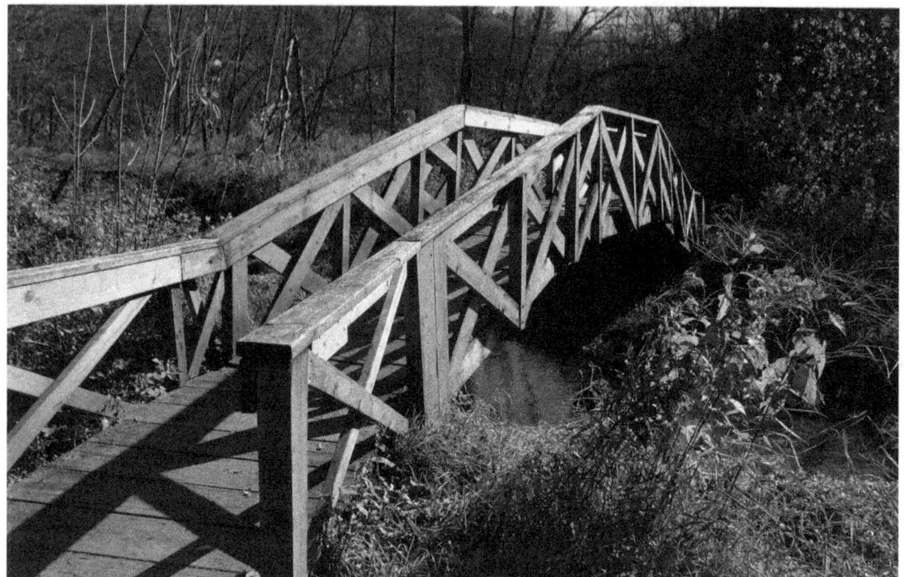

This wooden arch hiking bridge crosses Trout Run Creek in Whitewater State Park. *Photo by Steve Gardiner.*

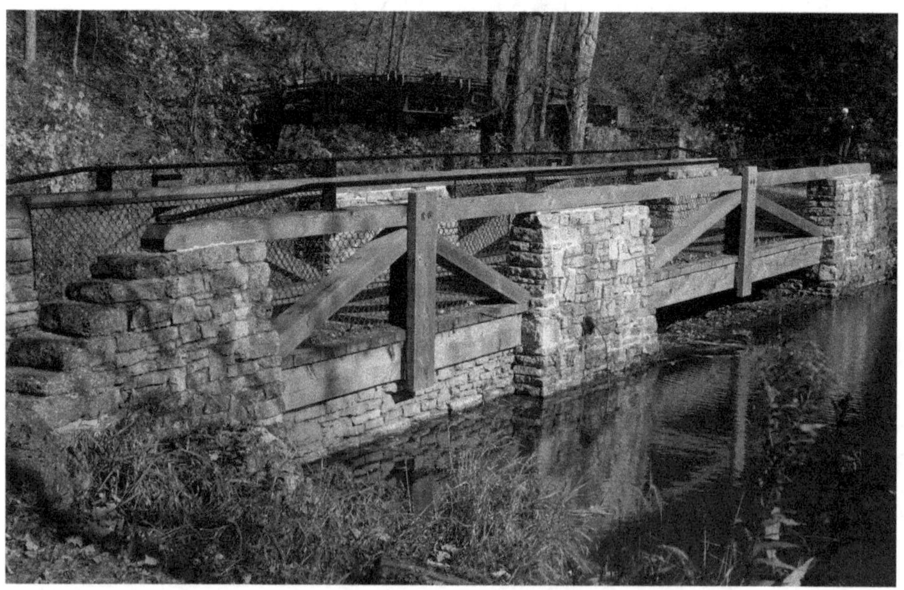

Near the beginning of the trail up Chimney Rock in Whitewater State Park, hikers cross this stone bridge and then turn left to cross the wooden arch bridge in the background. *Photo by Steve Gardiner.*

the Chimney Rock Footbridge, also built in 1935 by the CCC. The eighty-six-foot-long bridge is supported by timber beams and has a six-foot-wide timber plank deck.

Both of these bridges are owned by the Minnesota Department of Natural Resources and are part of the Whitewater State Park CCC/WPA/Rustic Style Historic Resources District.

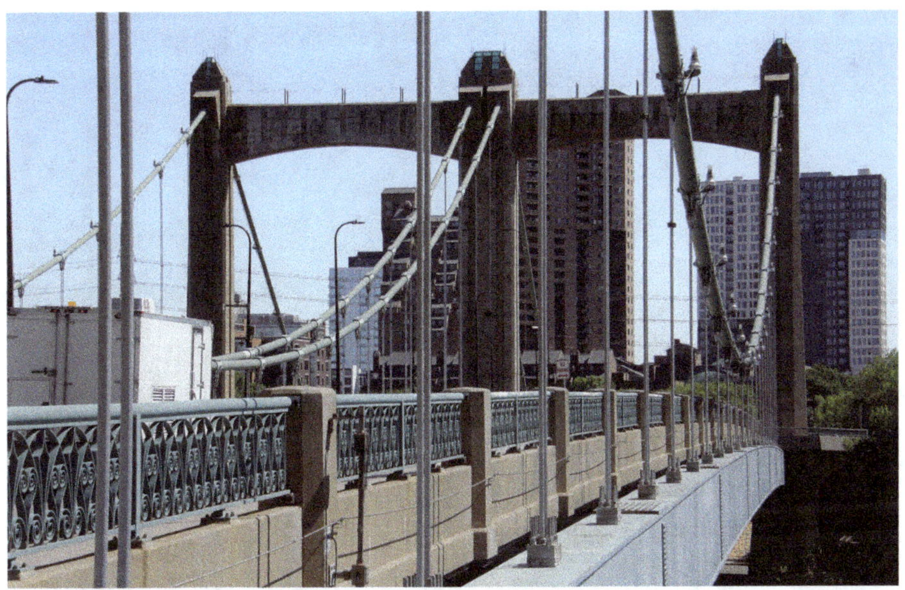

The Father Louis Hennepin Bridge, more commonly known as the Hennepin Avenue Bridge, is the fourth bridge on this site. The suspension bridge connects downtown Minneapolis with Nicollet Island. *Photo by Steve Gardiner.*

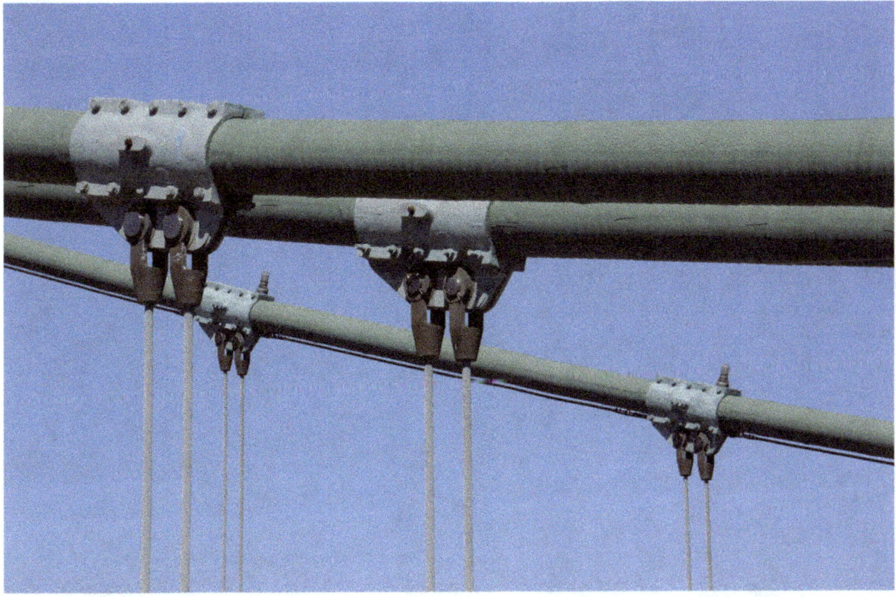

This is a close-up look at the points where the suspenders or hangers from the bridge deck connect to the suspension cable on the Hennepin Avenue Bridge. *Photo by Steve Gardiner.*

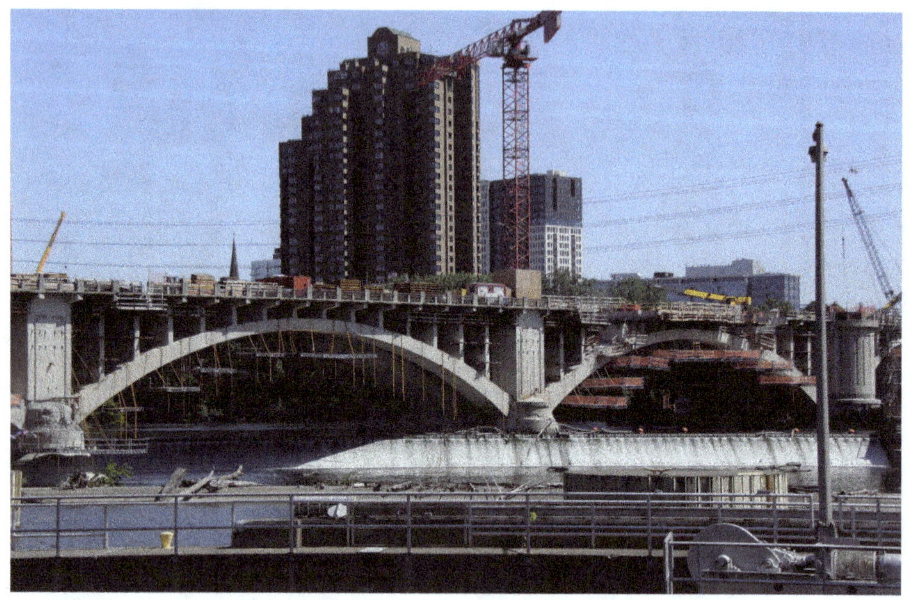

Equipment and materials cover the Third Avenue Bridge during major reconstruction on June 14, 2021. *Photo by Steve Gardiner.*

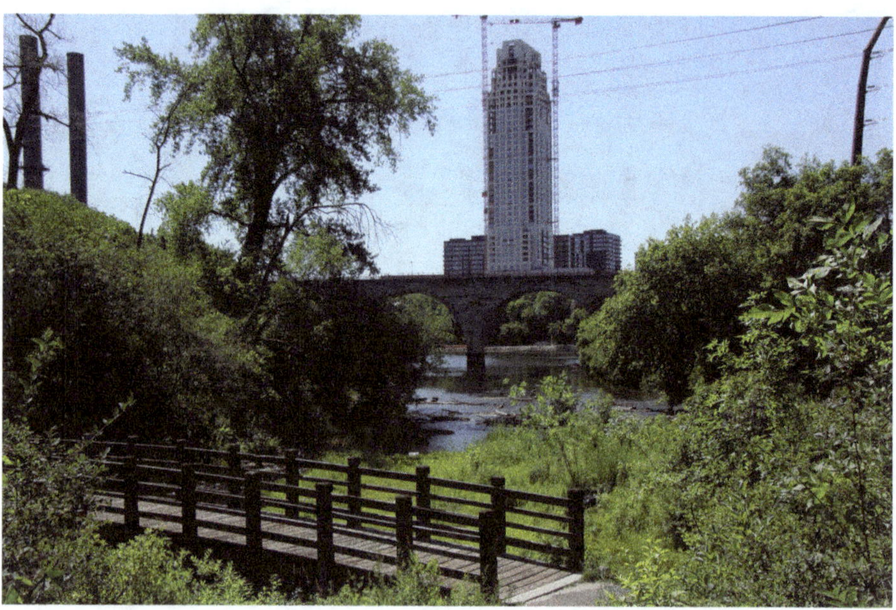

A footbridge gives walkers nice views of the Stone Arch Bridge in downtown Minneapolis. *Photo by Steve Gardiner.*

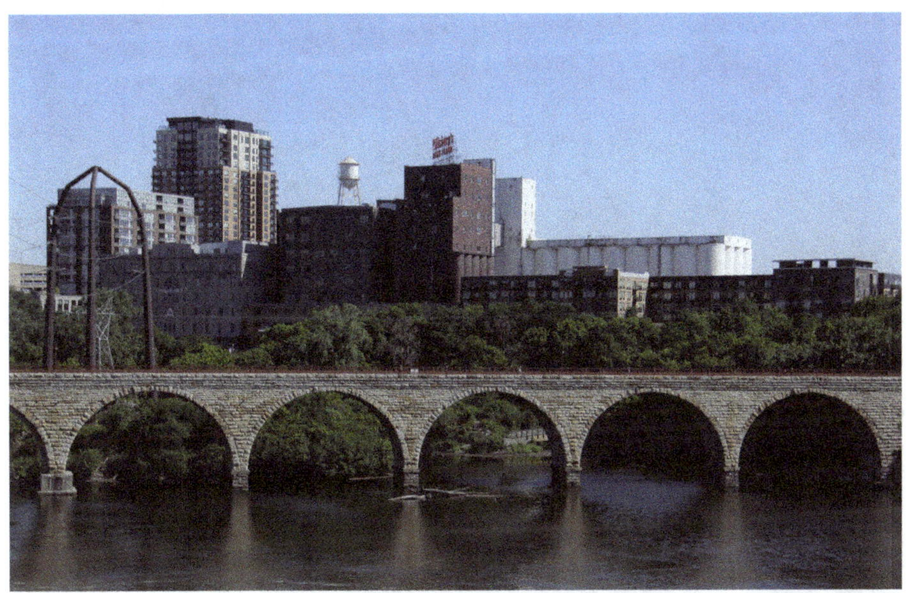

The Stone Arch Bridge, built in 1883 by the Great Northern Railroad, is currently owned by the Minnesota Department of Transportation and is a popular destination for walkers and bikers in downtown Minneapolis. *Photo by Steve Gardiner.*

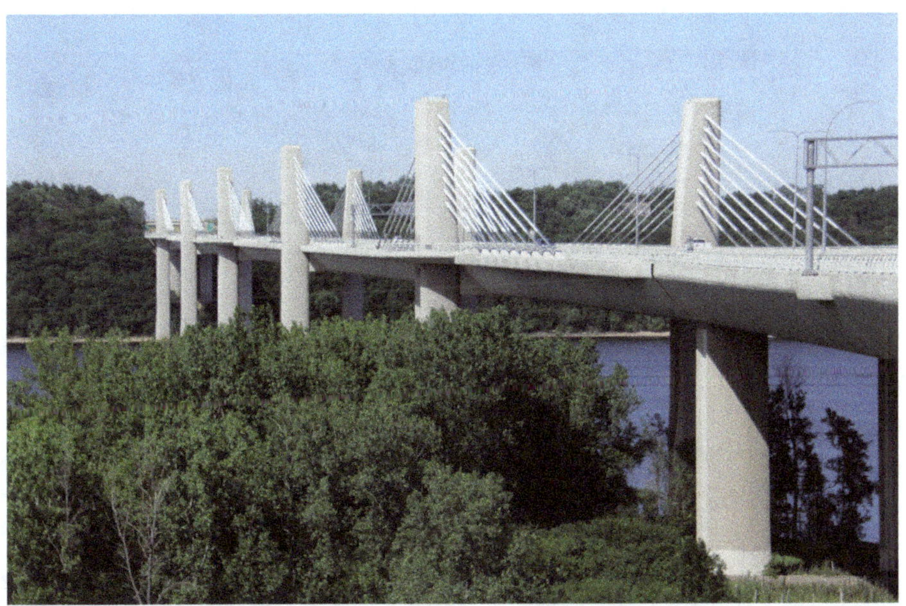

The St. Croix Crossing bridge spans the St. Croix River, which serves as most of the border between Minnesota and Wisconsin north of Prescott, Wisconsin, where the St. Croix River meets the Mississippi River. *Photo by Steve Gardiner.*

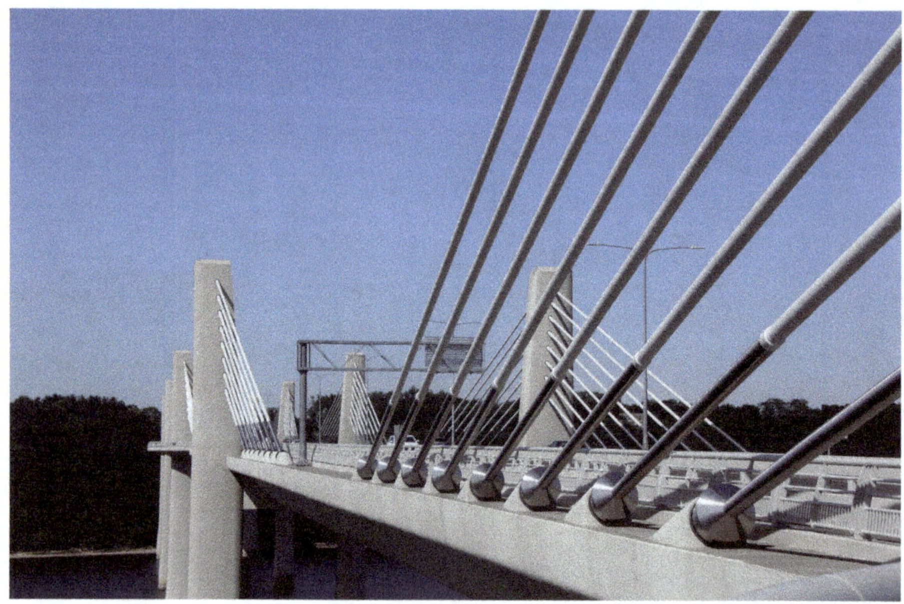

The St. Croix Crossing Bridge near Stillwater carries four lanes of traffic over the St. Croix River. It is an extradosed bridge, meaning it has a girder span as well as cable stays stretching from the towers to the bridge deck. This photo shows the points where the cables connect to the bridge decking. *Photo by Steve Gardiner.*

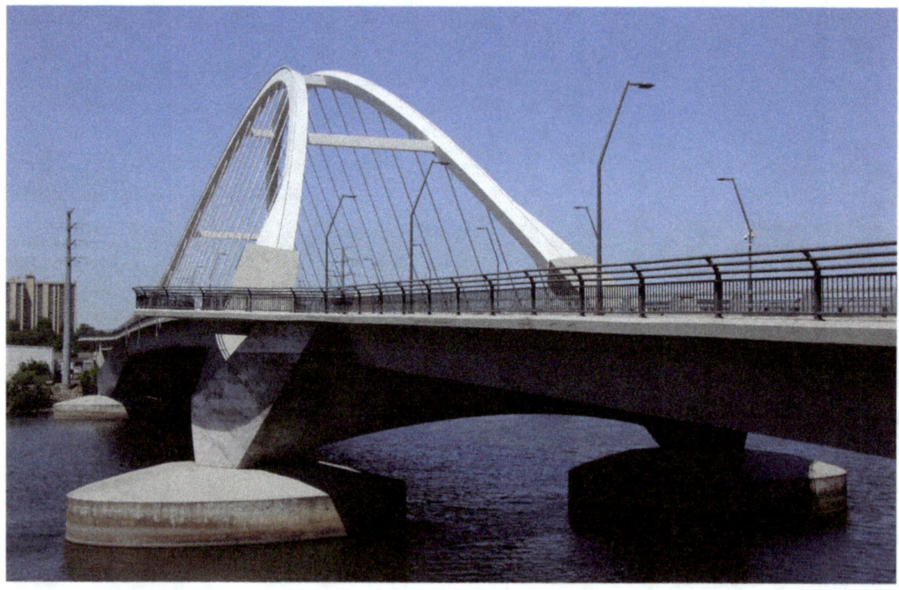

The Lowry Avenue Bridge is a steel tied-arch bridge finished in 2012. The arches of the bridge are often lighted in various colors at night. *Photo by Steve Gardiner.*

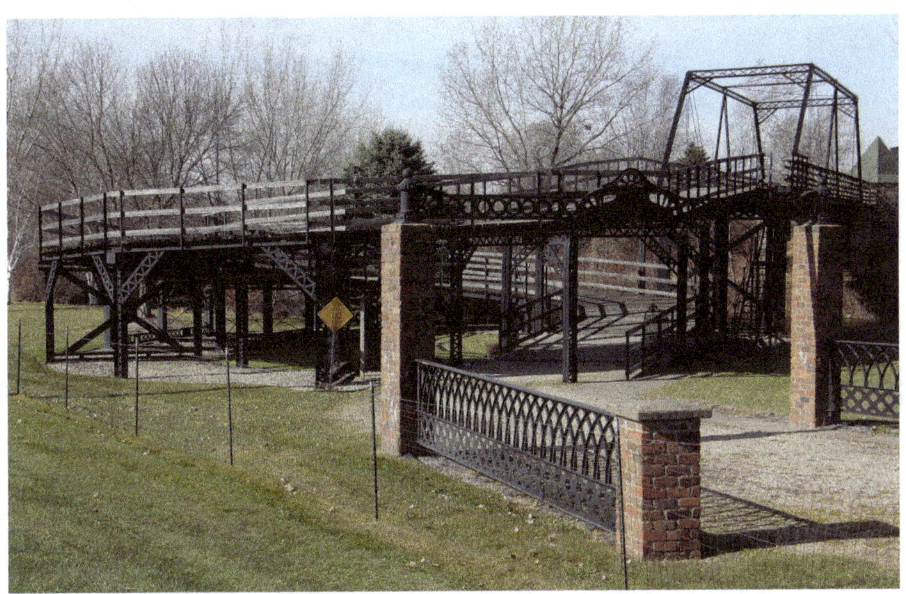

The Spiral Bridge in Hastings lasted fifty-six years and shuttled travelers into downtown Hastings. The original bridge was dismantled in 1951, but this replica sits just north of 220 Street East about ten miles south of Hastings. *Photo by Steve Gardiner.*

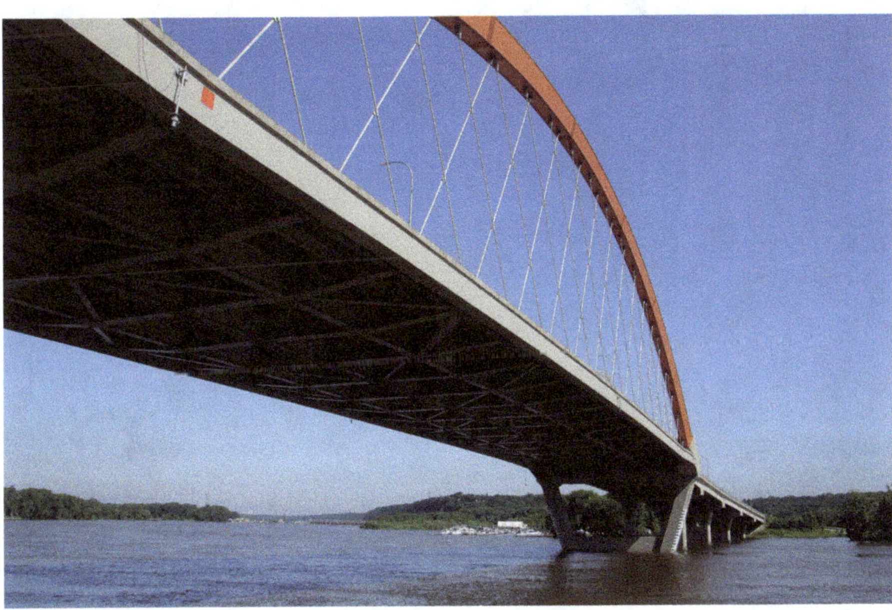

The construction of the new Hastings Bridge, which opened in 2013, included adding artwork, biking/walking paths and public spaces around the bridge. *Photo by Steve Gardiner.*

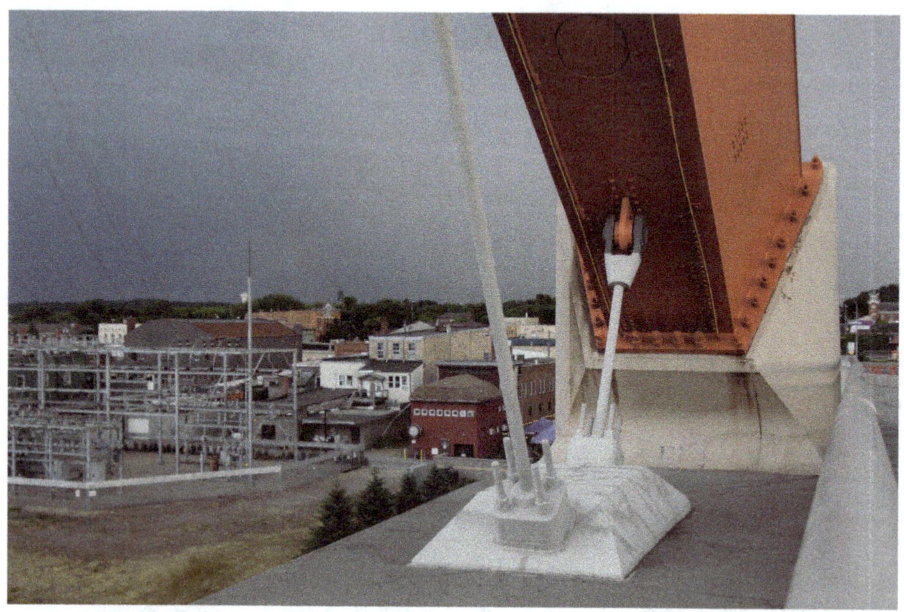

The Hastings Bridge is a tied-arch bridge. This photo shows the anchor of one of the arches and the point where one of the cables from the arch joins the bridge deck. *Photo by Steve Gardiner.*

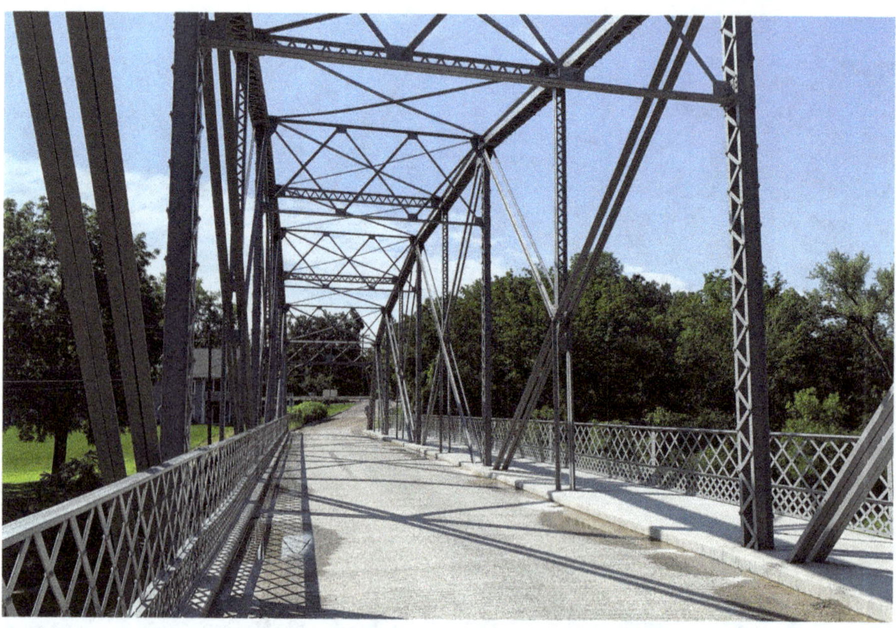

The Third Street Bridge in Cannon Falls was built in 1910 and received significant reconstruction in 2002 and again in 2021. It is owned by the City of Cannon Falls and was listed in the National Register of Historic Places in 1989. *Photo by Steve Gardiner.*

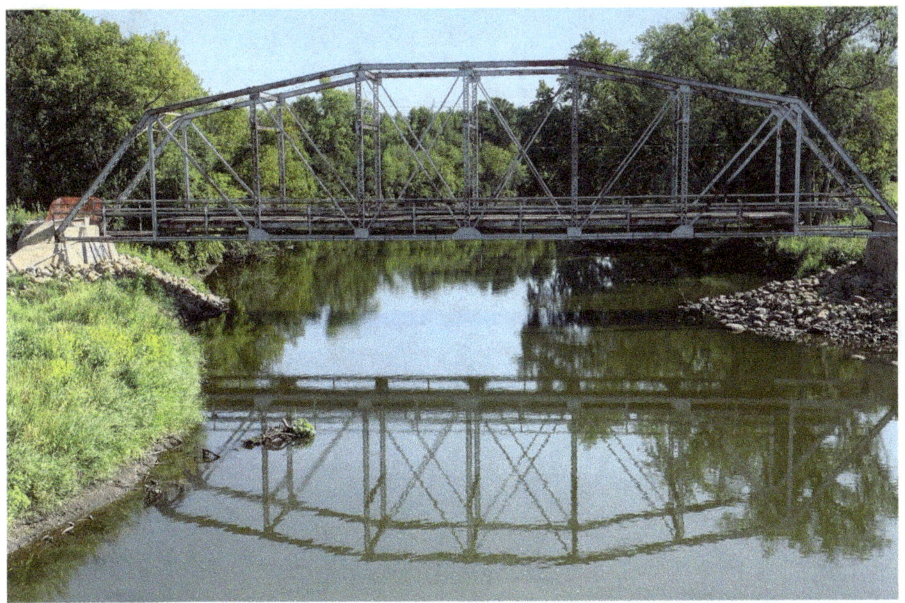

The abandoned Waterford Bridge, a steel through truss bridge, is reflected in the surface of the Cannon River on August 5, 2022. It was built in 1909 and is the subject of an ongoing restoration project to preserve the historic architecture of the bridge and to establish a scenic trail between the Mill Towns Trail System and the Dakota County Trail System. *Photo by Steve Gardiner.*

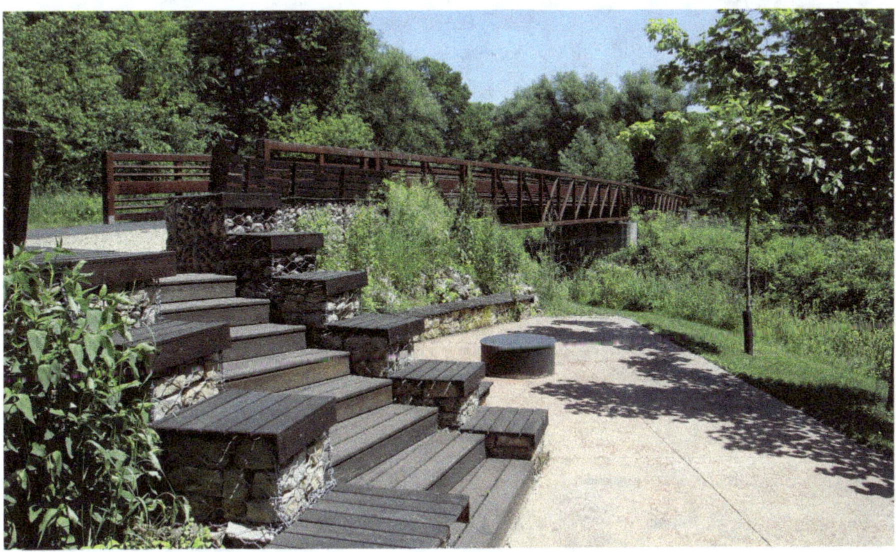

Cyclists on the Cannon Valley Trail between Cannon Falls and Red Wing can enjoy a break at the Marshall Memorial Rest Area and the bridge that crosses Belle Creek at Mile 11.4 just east of Welch. The rest area was funded by the estate of Albert and Elizabeth Marshall of Red Wing. *Photo by Steve Gardiner.*

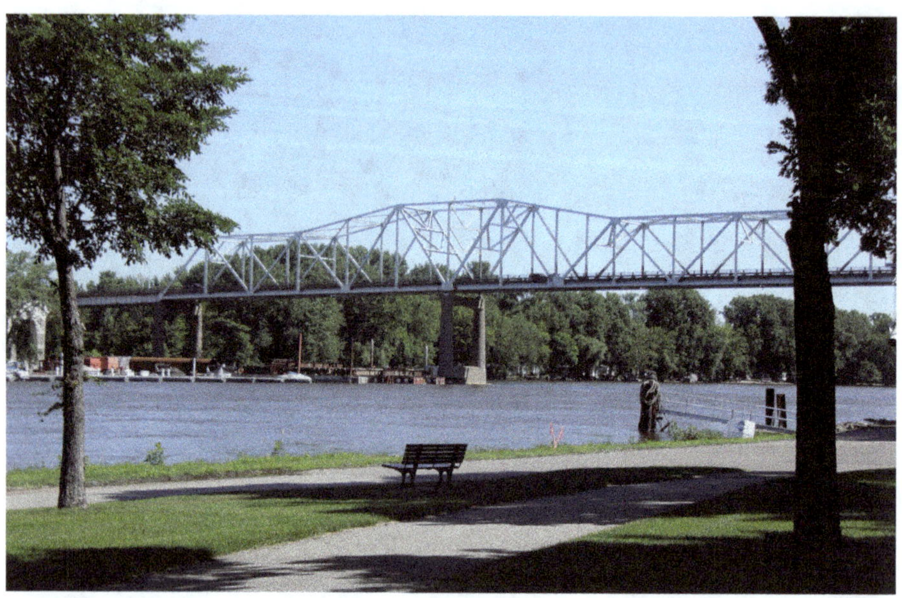

The Eisenhower Memorial Bridge, frequently shortened to the Eisenhower Bridge by locals, as viewed from Levee Park in Red Wing on July 5, 2018. The bridge was taken down in February 2020 and replaced by the Eisenhower Bridge of Valor. *Photo by Steve Gardiner*.

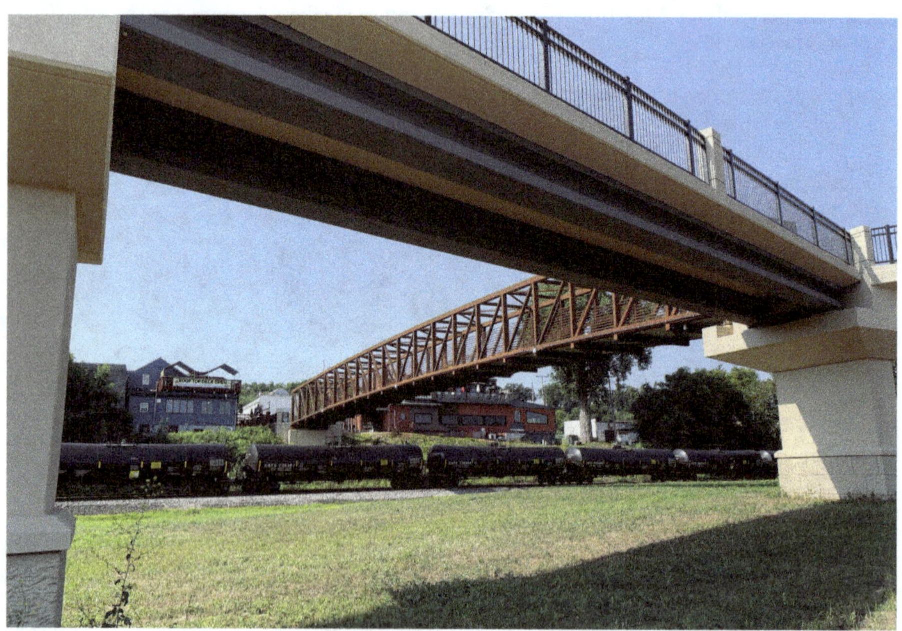

The Red Wing Riverview Skyway is a walking/cycling bridge that connects the West End District to Bay Point Park and the Upper Harbor in Red Wing. The bridge, which opened in October 2021, has two sections—one crossing the railroad tracks to a tower and a second section from the tower down to the sidewalk level. *Photo by Steve Gardiner*.

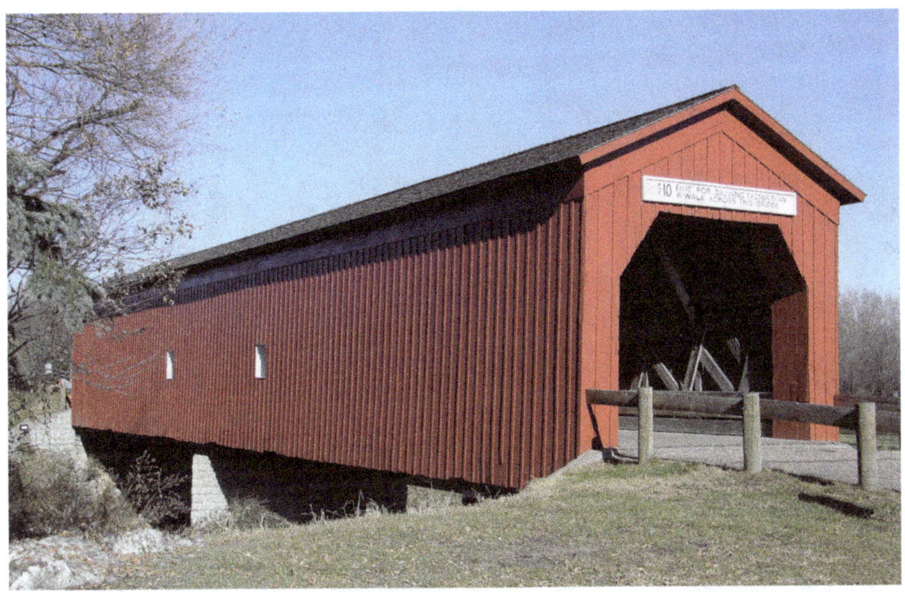

The only existing covered bridge in Minnesota is part of Zumbrota Covered Bridge Park, which features walking paths, a swimming pool, camping sites, the Zumbro River and plenty of open spaces. *Photo by Steve Gardiner.*

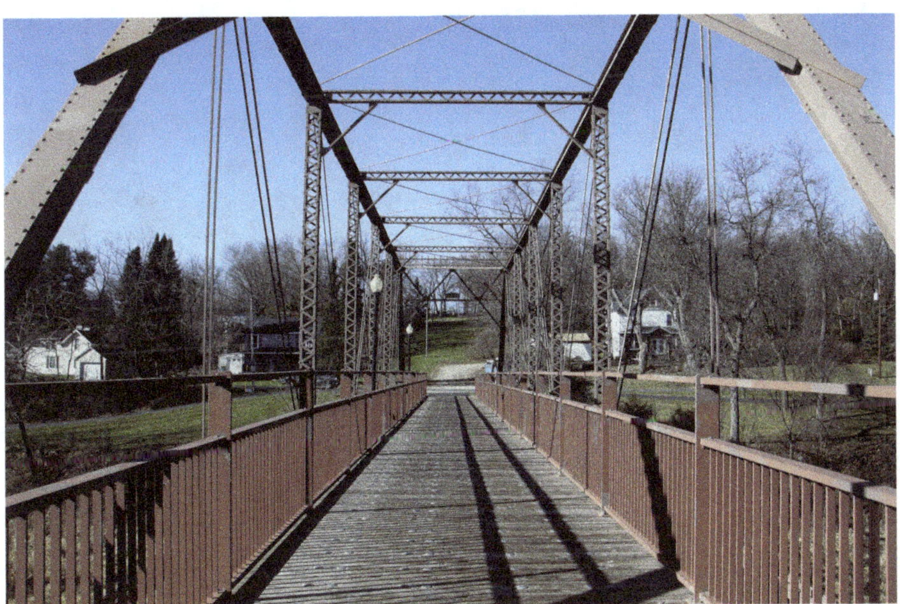

The historic Walnut Street Bridge in Mazeppa, seen here on November 2, 2020, is an example of a through truss bridge with a steel bridge deck, covered by timber, supported by the truss overhead. It was built in 1904 and is now a pedestrian bridge. *Photo by Steve Gardiner.*

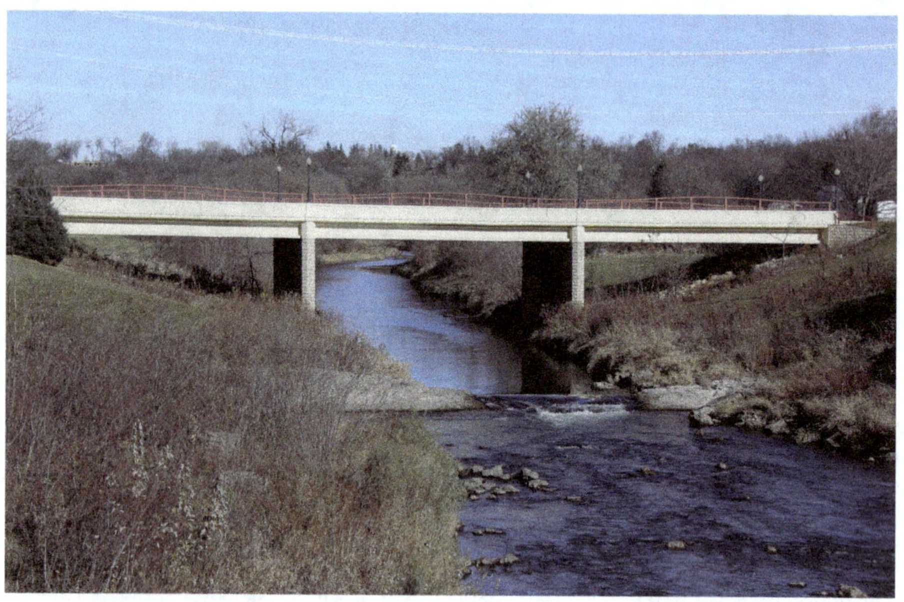

The Maple Street Bridge in Mazeppa shows the abutments where the bridge is anchored to the upper riverbanks and the two piers that support the bridge on each side of the North Fork of the Zumbro River. *Photo by Steve Gardiner.*

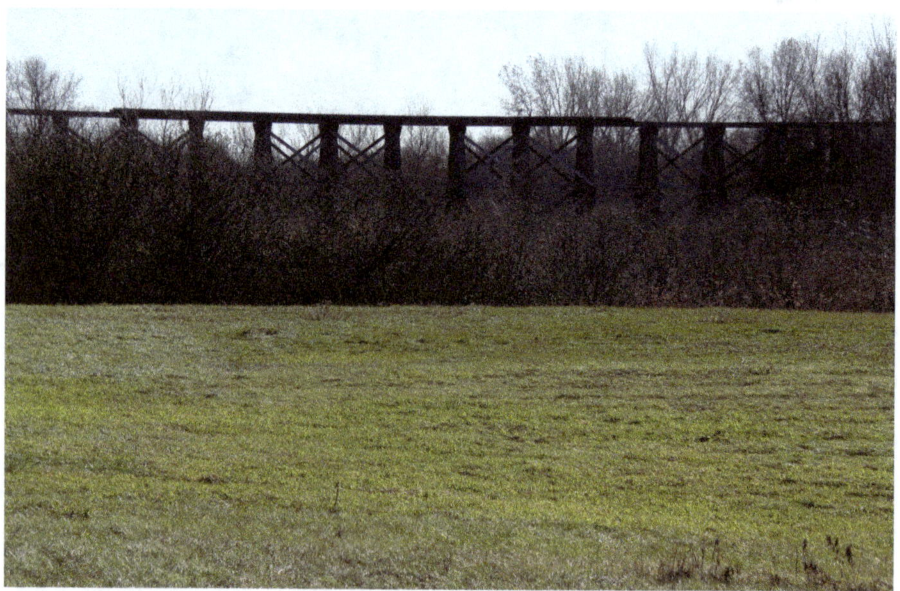

When this abandoned trestle bridge in Kenyon was built by the Milwaukee Railroad in 1903, it was 450 feet long and was built on a curve. The railroad tracks and sections of the bridge were removed in 1980. *Photo by Steve Gardiner.*

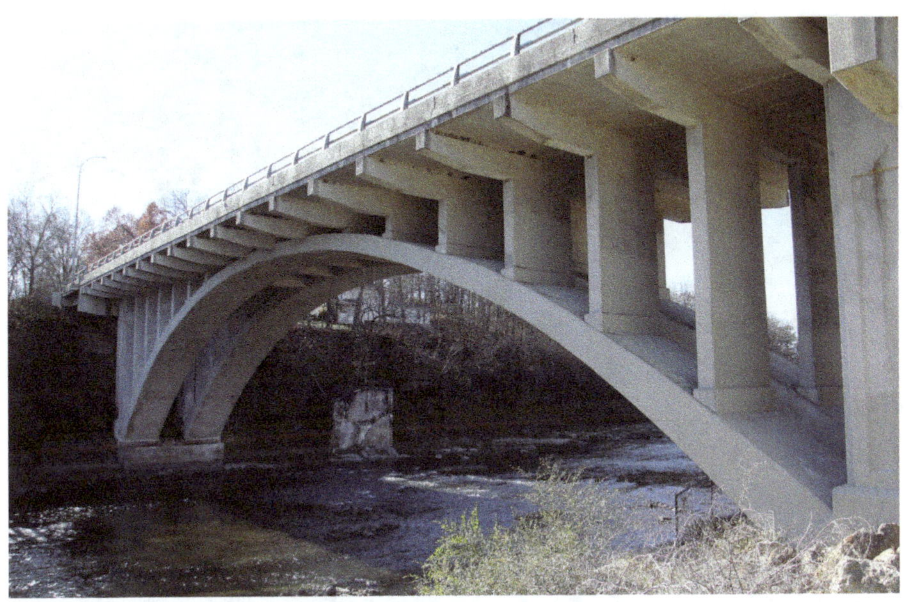

The Oronoco Bridge was built in 1918 and is a concrete arch bridge that supports County Road 18 over the Middle Fork of the Zumbro River in the city of Oronoco. *Photo by Steve Gardiner*.

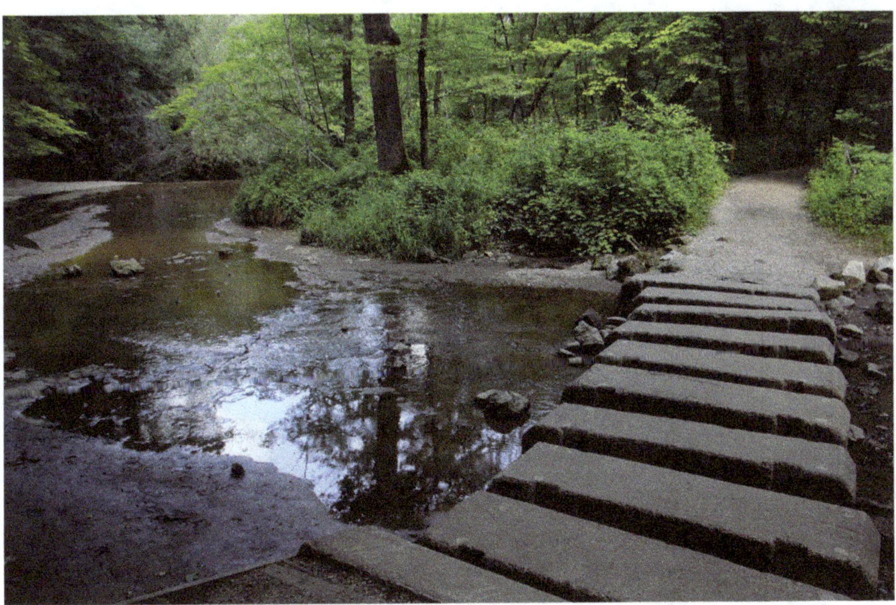

Flat stones were often stacked to build crude bridges similar to these concrete blocks seen at Nerstrand Big Woods State Park on July 31, 2018. *Photo by Steve Gardiner*.

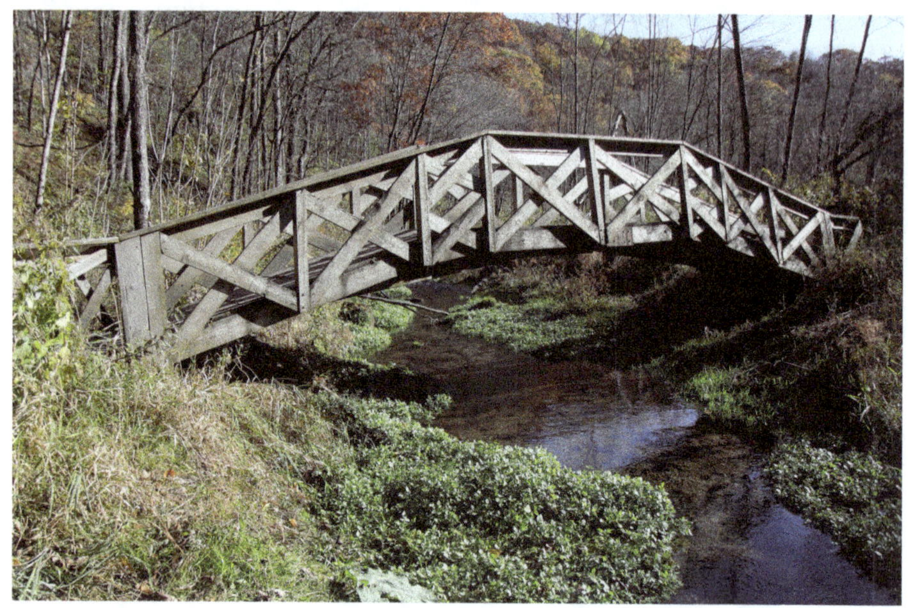

Hikers use this bridge to cross Trout Run Creek in Whitewater State Park. *Photo by Steve Gardiner.*

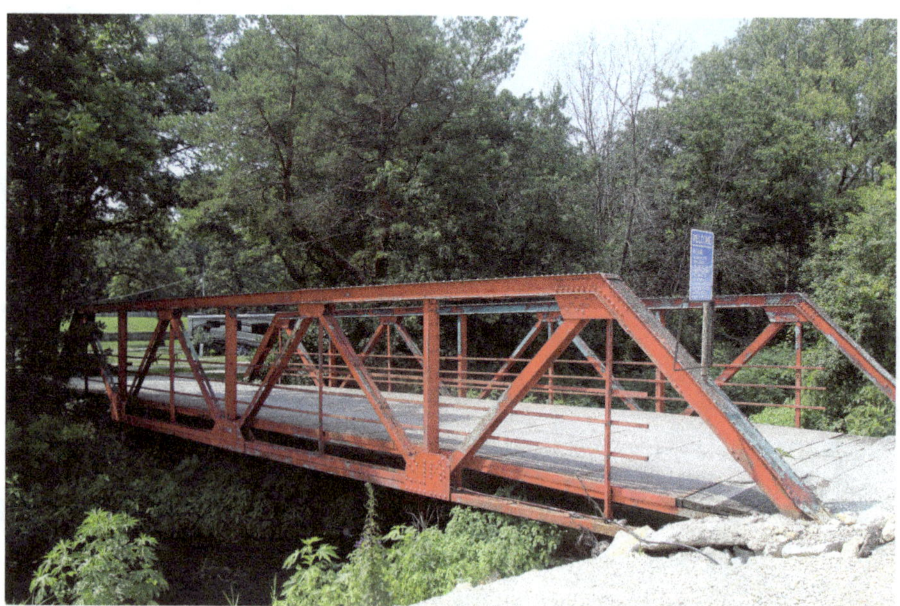

This Warren pony truss bridge serves as the entrance to Ferguson's Willow Creek Campground in Rochester. *Photo by Steve Gardiner.*

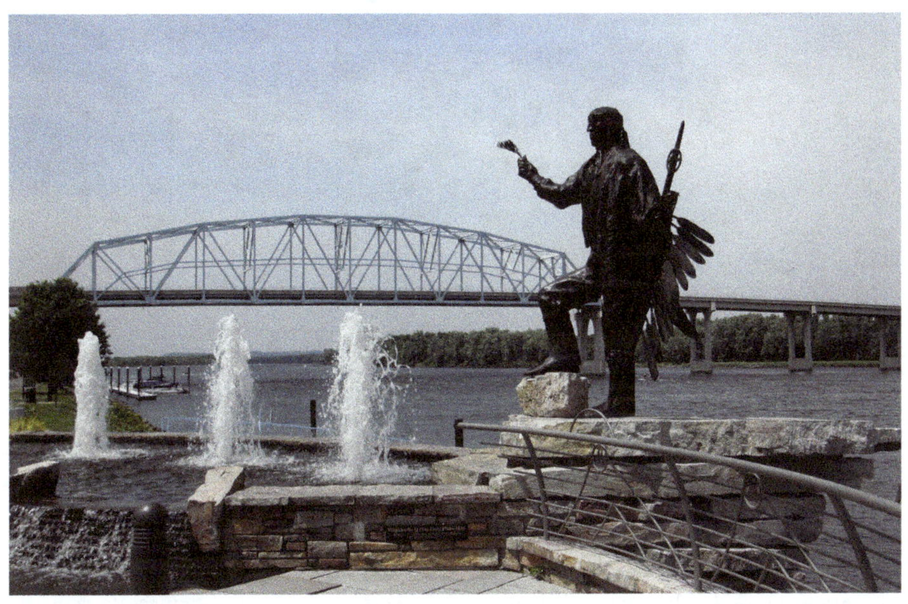

The view of the bridge at Wabasha, Minnesota, features a large fountain and a statue of Chief Wapahasha II in front of the National Eagle Center. *Photo by Steve Gardiner.*

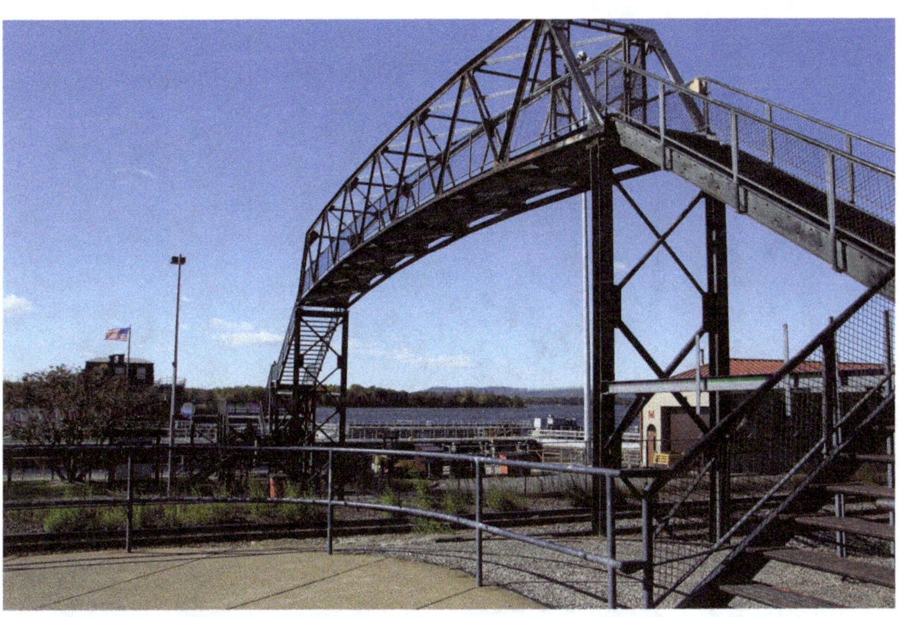

This footbridge spans the railroad tracks at the Wisconsin end of Lock and Dam 4 on the Mississippi River downstream from Wabasha. *Photo by Steve Gardiner.*

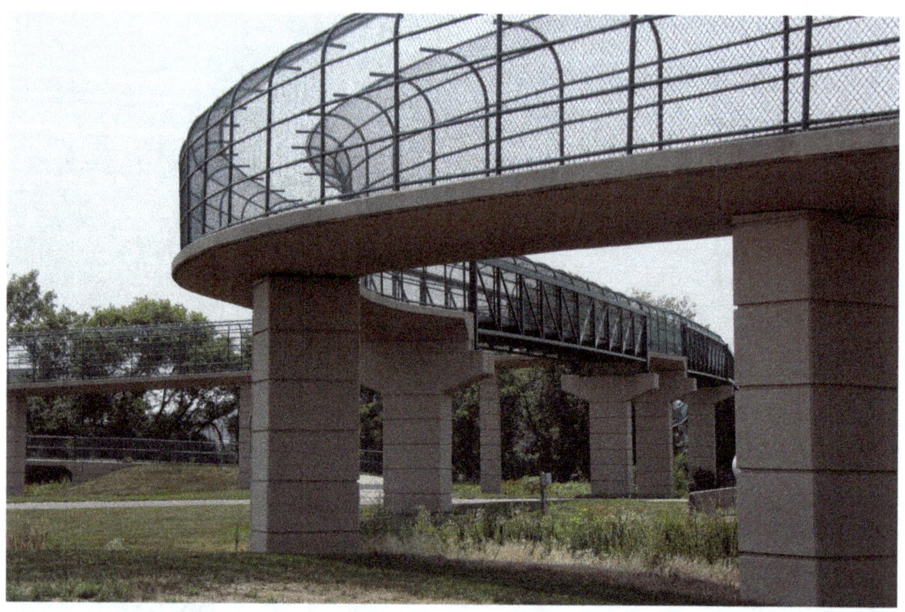

The Arianna Celeste Macnamara Bridge serves walkers and bikers as a connection between the Cascade Creek Trail and the Douglas-Cascade Trail by crossing over U.S. Highway 14, the railroad tracks and Seventh Street NW in Rochester. *Photo by Steve Gardiner.*

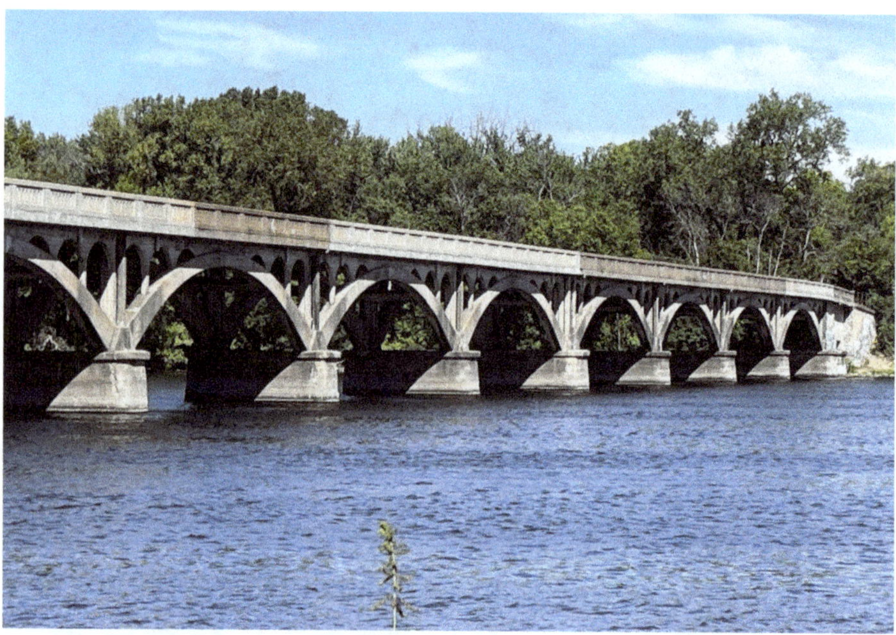

The John A. Latsch Wagon Bridge in Winona was opened in 1917 and rebuilt in 1947 and 2004. It replaced a wooden bridge in the same location. *Photo by Steve Gardiner.*

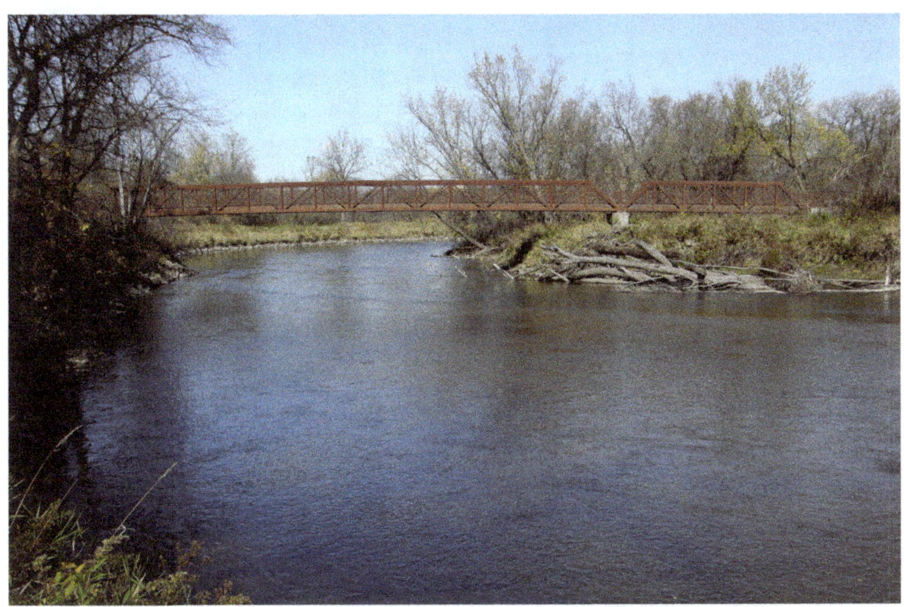

Built in 1910, the historic Zumbro Bottoms Iron Bridge, also called the Funk Ford Bridge, shown here on October 13, 2020, has been closed to automobile traffic but is used by horse riders and walkers. *Photo by Steve Gardiner.*

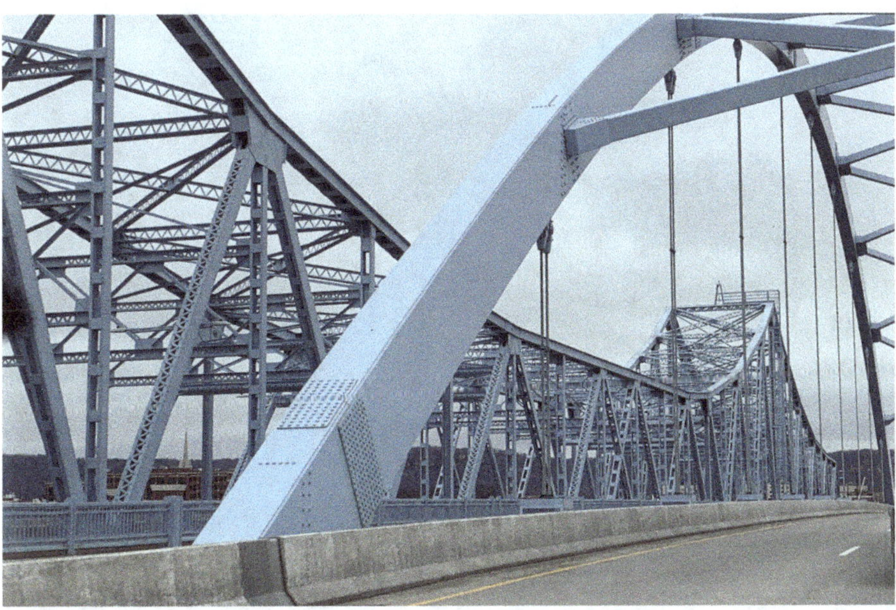

The two Big Blue Bridges, one an arch bridge and the other a through truss bridge, form the Mississippi River Bridge that connects La Crescent, Minnesota, with La Crosse, Wisconsin, using two lanes of traffic in each direction. *Photo by Steve Gardiner.*

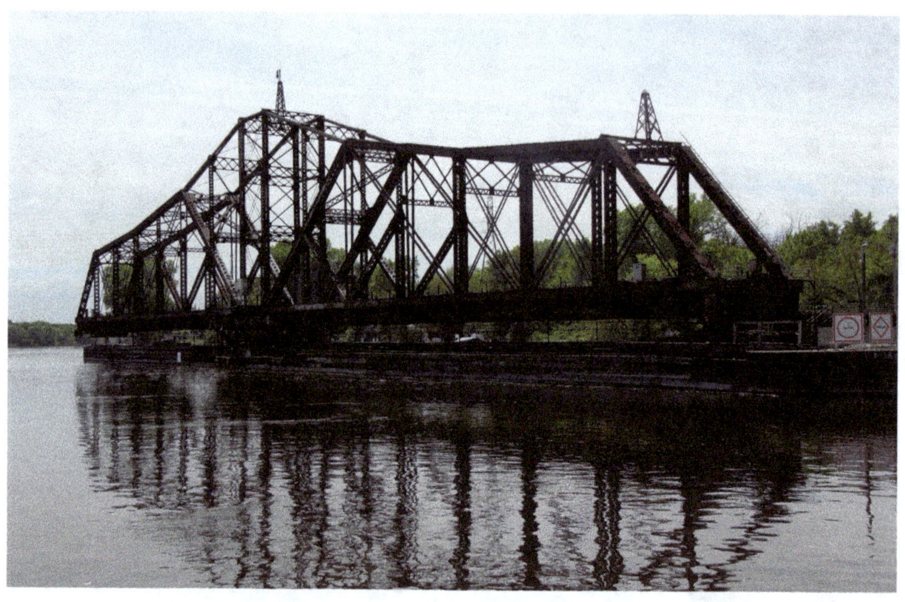

The railroad swing bridge between La Crescent, Minnesota, and La Crosse, Wisconsin, is shown in the open position with the swing section running parallel to the Mississippi River. *Photo by Steve Gardiner.*

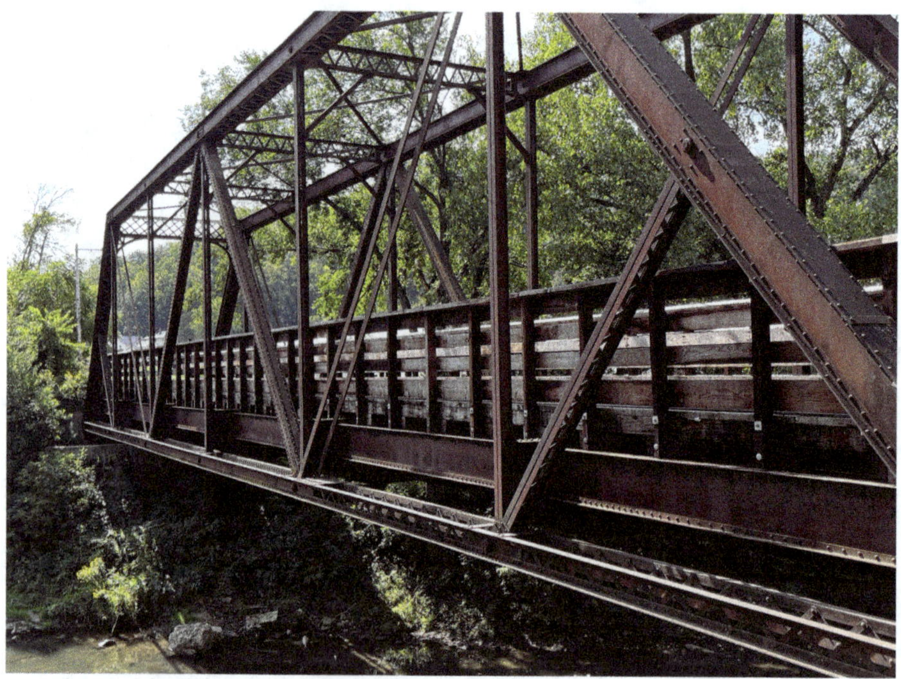

The Root River State Trail Pedestrian Bridge in downtown Lanesboro serves as a launching point for many walks and bike rides on the paved trail. *Photo by Steve Gardiner.*

Chapter 7

LA CRESCENT

A Bridge Gone Blue

It was 1:30 a.m. on August 9, 1935, when a car drove onto the Mount Vernon Street Swing Bridge. The four occupants of the car had spent the evening at a La Crescent, Minnesota nightclub and were returning to La Crosse, Wisconsin, when the car struck a bridge beam. The western span of the bridge instantly collapsed, sending the car plunging front-first into the Mississippi River.

The driver, Captain Fisher F. Blinn, thirty-three, resident engineer on the Trempeleau dam for the War Department, and front-seat passenger, Marceline Patro, twenty-five, of Minneapolis, were able to get out of the car and reach a beam of the collapsed bridge. The two passengers in the rear seat—Francis Landrieau, thirty-three, engineer on the Genoa Dam below La Crosse, and his wife, Ethel Landrieau, twenty-five—were not able to escape.

Louise Koenig of Milwaukee was camping at Pettibone Park on Barron Island with her sisters and some friends. She spoke with a reporter from the *Winona Republican Herald* that morning.

"There was a big crash and then a blue streak shot across the sky," Koenig said. "I believe the blue streak of light was caused by the electric wires. Then the bridge seemed to fold up and sink down. I heard a terrible shriek, and when I got to the edge of the river one of the men was pulling a girl on to a beam which had sagged into the river."

Koenig said she took off her dress and swam out to the car. She said she "tried to get the door open but the current was so swift I had to give up."

The man and woman were on the beam half an hour, according to Koenig. The woman was bleeding from a wound on her neck and was screaming, "Please help. Can't somebody get the car door open?"

The other girls from the campground went to the road and flagged down cars, warning them about the damage to the bridge. One car sped past them, stopping just short of the gap in the bridge.

"Then the police boat arrived," Koenig told the *Republican Herald*. "Patrolman Boma walked down one of the sagging girders and helped the man and girl, and soon they were put into a boat and taken to the La Crosse side. A short time later, the boat returned and took out the two bodies."

The wreck would have significant impact on bridges throughout the region.

La Crescent Swing Bridge

For most cities along the Mississippi River, freight took precedence over passengers, and the railroad bridges were built before vehicle bridges. The same happened at La Crescent.

The first railroad to reach La Crosse was the La Crosse and Milwaukee in 1858. Goods needed on the Minnesota side of the Mississippi had to travel by boat from La Crosse to Winona or La Crescent.

About that time, Thomas McRoberts, interested in promoting La Crescent, started a ferry service. The Minnesota legislature gave him exclusive rights to the ferry at La Crescent, and it didn't take long for McRoberts to take advantage of that situation and raise his rates high enough that farmers and businessmen were complaining. In response, the Common Council in La Crosse removed his ferry permit, and he was forced to do business more fairly, according to the La Crosse Public Library Archives.

In 1876, demand for moving goods had reached the point that the Chicago, Milwaukee, St. Paul and Pacific Railroad built a swing bridge between La Crescent and the north side of La Crosse. It was a Whipple through truss bridge that was 938 feet long with a main span of 360 feet.

It was better for a train bridge to cross at the level of the ground on both sides of the river so the train could move easily across. A bridge at that level would, however, block river traffic, so the swing span, which turned on a pier with the post at the center of balance for the span, solved the problem, although many boat captains hated the swing bridges. They viewed the center pier, leaving only a few yards' clearance on each side of a barge, as a navigation hazard.

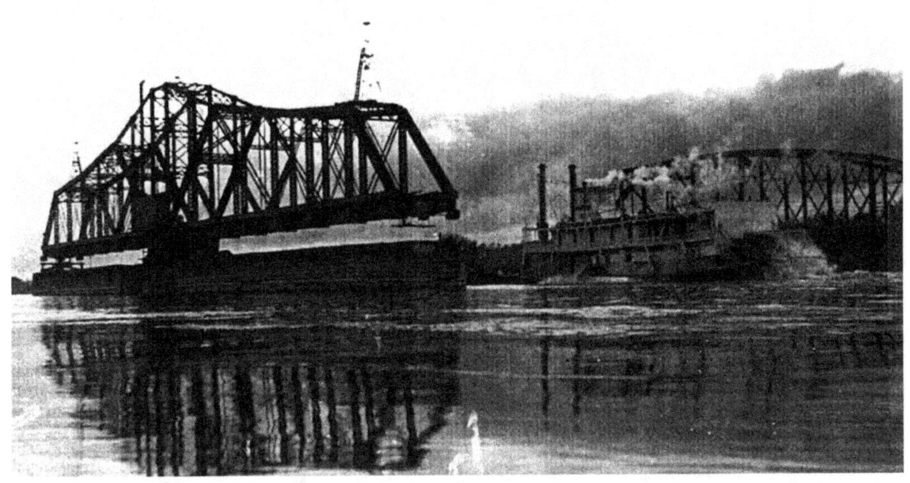

The Swing Bridge, shown in the 1880s, spans the west channel of the Mississippi River, which is shared by Wisconsin and Minnesota. The bridge was replaced by a new swing bridge in 1901. *Courtesy of the La Crescent Area Historical Society.*

A swing bridge required an operator on duty to open the bridge when a boat arrived and close it for oncoming trains. When the swing bridge is closed, vehicle or train traffic can pass directly through, just like on any other bridge. To open the bridge, the operator would first stop all traffic with lights or barriers and then turn the swing section ninety degrees, which would open the channel for boats to pass through. Boats heading north or upstream would pass on the Wisconsin side of the center pier, and boats heading south or downstream would pass on the Minnesota side of the center pier. After the boats passed, the operator would return the swing section to the closed position, and bridge deck traffic could resume.

The La Crescent Swing Bridge of 1876 lasted until it was replaced with another swing bridge in 1901. The new version, also called the La Crescent Swing Bridge, is a Pratt through truss bridge with a total length of 1,045 feet and a main swing span of 359 feet.

"The swing span pivots on a 26-foot diameter drum that sits atop 52 steel rollers, which bear its weight when open," explained the August 1, 2014 *La Crosse Tribune*. "Complicated as it sounds, the design was favored because it was less expensive than bascule lift bridges, and had fewer moving parts."

The bridge underwent significant rehabilitation in 1952, changing it from steam power to electrical. The La Crescent Swing Bridge is still open to railroad traffic and uses the swing span for boat traffic; however, after more

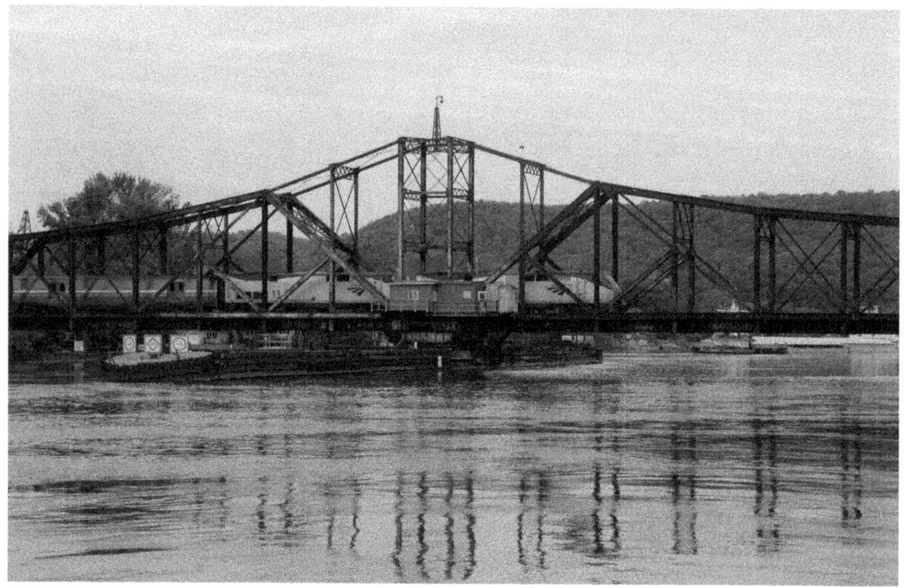

A train crosses the La Crescent Railroad Swing Bridge as a tow and barges wait upstream. When the train passes, the swing section will turn and allow the tow and barges to pass through. *Photo by Steve Gardiner.*

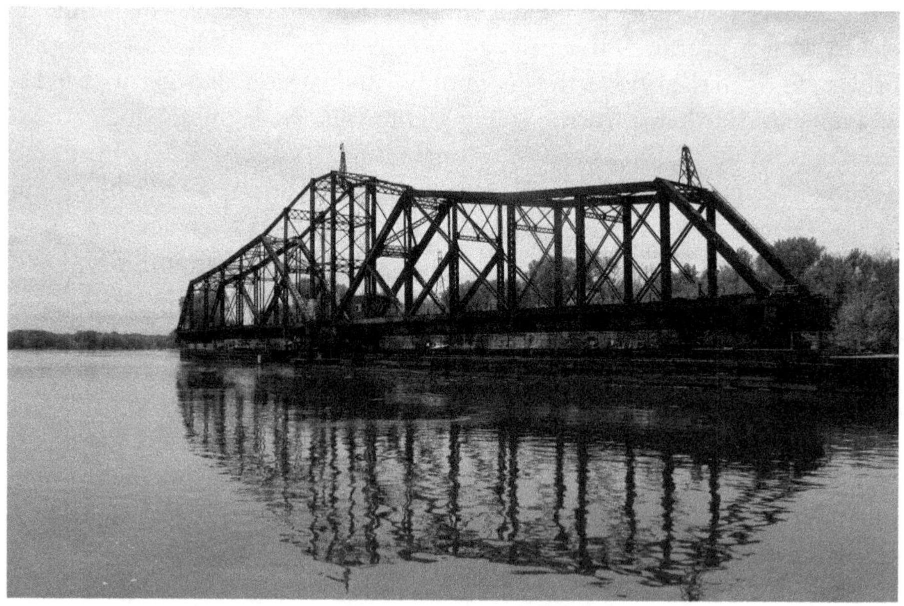

In this photo, the Swing Bridge is pivoted ninety degrees and is parallel to the river shore, open to allow boat traffic to move through. *Photo by Steve Gardiner.*

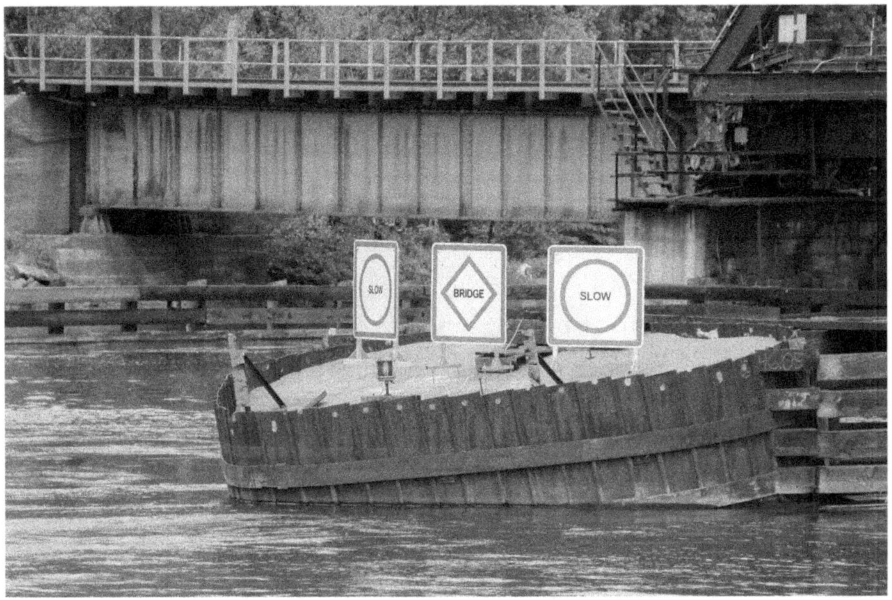

Bridges provide convenient access across rivers and streams, but they can also create boating hazards, as suggested by these warning signs on the La Crescent Railroad Swing Bridge. *Photo by Steve Gardiner.*

than a century of use, the U.S. Coast Guard has discussed the need for an upgrade or replacement of the bridge.

"The bridge wasn't really built with modern navigation in mind," said Roger Wiebusch, bridge administrator for the Coast Guard, in the May 27, 2009 issue of the *La Crosse Tribune*. "The bridge stayed the same, but navigation got bigger."

Mount Vernon Street Swing Bridge

With a railroad bridge in place, La Crescent and La Crosse needed a vehicle bridge. While most cities upriver had built high bridges at about this time, La Crosse opted for a vehicle bridge that, like the railroad bridge, featured a 430-foot swing span.

The swing span, at the time one of the longest in the country, was a polygonal Pratt through truss and was built by the Clinton Bridge & Iron Works of Clinton, Iowa. The bridge went from the foot of Mount Vernon Street to Barron Island, often referred to as Pettibone Island, where a pontoon bridge crossed the west channel to La Crescent. The pontoon bridge was replaced by a single-span steel bridge in 1904.

The Mount Vernon Street Swing Bridge, sometimes called the Wagon Bridge, was opened to traffic on December 22, 1890, and dedicated on July 4, 1891, the same day that the new city hall in La Crosse was dedicated. It operated as a toll bridge until 1919.

"I LOST CONTROL OF the car and we crashed into the steel girder," Fisher Blinn told the *La Cross Tribune* on August 9, 1935. "The smash didn't seem so terrific, but we immediately began to fall. The impact had caused the huge steel section to snap and the car and bridge plunged into the Mississippi."

Emergency crews were sent out to cut live wires, leaving La Crescent without power or telephones. It would take most of the day to restore those services.

With the bridge shut down, car traffic was directed north to Winona, but the weight limit on that bridge meant trucks were sent south to Lansing, Iowa. The *Republican Herald* reported that guards would be stationed at both ends of the Winona bridge to enforce the weight restrictions.

Police, after rowing out to save Blinn and Patro and again to recover the bodies of Francis and Ethel Landrieau, learned that just prior to the collapse, three large heavy trucks had crossed the bridge. One hour earlier, a Greyhound bus filled with passengers had passed over the bridge.

One early report stated that the Landrieaus' two small children were in the car with them. However, they were safe, unaware of the deaths of their parents.

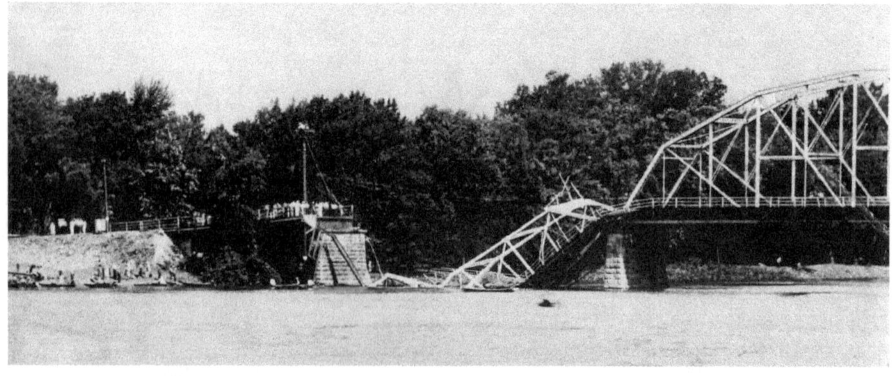

Photo showing the collapse of the Mount Vernon Street Bridge, August 9, 1935. *Courtesy of the La Crescent Area Historical Society.*

This was the accident that had inspired Winona to build the first Main Channel Bridge and remove its High Wagon Bridge. The response was even more urgent in La Crosse. That afternoon, an editorial in the *La Crosse Tribune* stated that it was time for the Mount Vernon Street Swing Bridge to go.

"The move for a new bridge could be started on no better day than that on which the bodies of two persons were retrieved from the water—drowned because a forty-year-old bridge can no longer stand up under the strain of modern day traffic."

Cass Street Bridge

Having the bridge closed not only put pressure on La Crosse and La Crescent, but communities like Caledonia and Lanesboro were also feeling the loss. The La Crosse Chamber of Commerce quickly formed the La Crosse Bridge Committee. They considered many possible bridge designs and even a proposal for a tunnel under the Mississippi River and finally settled on a central-span cantilevered bridge high enough for river traffic to pass beneath. The committee hired the Minneapolis Street Bridge Company to build the new bridge.

The design would need multiple piers, some that would require crews to work inside cofferdams as deep as forty feet below water level. The structure utilized several Warren deck truss spans on each end to rise up to the central span, which is sixty-seven feet above river level. This plan also meant changing road patterns on Barron Island and into downtown La Crosse.

The Warren cantilevered truss span is supported by a steel through truss. The upper chord of the truss has a twin peaks look, which influenced the Main Channel Bridge built three years later in Winona. That shared look was a product of the collaboration between the two cities on the important matter of building major bridges across the Mississippi River.

"The Wisconsin highway department is cooperating with the Minnesota department in the project and has loaned to Minnesota plans of the recently completed La Crosse bridge after which the Winona structure is to be patterned in part," reported the *Winona Republican Herald* on November 11, 1939.

It took four years of hard work, but on September 23, 1939, Wisconsin governor Julius Heil and Winona mayor Floyd R. Simon headlined a ceremony opening what would be called the Cass Street Bridge, just a few hundred feet downstream from the Mount Vernon Street Bridge.

THE CASS STREET BRIDGE connected via roads across Barron Island to the steel through truss West Channel Bridge that was built in 1931. After more than eighty years in service, that bridge was replaced by two parallel concrete girder bridges. The first, with one lane of traffic in each direction, was built in 1992. The second, also with two lanes, opened in 1993 and allowed for two lanes of traffic in each direction. The bridges carry U.S. 14 and U.S. 61 across the West Channel of the Mississippi River and the Minnesota/Wisconsin state line.

CAMERON AVENUE BRIDGE

With two lanes of traffic, one in each direction, the Cass Street Bridge worked well until traffic increased and officials felt two lanes in each direction would be better.

They decided to place the Cameron Avenue Bridge just downstream of and parallel to the Cass Street Bridge and use a through arch design with the 475-foot main span deck suspended from the arches, a system called tied arch. The Cass Street Bridge now carries traffic westbound from La Crosse to Barron Island, and the Cameron Avenue Bridge brings traffic eastbound from Barron Island to downtown La Crosse.

In mid-December 2003, the arch structure was built on scaffolding on barges and then floated into place and lowered onto the support columns. In order to accomplish this, the Cass Street Bridge and the Mississippi River needed to be closed for one day while the arch was installed.

"This is a major event, a little history here in La Crosse," Gary Snyder, bridge project supervisor, told the *Tribune*. "It's a milestone."

Snyder, who had supervised many bridge projects throughout the area, said he was planning to retire after thirty-five years with the Wisconsin Department of Transportation, but when he was offered the Cameron Avenue Bridge Project, he said, "You don't just turn down the project of a lifetime."

The significance of the bridge was clear to Snyder.

"They just don't get bigger than this," he told the *Tribune*. "It's exciting—the massiveness of the whole thing."

The $40 million bridge opened on November 17, 2004.

After the Cameron Avenue Bridge opened, the Cass Street Bridge was closed for a round of repairs, and all traffic was routed onto the new Cameron Avenue Bridge. The Cass Street Bridge was wrapped in

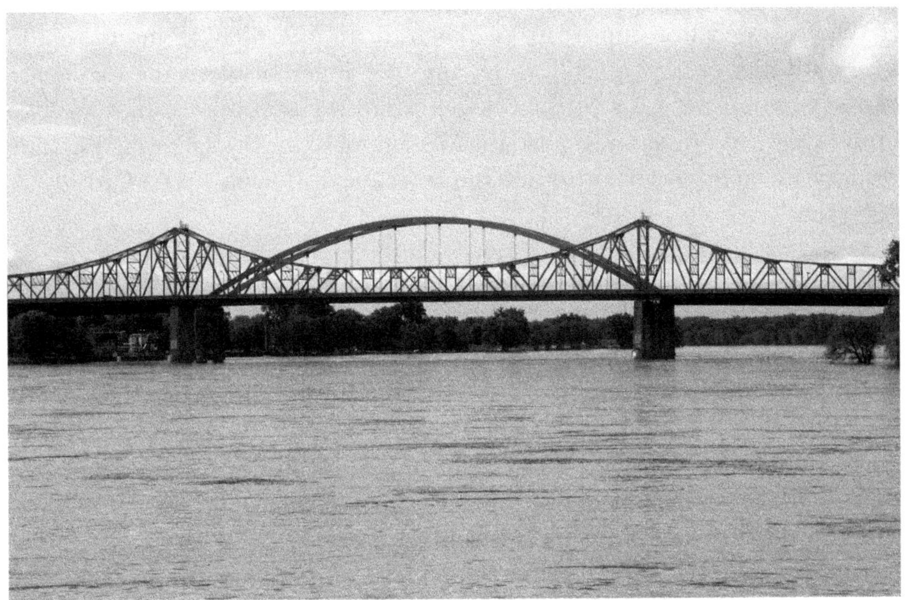

From a distance, the two bridges at La Crosse, Wisconsin, appear to be one, but the Cass Street Bridge is a truss bridge and the Cameron Avenue Bridge is an arch bridge. *Photo by Steve Gardiner.*

tarps while workers blasted off lead-based primer paint and repainted the bridge blue to match the new Cameron Avenue Bridge. Each day's schedule included blasting followed immediately by painting before a new layer of rust could begin forming. The tarps helped keep the lead paint from ending up in the river.

The $9 million renovation also included replacing the steel grid deck with a concrete deck, rebuilding the approaching roadways, upgrading lighting and installing a new pedestrian staircase, according to the June 27, 2006 *La Crosse Tribune*, the day the bridge reopened to traffic.

With the collapse of the I-35W bridge in Minneapolis on August 1, 2007, Wisconsin governor Jim Doyle ordered an immediate inspection of all truss bridges in the state. Both of the La Crosse bridges were reviewed and deemed safe, according to the *Tribune* on August 23. As part of a regular two-year inspection cycle, both bridges were inspected the following year, a process that seemed more urgent following the closure of the Main Channel Bridge in Winona June 3–14 because of concern over the bridge's gusset plates. The 2008 inspection determined that the Cass Street Bridge's gusset plates were in excellent condition and that both bridges were structurally safe and sound.

When viewed from upstream or downstream, the arch of the Cameron Avenue Bridge seems to settle nicely into the valley between the two peaks of the truss on the Cass Street Bridge, giving the appearance that the two bridges are one. Sometimes called the Mississippi River Bridge or the Big Blue Bridges, the pair have blended into the cityscape of downtown La Crosse.

COFFEE STREET BRIDGE

Built in 1893 by the Chicago Bridge Company, the bridge was originally designed as a wagon bridge to carry Coffee Street in downtown Lanesboro across the South Branch of the Root River. It has a Pratt through truss steel main span and a steel girder approach span on the north end. The main span is 119 feet long, and the approach span is 20 feet long.

The bridge supported vehicle traffic until the early 2000s. At that time, the Coffee Street Bridge Enhancement Group met with the city and proposed making it a pedestrian bridge between downtown and the Bass Pond parking lot.

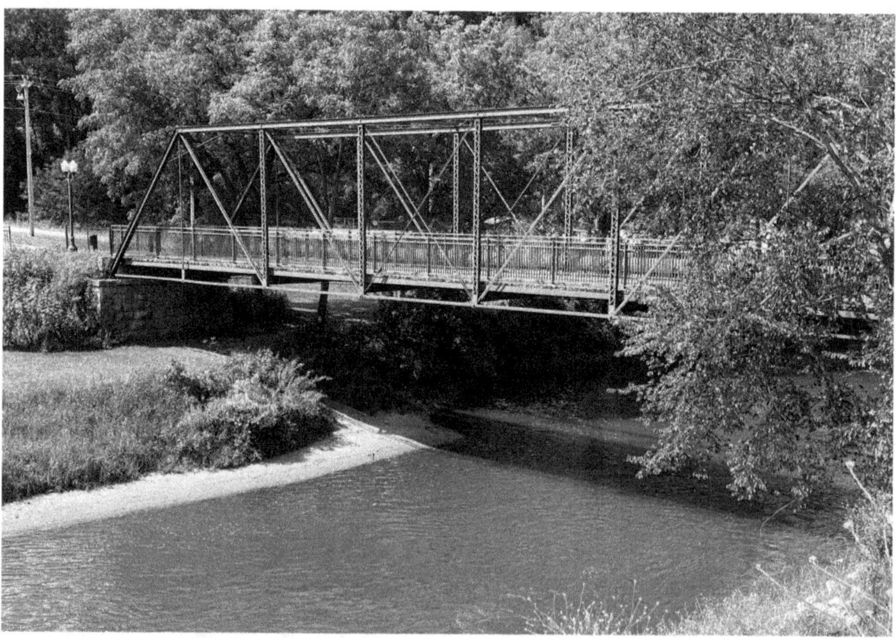

The Coffee Street Bridge, also known as the Iron Wagon Bridge, in downtown Lanesboro is a single-span through truss bridge built in 1893 by the Chicago Bridge Company. It crosses the south branch of the Root River. *Photo by Steve Gardiner.*

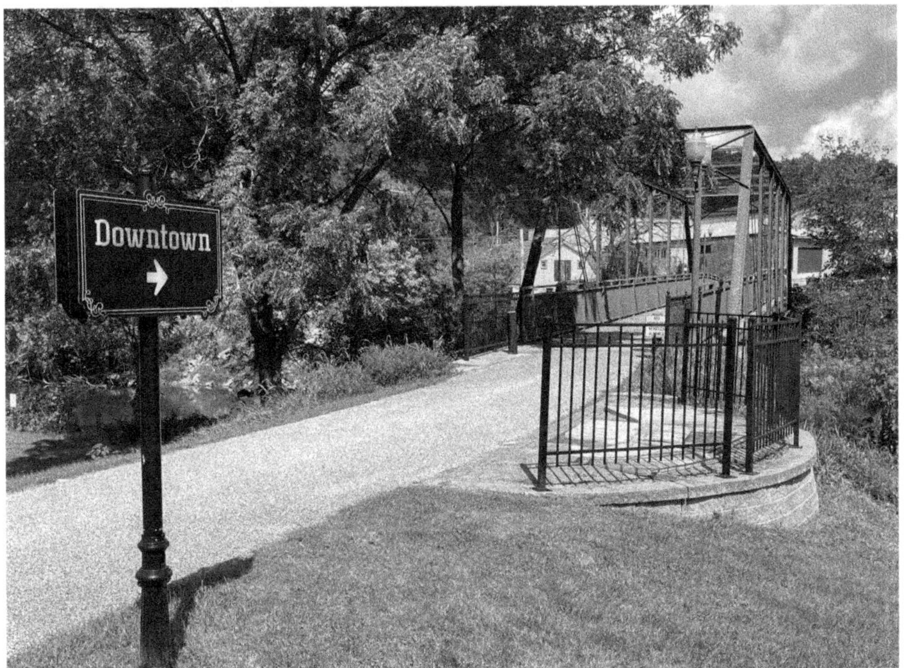

Owned by the City of Lanesboro, the Coffee Street Bridge was rehabilitated in 2002 and opened to pedestrian traffic. Improvements included a new deck, a new steel railing and decorative lighting. *Photo by Steve Gardiner.*

"The bridge was converted from vehicular to pedestrian use," according to the MnDOT Historic Bridge Report. "Additional work included installing a new wood deck to replace the non-historic concrete deck that was in place, reconstruction of the northeast approach span, stabilization of the stone abutments, repainting the structure, and replacing the original rail with a new steel railing. Decorative lighting was installed at either end of the structure."

The rehabilitation project was completed in 2002.

Root River Pedestrian Bridge

In 1872, the Southern Minnesota Railroad built 165 miles of track from La Crescent to Winnebago through very difficult terrain requiring many bridges. Over the years, more miles were added to the line, and it was sold several times to other railroads. In 1979, the Chicago, Milwaukee, St. Paul and Pacific Railroad owned the tracks through the Root River Valley and

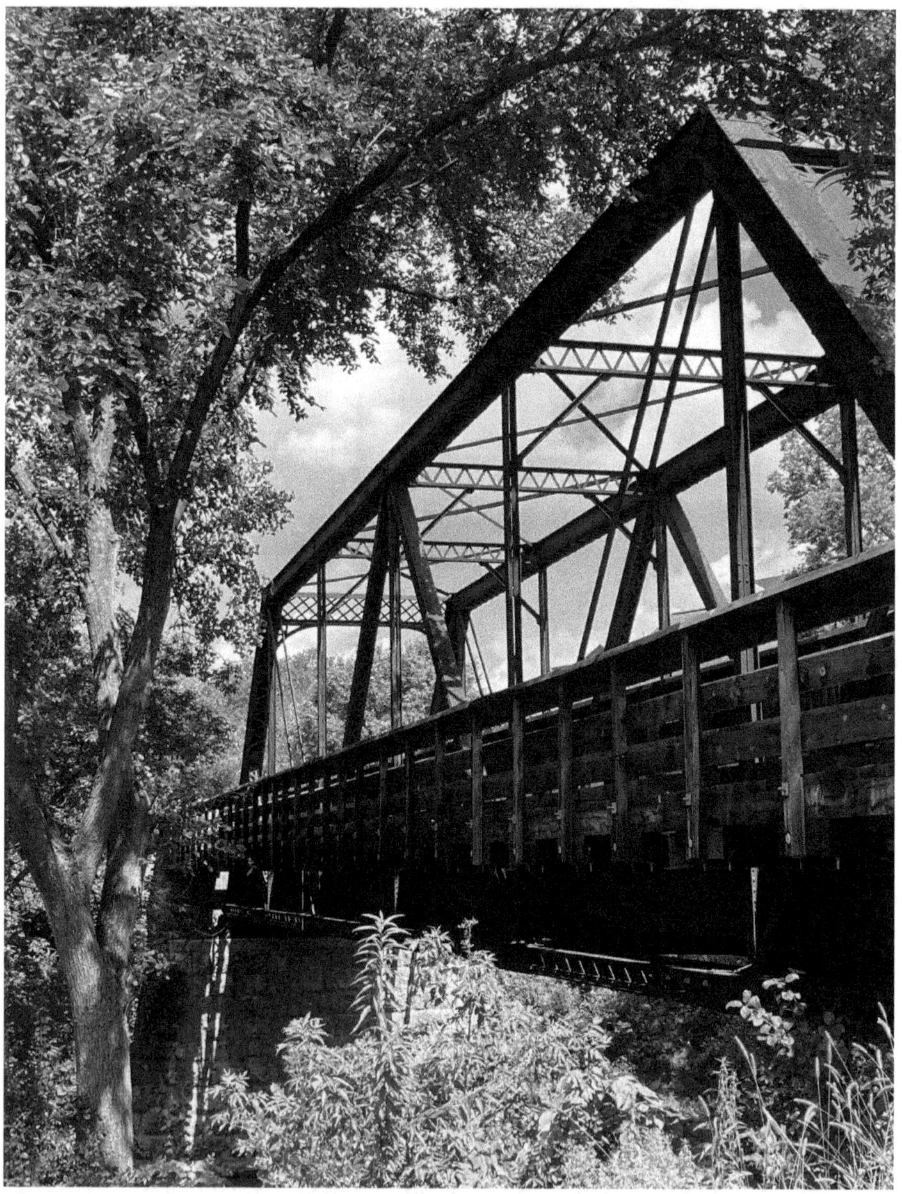

Above: The Root River State Trail Pedestrian Bridge, also known as Root River Bridge #3, is just off Parkway Avenue South in Lanesboro. It is a Warren through truss bridge built in 1910. *Photo by Steve Gardiner.*

Opposite: Cyclists on the Root River State Trail cross this old railroad bridge, known as Root River Bridge #5, between Lanesboro and Whalen. *Photo by Steve Gardiner.*

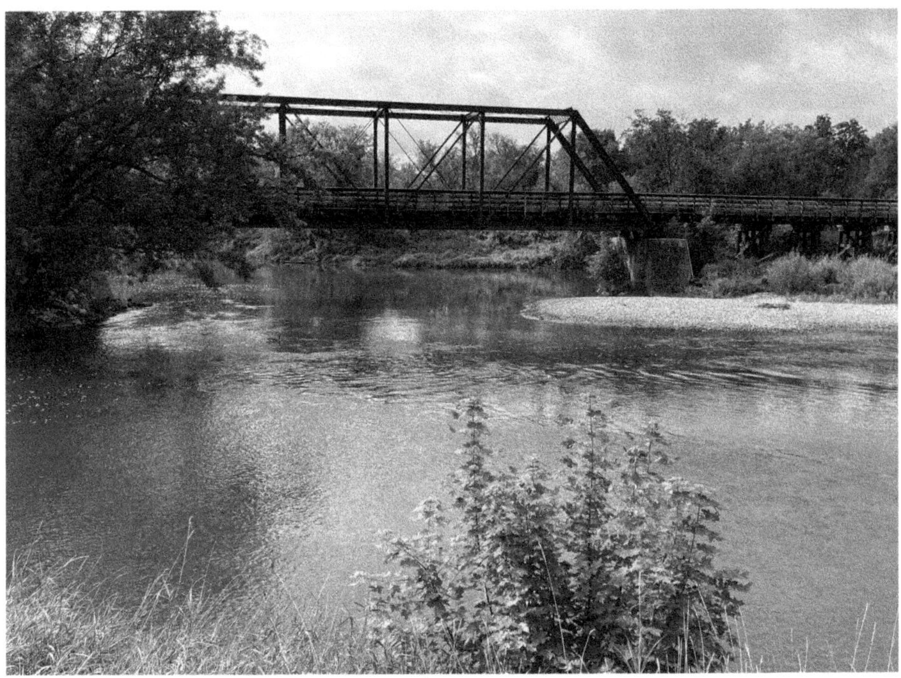

abandoned them. This opened the door to an opportunity under the Rails-to-Trails movement to convert the railbed into a bicycle trail. With the Elroy-Sparta Trail in Wisconsin as inspiration, the Root River State Trail officially opened in 1986.

The trail is flat or gentle hills and is paved. It allows bicyclists to cross many old railroad bridges as the Root River winds back and forth across the valley.

One of the first bridges most riders see is the Root River Pedestrian Bridge in downtown Lanesboro. It is a Warren through truss bridge built in 1910 and is 135 feet long.

Heading east toward Whalen, cyclists cross another old railroad bridge at the edge of Lanesboro. It is called Root River Bridge #4 and is a Pratt pony truss bridge built in 1899 and rebuilt with relocated pieces in 1911. Its longest span is 100 feet, and the total length of the bridge is 310 feet.

Continuing east, cyclists soon cross Root River Bridge #5, built in 1899 and rebuilt in 1916. It is a Pratt through truss bridge with a main span of 135 feet and a long approach span, giving the bridge a total length of 425 feet.

Many other old railroad bridges are part of the Root River State Trail, which is forty-two miles long, extending from Houston through Rushford, Peterson, Whalen, Lanesboro and on to Fountain.

CONCLUSION

For centuries, bridges have served as aids to transportation, helping us move easily and quickly across canyons, rivers and rough terrain that would otherwise make our lives more difficult and challenging. They modify landscapes and alter the way humans relate to a place.

In that same time, bridges have also served as metaphors. Countless speakers and writers have used bridges as symbols to help us make transitions.

Bridges have been seen as connections between one idea and another, between one person and another, between one group and another, between one culture and another. Bridges are used as a connector between one time in history and another or the beginning of one cycle and the end of another.

As metaphors, bridges are normally employed when there are two choices—a now and a future, a here and a there, an old idea and a new idea, a current situation in life and a new situation in life. Using a bridge metaphor signifies a start, a movement toward something or somewhere different and serves as a means of getting there.

Many people have dreams about bridges, and psychologists have offered different interpretations of the meanings of those dreams based on how long the bridge appears, how high the bridge is above the water below, how solid the bridge seems or how many other people are on the bridge. Other interpretations might depend on if the dreamer reported falling off the bridge or not being able to reach the far end of the bridge. Still different interpretations might be reached if the dreamer is traveling under the bridge on foot or in a boat as opposed to moving across the bridge. Bridges may serve as connections between the conscious and unconscious parts of the mind.

Religious speakers and writers have long used bridges as symbolic connectors between the material world and the spiritual world, between God and man or between this life and the hereafter. They may represent the differences between the heart and the soul, between a good life and a bad life.

Bridges have also been seen as physical symbols for a certain location. The Tower Bridge represents London, England. The Golden Gate brings to mind San Francisco. The Harbour Bridge is a symbol of Sydney, Australia.

Bridges seem to work well as metaphors because they are built on solid foundations and then span a distance, bringing together the two sides that have previously been apart or have been separated by some barrier or challenge.

Like the physical bridges that help us across chasms in our travels, metaphorical bridges are generally seen as positive. They frequently represent human progress, human aspirations, powerful connections and communication and hope.

Bridges in Language

The English language is filled with phrases that use *bridge* as an image:

- A bridge too far: a goal or plan that is likely too difficult to accomplish
- To build bridges: to create or improve relationships between individuals or groups of people
- To burn your bridges: to make a decision that can't be reversed or corrected in the future or to eliminate the possibility of returning
- Cross that bridge when you come to it: to deal with a problem or situation at the appropriate time in the future as opposed to in advance
- To bridge the gap: to find a temporary solution to a problem until a more permanent solution can be found
- Like water under the bridge: a problem that has been solved and moved into the past
- I've got a bridge to sell you: a statement meaning the speaker believes that the listener is gullible

Many famous quotations include the concept of a bridge:

- "Compassion removes the walls of mistrust and builds bridges of hope, trust, and beliefs." Amit Ray
- "A word is a bridge. It is a wave of light and sound that spans the perceived distance between one thing and another." Thomas Lloyd Qualls
- "Bridges are made with intention. They make it possible to go between two places that were previously difficult to access." Gudjon Bergmann
- "Action is the bridge between thought and reality." Richie Norton
- "A picture is nothing but a bridge between the soul of the artist and that of the spectator." Eugène Delacroix
- "Rather than focusing on the obstacle in your path, focus on the bridge over the obstacle." Mary Lou Retton
- "Love is that condition in the human spirit so profound that it empowers us to develop courage; to trust that courage and build bridges with it; to trust those bridges and cross over them so we can attempt to reach each other." Maya Angelou
- "One of the hardest things in life to learn is which bridges to cross and which bridges to burn." Oprah Winfrey

BRIDGES IN LITERATURE

Books, stories and poems are filled with images of bridges.

"An Occurrence at Owl Creek Bridge" is a short story written by Ambrose Bierce in 1890 and set during the Civil War. Peyton Farquhar, a Southern farmer, is standing on a bridge with his hands tied behind his back and a noose around his neck. Northern soldiers are preparing to hang Farquhar for attempting to interfere with them advancing into the area.

Farquhar looks down from the bridge into the water below, and his mind drifts with the stream as he feels himself falling. He loses consciousness and then realizes that his hands are loose and he is swimming away from the soldiers who are shooting at him from the bridge. He struggles to the bank of the river and makes his way home to his wife and family. Just as he is ready to hug his wife, he feels a sharp pain in his neck as he is brought back to reality, dangling from the rope on Owl Creek Bridge.

AMERICAN AUTHOR THORNTON WILDER won the Pulitzer Prize in 1928 for *The Bridge of San Luis Rey* (1927) about a rope bridge on the road between Lima and Cuzco in Peru. The bridge had been built by the Incas some one hundred years before, and it collapsed at noon on Friday, July 20, 1714, as five people were crossing it. All five fell to their deaths in the river below.

Brother Juniper, a Franciscan friar, was heading to the bridge to cross it and witnessed the accident. He wanted to understand how those five people happened to be on that bridge at exactly that moment, to see if he couldn't find some sense of God's Divine Providence in the tragic event. He set out to interview people who knew the victims, hoping to discover why they had arrived at the bridge when they did.

Wilder himself said that the book asks the question, "Is there a direction and meaning in lives beyond the individual's own will?"

IN HIS NOVEL *THE Bridge on the River Kwai* (1952), Pierre Boulle tells the story of British lieutenant colonel Nicholson and his men, who are captured in 1943 and taken to a Japanese prisoner of war camp under the command of Colonel Saito. Saito demands that Nicholson and his men build a railroad bridge. Nicholson refuses to participate, citing the Hague Convention ruling that officers should not be made to perform manual labor in POW camps. Saito locks Nicholson and the other officers in small iron boxes during the heat of the day. Nicholson remains adamant, and eventually, Saito backs down.

Released, Nicholson then wants to show what a good job the British troops can do, and his men rally and turn the bridge into a symbol of work ethic and national honor, making it a "masterpiece which was to prove the superiority of the West."

IN THE NOVEL *THE Bridges of Madison County* (1992), author Robert James Waller follows *National Geographic* photographer Robert Kincaid as he drives from his home in Washington State to Madison County, Iowa, on an assignment to photograph the covered bridges in the area. Having trouble locating one of the bridges, he stops at a farmhouse to ask directions. There he meets Francesca Johnson, whose husband and children are gone for a week to attend the state fair. Robert and Francesca get involved in a conversation that eventually leads to a four-day romantic affair. When Robert is ready to leave, he asks Francesca to go with him, but she declines. They both know that when he leaves, they will not see each other again; however, the love they found during their brief time together lasts a lifetime.

The book was a #1 bestseller and sold sixty million copies worldwide. In 1995, it was made into a movie of the same name starring Clint Eastwood and Meryl Streep.

IN 1940, ERNEST HEMINGWAY wrote the novel *For Whom the Bell Tolls*. In it, American Robert Jordan enlists in the Republican forces during the Spanish Civil War. He travels behind enemy lines to help a group of guerrilla fighters. In their camp, he meets Maria, and the two fall in love. The guerrillas plan to blow up a bridge, and Jordan will be an important part of that mission. As they prepare, several incidents make their success look doubtful, but eventually Jordan succeeds in blowing up the bridge. The explosion also kills Anselmo, one of the guerrillas with Jordan, and soon after, a Fascist soldier fires his rifle and hits Jordan's horse, which then tramples Jordan, breaking his leg.

With Fascist troops moving in, Jordan knows he must let Maria and the others go, and he must be left behind. As he awaits the approaching Fascist troops, he contemplates suicide but realizes he needs to fight to slow down the Fascists. He is left feeling a sense of harmony as the enemy troops approach.

BRIDGES IN ART

We constantly see images of bridges. They are frequently included in print and television advertising. They are portrayed in tourist brochures. A span across a river can be a captivating focal point in a photograph or painting.

Anyone who lives in Minnesota or Wisconsin near the Mississippi River understands the significance of bridges, so it is no surprise that many paintings from the region feature bridges as prominent components.

"A bridge is a device to overcome an obstacle such as a valley or a river," said Brian Szott, art curator at the Minnesota Historical Society in St. Paul, "so its purpose lends itself to a sort of symbolism."

In the April 24, 2021 edition of the *Red Wing Republican Eagle*, Szott cited bridges like the Aerial Lift Bridge in Duluth, the Spiral Bridge in Hastings (which no longer exists) and the Hennepin Bridge and the Stone Arch Bridge, both in Minneapolis, as marvels in their time. The uniqueness and beauty of those and other bridges made them suitable elements for artistic compositions, according to Szott.

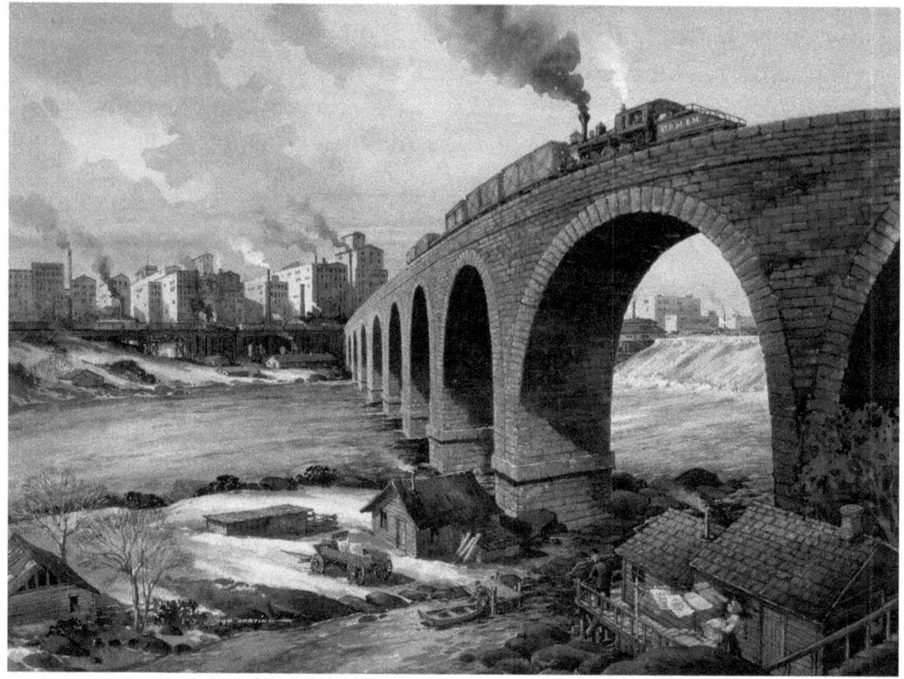

One of the most popular bridges in Minnesota, the Stone Arch Bridge in Minneapolis was captured in watercolor by Lloyd P. Hinton in 1920. *Courtesy of the Minnesota Historical Society.*

"All of them are engineering feats and are beautiful to look at," he said. "I don't think the symbolism is lost on artists, because bridges personify progress, and progress is a theme in American art."

As the art curator, Szott spends plenty of time with the paintings in the historical society's collection, and he has developed some favorites, including a few that contain bridges. One he admires is an 1888 painting by Alexis Fournier titled *Ft. Snelling*. "It's a large painting, maybe 12 feet long," Szott told the *Republican Eagle*. "It's such an ambitious painting, and the focal point is not the fort, but the bridge and what's taking place across the bridge."

In a landscape painting, most of the scene is the natural world, Szott said, and a painter might put in a bridge as a man-made element, a focal point in contrast with the rest of the landscape. Szott also noted that it is not just a matter of the artist's intent but also includes whatever symbolism the viewer brings to the painting.

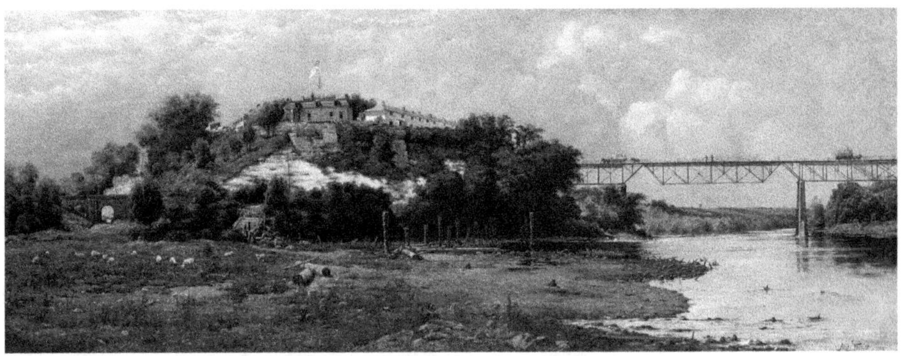

The bridge at Fort Snelling is the subject of this 1888 oil painting by Alexis Jean Fournier. An American flag flies over one of the buildings, and horse-drawn wagons cross the bridge. *Courtesy of the Minnesota Historical Society.*

"Historically, bridges were very important to the railroad," he added. "As a tool, bridges became incredibly important to the development of the West, starting right from the Mississippi River. We are so used to bridges today and we sometimes forget how important they were throughout our history."

INDEX

E

F

G

H

I

J

L

M

N

O

P

R

S

T

U

V

W

Z

ABOUT THE AUTHOR

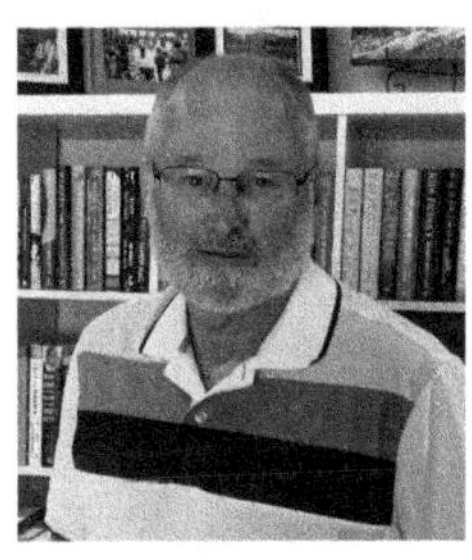

Steve Gardiner taught high school English and journalism for thirty-eight years in Wyoming, Peru and Montana. He was the 2008 Montana Teacher of the Year and holds a doctorate of education degree. He has published articles in the *New York Times*, the *Chicago Tribune*, the *Christian Science Monitor*, the *Denver Post*, *PBS NewsHour*, *Educational Leadership*, *Phi Delta Kappan*, *Education Week* and many others. In 2022, he published his book *Historic Disasters in Southeast Minnesota* with The History Press. Read more at www.quietwaterpublishing.com. He and his wife, Peggy, live in Lake City, Minnesota.

Other Books by Steve Gardiner

Adventure Relativity: When Intense Experience Shifts Time

Building Student Literacy Through Sustained Silent Reading

Devils Tower: A Climbers Guide (with Dick Guilmette)

Highpointing for Tibet (with John Jancik)

Historic Disasters in Southeast Minnesota

Mountain Dreams: The Drive to Explore, Experience, and Expand

Under the Midnight Sun (with John Jancik)

Why I Climb: Personal Insights from Top Climbers

www.ingramcontent.com/pod-product-compliance
Lightning Source LLC
LaVergne TN
LVHW010933100826
845153LV00001B/18
9781540258458